SOFTIMAGE®3D

DESIGN GUIDE

BARRY RUFF AND GENE BODIO

The Coriolis Group, Inc.
An International Thomson Publishing Company
14455 N. Hayden Road, Suite 220
Scottsdale, Arizona 85260

602/483-0192
FAX 602/483-0193
http://www.coriolis.com

Printed in the United States of America
ISBN 1-57610-147-9
10 9 8 7 6 5 4 3 2 1

Publisher

Keith Weiskamp

Project Editor

Michelle Stroup

Production Coordinator

Jon Gabriel

Cover Design

Performance Design

Layout Design

April Nielsen

CD-ROM Developer

Robert Clarfield

🌀 **CORIOLIS GROUP BOOKS**
an International Thomson Publishing company I(T)P®

Albany, NY • Belmont, CA • Bonn • Boston • Cincinnati • Detroit • Johannesburg
London • Madrid • Melbourne • Mexico City • New York • Paris • Singapore
Tokyo • Toronto • Washington

DEDICATION

To my wife Beth, who I love more than computers.
—Barry Ruff

To my loving wife Kip and daughter Desiree.
—Gene Bodio

SOFTIMAGE 3D
DESIGN GUID

SOFTIMAGE 3D
DESIGN GUIDE

ACKNOWLEDGMENTS

I'd like to take a moment to thank all the people that made this book happen, and also to let you, the reader, know that Gene, Phil, and I could never have completed this project without the assistance and input of all the individuals mentioned here.

First and foremost, our largest debt of gratitude goes to Phil LeMarbre who came in on the last three months of effort and pushed us through to publication. Phil acted as a contributing author on a number of chapters and provided figures for others; he single-handedly put the Softimage scene databases together for the CD-ROM; and researched, organized, and wrote the appendix. Phil is co-founder of PCA Graphics Inc., a father of five, and lives in Hopedale, Massachusetts. Phil, thanks for your time, patience, and diligence.

This being a book on Softimage, there are obviously a number of people in Montreal we need to thank. Moshe Lichtman, Claude Cajolet, Dan Kraus, John Carapella, Jean-Marc Krattili, and Mark Petit—thanks for keeping us in the loop and a special thanks for making Softimage the outstanding product that it is. To the beta crew, Raonull Conover, Sammy Nelson, Pierre Robidoux, Greg Smith, and all the other developers, support, and special projects folks we've had the pleasure to work with, many thanks, we're looking forward to Sumatra.

Since the inception of the project, the Coriolis Group has been an outstanding creative and technical team, striving with us to make this book happen. Thanks to Keith Weiskamp for believing in us and the project, to Sandra Lassiter for keeping us on target, to our proficient, efficient (and did I say fast?) copyeditors Chris Kelly and Susan Holly. Thanks to Robert Clarfield for all the great third-party wares and legwork on the CD-ROM, Tony Stock for his work on the cover, and Kelly Mero for pushing the product, and on the production side thanks to April Nielsen and Jon Gabriel for all their efforts.

Thanks to John Rix for reading our chapters in a painful manuscript form and still thinking enough of them to write a foreword for us. And, thanks to Robert Stein III for providing imagery in the color section. Thanks to Viewpoint for the use of 3D models, provided by Viewpoint DataLabs International, Inc., Orem, UT 801-229-3000, http://www.viewpoint.com. Kevin Gillespie at Hasbro Interactive kindly granted us permission to use images based on those previously created for Hasbro.

And finally, this leads me to the person who had the single most impact on this text. To Michelle Stroup our project editor, a heartfelt thank you. It's been a true pleasure working with Michelle. Her unswerving devotion to delivery and her constant understanding and flexibility are the elements that made this project happen.

CONTENTS

Chapter 4
Textures 55

Local And Global Textures 56

Global Texturing 64

UV Vs. Projection 71

Examples Of Multiple Map Layers 74

The Amorphous Sphere 78

UV Traveling Textures 79
Wrap-Up 81

SOFTIMAGE 3D
DESIGN GUIDE

See more examples of Gene Bodio's work at
www.PCAGraphics.com, which also provides continuing
Softimage information.

SOFTIMAGE 3D
DESIGN GUIDE

FOREWORD

Today, more and more artists and designers are specializing in modeling, animation, texturing, lighting, and rendering, and Softimage has the power to be the tool of choice for professionals in each of these areas. However, it can be a daunting task to become proficient in such a diverse software package. It is not enough to know that pressing a particular button will perform a particular operation; it is crucial to know how to combine all the functions in a logical and efficient way. The best way to get a handle on Softimage is by following tutorials that demonstrate how the functions and dialogs can create animated 3D scenes.

Since version 1.0, Softimage has grown in depth, and its feature set has expanded to include features like the Actor module, with its IK and dynamic simulations; and Mental Ray, to advance Softimage's rendering capabilities. Paint dialogs containing UV texture editing and 3D paint are among the many features that support the production of video games. New viewports like the Spreadsheet and Dopesheet help keep a handle on complex scenes, while expressions and channels provide even more avenues to control motion. Today, as new users sign on, they are faced with a deep and complex program.

This book is written from a production perspective by individuals who rely on Softimage to create—often under extremely tight deadlines—the imagery that we see on television and in film. Short production schedules necessitate trimming down the steps and cutting down on keystrokes—just a few extra steps can cause significant overhead in large-scale projects. This book continues where Softimage's tutorials leave off, leading you through a cross section of tasks that will familiarize you with many of the day-to-day techniques, all the while familiarizing you with keyboard hotkeys and shortcuts. Throughout the course of this book you'll discover a variety of ways to render, animate, model, develop game content, and successfully produce the highest quality material using Softimage.

3D animation has become an integral part of film, television, games, and print media. It continually revitalizes and inspires creators with richer, more complex visions. As 3D animation matures and becomes accessible to a broader range of artists, what will differentiate the great from the mundane will not be the amazing technology, but what the technology communicates, as well as the emotional effect it has on the viewer. This is the unchanging measure of all art forms. Every 3D artist should work to illuminate the viewer, to illustrate a world previously unknown. Let this book be one of the first steps towards learning a tool that can help you realize those visions.

John Rix
Technical Director, Advanced Graphics
Electronic Arts Inc.

PART 1

Exploring Softimage

MODELING 1

Key topics:

- **Extrusion**

- **Modeling relations**

- **Trimmed NURBS**

- **Polygon tools**

Modeling is the first step in creating your 3D scenes. In this chapter and the next, we'll cover some of the common techniques and practices used to build useful and dependable objects. We'll create efficient models quickly and easily, using Softimage's wide range of tools for manipulating 3D geometry. Selecting the appropriate tool and using it properly is more than half the battle when modeling.

The best way to learn anything about Softimage is by trying it for yourself. In the following sections, you'll go through some hands-on examples of how to use extrusion, guided extrude surfaces, revolves, and trimmed NURBS, while taking advantage of Softimage's powerful modeling relations features. Then, on to some practical polygon modeling: creating a human hand in 10 easy steps.

Some of the examples in this chapter will begin by loading in elements or scenes from the CD-ROM enclosed with this book. Do this by pressing F1 to enter the Model module and then select **Get|DB Manager**. Navigate to your databases, and select the **Link DB** button. In the Set Database window that appears, use the Path Browser to locate the Chapter1 database. Highlight Chapter1, and select **Link**. Now, you will be able to retrieve elements directly from the Chapter1 database.

Extrusion

Extrusion is one of the most basic of modeling tools. It creates a surface by moving a curve along another curve and creating geometry along that path. In this section, you'll create some quick extruded surfaces and play with their parameters of construction to better understand the variety of surface types you can create with the extrusion tools.

To begin, select **Preferences|Create Modelling Relation**. Modeling relations allow you to maintain information about how a surface was constructed. A relationship between curves and the surfaces they create is kept so that altering a curve will automatically reconstruct the surface with modified generation parameters. Modeling relations will be used extensively throughout this chapter.

Extrusion Along A Path

You can extrude a selected curve along another curve or any axis. Select **Get|Primitive|Circle**, and in the open Create Circle window, change Radius to 1; leave Step at 8; select NURBS, Quadratic; then click on OK. This circle will be used as a generation curve for your extrusion. By extruding the circle down a path, you will create a simple tube- or pipe-like object.

To create the extrusion path, select **Draw|Curve|NURBS**, and in the Front view, draw an open three-leaf clover form around the generator curve. (See Figure 1.1.) The generator curve should remain at the 0,0,0 location. The origin is the point that will travel along the extrusion path, dragging the generator along and sweeping out a surface in space. So, in this example, to create a tube that is centered around the extrusion path, the generator should encircle the origin.

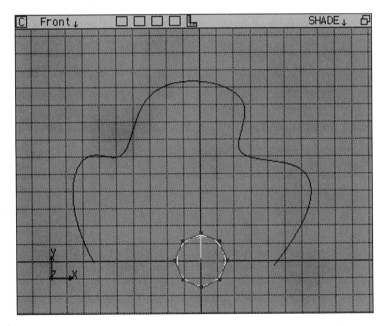

Figure 1.1 Wireframe view of the generator curve and extrusion path.

Highlight the generator curve, and select **Surface|Extrusion**. In the Extrusion window shown in Figure 1.2, select NURBS, On Curve; do not choose Close; then click on OK. (Note that bevelling is not available for NURBS.) View the extruded object in the

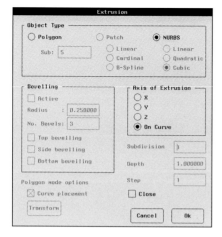

Figure 1.2 The Extrusion dialog box.

shaded Perspective window. If the normals on the extruded object are inverted, highlight the generator curve, and select **Effect|Inverse**. After a slight calculation delay, the normals on the extruded object should be corrected. Because you created a modeling relation between the generator curve and the extruded object, you can manipulate (scale, rotate, translate) the generator curve, and the extruded object will interactively change. Try moving some of the generator's control vertices, and watch as they are updated on the extruded object.

As mentioned previously, the generator curve should remain at the 0,0,0 location. This has nothing to do with the center point of the generator curve. To prove this, drag the generator curve around on the XY plane, and see how the extruded object reacts to the displacement of the generator curve. Now, move the generator in the Top view along the XZ plane. Try rotating the generator. Experiment until you feel comfortable with how the extrusion object reacts to the position of the generator.

In most circumstances, your generator will be centered around or positioned on the origin. To create sheared and displaced extrusions, however, you can manipulate the generation curve as needed. Delete the circle and extrusion object to start fresh for the next example.

Extrusion Along An Axis

Middle-click on **Get** to create another circle at the origin. Accept the previous circle construction values, and select **Surface|Extrusion** to open the Extrusion window. Select Polygon, and set Z as the axis of extrusion, Subdivision to 1.0, and Depth to 10.0. Make Bevelling active for Top and Bottom, and set the bevel number to 1. Subdivision controls the number of divisions created along the chosen axis, while Depth controls the length (in units) that the object will be extruded along the selected axis.

This function creates nicely bevelled extruded objects. Unfortunately, it doesn't work with NURBS. Delete the extrusion, and highlight the circle once again. Middle-click on **Surface** to reopen the Extrusion window. Change the Radius of the bevel to .5, and see how this changes the extrusion. Delete the resulting extrusion before moving on.

Guided Extrude

Select **Draw|Curve|NURBS**, and in the Front view, draw an *M*-shaped structure over the circle. Duplicate the new curve, and in the Top window, translate it back 6 units in the Z axis. Edit the newly translated curve, and move the middle control point up to form an arch out of the *M* curve. (See Figure 1.3.) Guided Extrude will take the generator curve, which it calls the *cross section*, and run it between the two NURBS, scaling the circle to match the distance between the curves to create an extruded surface.

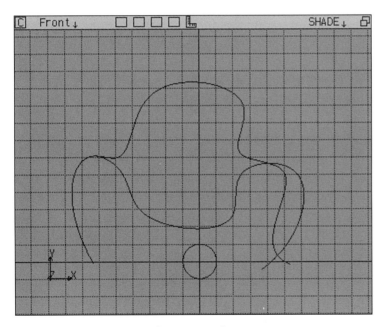

Figure 1.3   Wireframe view of extrusion paths.

Select **Surface|GuidedExtrude**, and in the GuidedExtrude window, choose Scale Width Only. When queried, left-click on the circle for the cross section, then the back curve for the left guide, and, finally, the front curve for the right guide. View the extruded object in the shaded Perspective window. Middle-click on **Effect** to invert the normals, if needed. The resulting shape, seen in Figure 1.4, resembles a stylized plastic chair. Unfortunately,

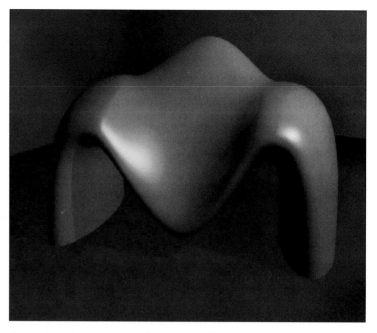

Figure 1.4 Rendered view of the extruded form.

modeling relations do not work with Guided Extrude, so you cannot rebuild this shape by editing the cross section.

A Strange Flower Pot

The next sections will use a number of core modeling tools, including revolutions and trimmed surfaces. In addition to surface creation, we will also cover some important techniques for working with curves. The exercises will build on one another to create a strange sample object to experiment with. Modeling relations will allow you to modify the final object in a variety of ways.

Surface Of Revolution

This function creates a 3D object by revolving a curve, or face, about an axis. Select **Get|Scene**, and load the scene "revolve" from the Chapter1 database. Hide everything in the scene except the curve nurbs1. Make sure Create Modeling Relation is toggled on (this function is found under **Preferences**). Highlight the nurbs1 curve, and select **Surface|Revolution**. In the Revolution window under Object Type, check NURBS and Quadratic; under

Axis of Revolution, check Y; and leave the rest at default settings. (See Figure 1.5.)

View the revol1 object that is to become the flower pot in the shaded Perspective window. (If the normals are reversed, highlight nurbs1, and select **Effect|Inverse**.) One method of adjusting the complexity of this selected object is to choose **Info|Selection** to open the NURBS Surface Info window. In this window, the Curve settings control the number of subdivisions in both the U (horizontal) and V (vertical) directions. The Step parameters control the smoothness of the individual curves in both the U and V directions. Change both Step values to 1, and create linear NURBS. Experiment with these values, and when finished, reset the values to the following: Curve, U=1, and V=1; Step, U=3, and V=10.

When performing camera functions (zoom, orbit, and so on) in the shaded Perspective window, the program defaults to wireframe during movement. To make Shade mode continuous, choose Setup (at the top of the Perspective window), and select Shade. This will keep the Perspective window in Shaded mode, even when you are interacting with models.

Because you have created modeling relations, scaling, rotating, or translating nurbs1 will interactively change the shaded revol1 object. To create an opening in the top of your revol1 pot, highlight nurbs1, and select **Edit|Move Point**. Translate the top control point left 1 unit on the X axis. This creates the hole in the top of the pot, but as you can see in Figure 1.6, it appears flat and unfinished. A small rounded bead around the perimeter of this hole will add some depth to the object and create a more finished look. The function Extrude on an extracted curve will accomplish this task.

Extrude On An Extracted Curve

The first step in creating the bead is to make a generator curve. This will be the shape of the bead that gets extruded around the lip of the pot. Select **Get|Primitive|Circle**, and in the Create

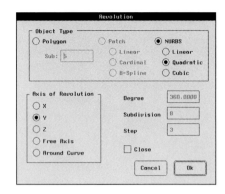

Figure 1.5 The Revolution dialog box.

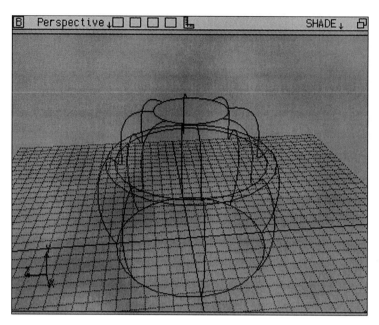

Figure 1.6 Wireframe view of the revolved pot.

Circle window, choose NURBS, Quadratic; set the Radius to .25 and Step to 4; then select OK. Highlight only revol1, and select **Draw|Extract**. In the Top view, click on the perimeter of the hole. This opens the NURBS Extract Curve window. Move the slider bar to make sure the correct curve is highlighted, then select Extract and Exit. (See Figure 1.7.) In the Schematic window, left-click on Plain Mode, and toggle Model Mode on. Note that nurbs2 has a modeling relation with revol1.

To make the bead, highlight circle1, and select **Surface|Extrusion**. In the Extrusion window, check off NURBS and On Curve (Close should be checked by default), and click on OK. The final step is to choose the path of extrusion by left-clicking on nurbs2. If the new extru1 bead has reversed normals, highlight circle1, and select **Effect|Inverse** to take care of the problem. Because model relations are still active, manipulate the size and shape of circle1 until you achieve the desired look. (See Figure 1.8.) Watch the bead update in the shaded Perspective window. To add more detail to the model, the next step is to create holes in the side of the pot. This will be accomplished with the trim function.

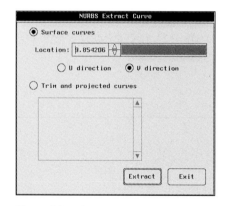

Figure 1.7 The NURBS Extract Curve dialog box.

Figure 1.8 Shaded view of the extruded bead.

Trimmed NURBS

Select **Get|Primitive|Circle**, and in the Create Circle window, choose NURBS, Quadratic; set Radius to 2; set Step to 8; and click on OK. In the Front window, position circle2 on the lower part of the pot. Highlight revol2, select **Draw|Trim NURBS Surface**, then left-click on circle2. This opens the Trim NURBS Surface window. (See Figure 1.9.) The blue line in the Top view shows the direction circle2 will be projected. Select Parallel, Z axis, Local, and Remove for the trim operation. To make sure the setup is correct, select Preview. In the Top view, notice the projection splines on the object along the Z axis. Everything looks good, so select OK to confirm the trim. The operation has created a new object (revol3), which contains the holes. Highlight revol2, and select **Display|Hide|Toggle &! Deselect Hidden** to hide the original revolve. Now, revol3 and the holes should be visible.

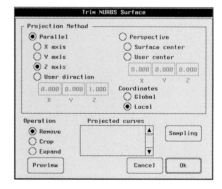

Figure 1.9 The Trim NURBS Surface dialog box.

Changes in the hole circle (circle2) will be updated in revol3. Select and scale circle2, and watch the trimmed hole in revol3 change. Choose **History|Undo** to return to the original circle2. Translate circle2 up on the Y axis until it intersects the constricted area of revol3. To increase the speed of this operation, select Setup (at the top of the Perspective window), and choose Wire Frame.

The holes look two-dimensional and give the pot an unfinished look. Let's quickly add a bead similar to the lip of the pot. Begin by extracting a curve from the hole perimeter. Highlight only revol3, select **Draw|Extract**, and left-click on the hole perimeter in the Front window. In the NURBS Extract Curve window that opens, highlight trim#2, and select Extract and Exit. This creates the new curve, nurbs3. To make the trim bead, highlight only circle1, and select **Surface|Extrusion**. In the Extrusion window, check off NURBS and On Curve (Close should be checked by default), and click on OK. Left-click on nurbs3 for the path creating extru2. (See Figure 1.10.)

The base of the object needs a rim to sit on—perhaps a square bead. Highlight revol3, and select **Draw|Extract**. In the Front window, left-click on the perimeter curve at the base of the pot. In the open NURBS Extract Curve window, select Extract and Exit (creating nurbs4). To construct the generator curve, select **Get|Primitive|Circle**. In the Create Circle window, select

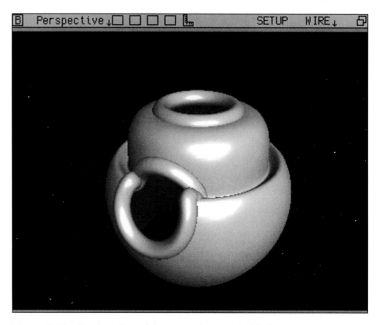

Figure 1.10 Shaded view of the pot with a beaded hole.

NURBS, Linear; set Radius to 1, and Step to 4; and click on OK. Rotate the new object (circle3) -45 degrees on the Z axis. Select **Surface|Extrusion**, and in the Extrusion window, choose NURBS and On Curve, then click on OK. When queried for a path, left-click on nurbs4, creating extru3 (the base of the pot).

Now, to perform one final operation on the pot, we'll create a smile between the hole and the base by using curve on surface.

Curve On Surface

Select **Draw|Curve|NURBS**, and in the Front window, draw a smile between the base and hole on the side of the pot. Select **Draw|Open/Close** to close the new curve (nurbs5). In the NURBS Open/Close window, accept Normal, and click on OK. Adjust the curve as necessary to create the perfect smile.

When satisfied with the curve, highlight only revol3, and select **Draw|Project on NURBS Surface**. Left-click on nurbs5—the smile curve—to open the Project on NURBS Surface window. In that window, check off Parallel, Z axis, and Local, then select Preview. Within the Projected curves box, highlight only PROJ # 2 (work with the curve closest to the camera), and click on OK. A new curve has now been incorporated into revol3.

With revol3 still highlighted, select **Draw|Extract**, and in the Top window, left-click on the projected smile curve. In the NURBS Extract Curves window, select Extract followed by Exit. You have created nurbs6—the smile curve on the surface. The current scene is pictured in Figure 1.11.

The final object needed to create the smile is a generator curve. Select **Get|Primitive|Circle**, and in the Create Circle window, choose NURBS, Quadratic; set Radius to .25, and Step to 3; and click on OK. Select **Surface|Extrusion**; choose NURBS, On Curve, and Close; and then click on OK. Left-click on nurbs6 to create extru4, a set of smiling lips. Invert the normals, if necessary. Then, using modeling relations, adjust circle3 or nurbs6 until you get a satisfactory smile.

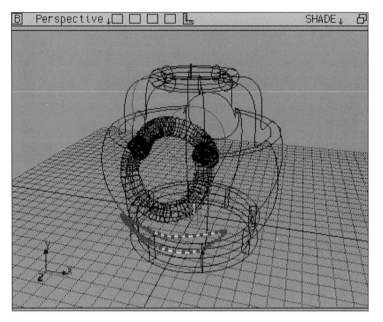

Figure 1.11 View of the current scene.

That completes the strange flower pot, shown in Figure 1.12. Examine the multitude of modeling relations in the Schematic view. All these relations are active, so you can go back and fundamentally change the shape of the pot and its parts while maintaining all the other work you've done. When you've

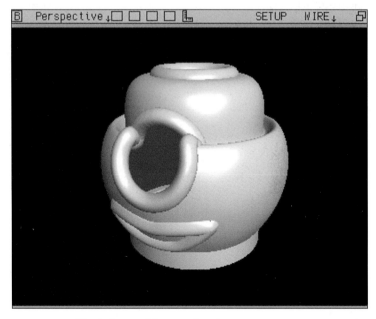

Figure 1.12 Shaded view of the completed pot.

finished admiring your handiwork, select **Delete|All**, and we'll move on to create a hand model.

Polygonal Human Hand

In this section, you will construct a simple human hand. The aim is to create a hand with a basic amount of geometry that you can easily manipulate. A secondary goal is to make the hand quickly. The construction is broken down into 10 steps, and the entire process will cover a variety of tools for polygonal modeling.

To guide your work, load the scene "hand" from the Chapter1 database, and move the elements out of your way, but keep them close enough to compare your work as you progress through the steps of construction. Each step will copy and extend the previous one, so you'll have a working history of your construction, similar to that in Figure 1.13.

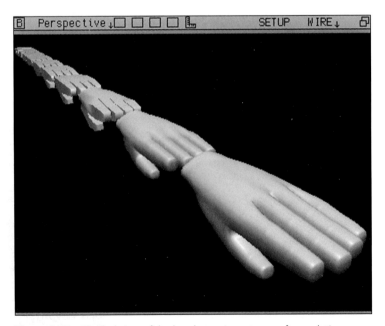

Figure 1.13 Shaded view of the hand at various stages of completion.

Start With A Cube

Select **Get|Primitive|Cube**, and set the length to 4. Scale the cube on the Y axis to .35. Select **Info|Selection**, and name the new object "palm_a".

Subdivide The Cube

Select **Duplicate|Immediate**, and make a copy of palm_a. Translate the new object (palm_a1) +5 units on the X axis. This leaves a 1-unit gap between the two cubes. You will subdivide palm_a1 to create an easy shape to pull fingers from. Select **Effect|Subdivision** to open the Polygon Subdivision window, and set the subdivisions as follows: X=0, Y=0, Z=3. Then, hit OK.

Create The Base Of The Fingers

Again, select **Duplicate|Immediate** to copy the object (palm_a1). Translate the new object (palm_a2) another 5 units on the X axis (middle-click in the TransX text box, and enter 10). Now you want to extend and scale in slightly the end polygons of palm_a2. To accomplish this, you have to select and tag the polygons. Switch from OBJ (object) mode to POL (polygon) mode by pressing F12. Select **Polygon|Select by Rectangle**, and highlight the end polygons in the Top view. The selected polygons will be highlighted in purple in the wireframe views. You will extend the polygons to create the fingertips.

Select **Tag|Rect**, and tag the front control points, which will be highlighted in red. Select **Polygon|Coplanar** to open the Coplanar window. Inside this window, set Inset to .1, Height to 2, and Discontinuity Angle to 60. Then, choose both Tagged Polygons Only and Apply After Transform, and click on OK. When asked to select a mesh, left-click on palm_a2. This action creates a new object (palm_a2_cplnr1) directly over palm_a2. Delete palm_a2, and rename palm_a2_cplnr1 as palm_a2. The next step is to create a denser mesh in the knuckle area.

Add The Knuckle

Use **Duplicate|Immediate** to copy the object (palm_a2). Translate the new object (palm_a3) another 7 units on the X axis (middle-click on the text box under TransX and enter 17). In POL mode, select **Polygon|Select by Rectangle**, and highlight the leading four polygons on palm_a3. Select **Duplicate|Immediate**, and translate these polygons slightly to the right on the X axis. Copy these polygons again (**Duplicate|Immediate**), and translate them slightly forward on the X axis once again. Return to OBJ mode.

Complete The Fingers

Copy (**Duplicate|Immediate**) palm_a3. Middle-click on the text box under TransX, and enter 24. Make POL mode active, copy the selected polygons (**Duplicate|Immediate**), then translate them approximately 1 unit on the X axis. At this point, start to narrow the fingers by scaling down slightly on all three coordinates (UNI).

Time to create another finger joint. Copy the highlighted polygons twice, moving them slightly forward on the X axis each time. Middle-click on **Duplicate** to create the last section of the fingers. Translate the polygons 1 unit on the X axis, and scale slightly down on all three coordinates (UNI). You may need to scale down more on the X axis. To create the end of the fingers, middle-click on **Duplicate**, move the polygons slightly forward, and scale them down in X to produce a more rounded ending. (See Figure 1.14.) Return to OBJ mode.

Begin The Thumb

Middle-click on **Duplicate** to copy palm_a4. Middle-click in the text box under TransX and

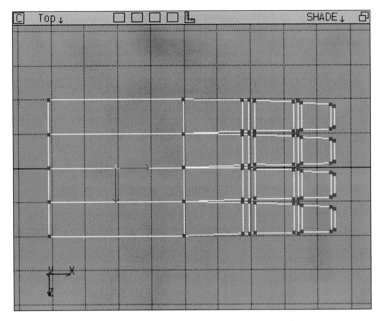

Figure 1.14 Wireframe view of the half-completed hand.

enter 33 (moving palm_a5 forward). You can now start building the thumb. Using the Top view, position palm_a5 to allow work on the bottom of the first segment (assume this is a left hand with the thumb pointing down the Y axis).

To begin thumb construction, you must add two points on the side of the base of the hand, between the first two isoprams—one on the top and the other on the bottom. Select **Edit|Add Point**, and left-click on the middle of the first two isoprams—once on top and then again on the bottom. (If the points are not visible, select **Show|Points**.) These two added points need an edge between them. To add the edge, select **Polygon|Edge**, and left-click first on one point and then the next. Check the Top view to make sure the edge is straight. Move the points, if necessary, to adjust the edge.

Select the polygon on the left-side base of the hand—up to the start of the index finger—and make sure this is the only polygon selected. Enter POL mode, copy the polygon, and translate the new polygon down the Y axis approximately 1 unit. Enter TAG mode, and clear any leftover tags from previous operations. View palm_a5 in the Front window, and tag the front two points of the just lowered polygon. Translate the tagged points .5 units back on the X axis. Deselect these points (middle-click on the rectangular tag), and tag the back two points of the lowered polygon. Translate these points forward on the X axis .5 units and up on the Y axis until a straight line is formed. Return to OBJ mode.

Create The Thumb Tip

Copy palm_a5, and move the new object (palm_a6) forward on the X axis. From the Top view, select the most forward polygon within the newly formed thumb region. Return to POL mode, and begin work on the first thumb joint. Copy the polygon, rotate it on the Z axis until the polygon points down at a 45-degree angle, and drag the polygon down on the Y axis to just below the parent polygon. Then, drag the polygon away from the hand, and scale to size. This completes the first thumb joint area.

Copy the polygon again, rotate it on the Z axis until horizontal, translate down on the Y axis until the polygon is just below the parent polygon, translate 1 unit on the X axis, and scale down slightly. You have one more joint to build. Copy the polygon twice, moving it slightly down on Y each time. To build the thumb tip, copy the polygon, move it on the X axis back .5 units and down on Y about .7 units, and scale the polygon down slightly. For the last time, copy the polygon, move it just slightly forward, and scale down to produce a rounded thumb as in Figure 1.15. Return to OBJ mode.

Make The Wrist And Determine The Finger Lengths

Copy palm_a6, and move the new object (palm_a7) forward on the X axis. Return to POL mode, and prepare to work on the wrist. Make sure no polygons are selected, then select the end polygons in the wrist area. Copy the polygon, move it back on the X axis .5 units, and scale on the X and Z axes until the size appears correct. To finish the wrist, copy the polygon once more, translate back on the X axis 1 unit, and scale it .25 units on the X axis.

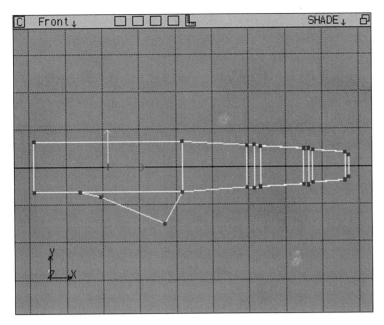

Figure 1.15 Wireframe view of the thumb.

Now that the wrist is done, start fine-tuning the fingers. The middle finger should be longer than the index and ring fingers. In TAG mode, tag the two joints and tip of the middle finger, select **ScaleX**, and scale the points out .5 units. Untag all points, tag the same points on the little finger, and scale them back on the X axis 1 unit. Return to OBJ mode.

Continue Fine-Tuning The Hand

Copy palm_a7, and move the new object (palm_a8) forward on the X axis. Continue fine-tuning the hand from the Front view. Tag the bottom points of the fingertips and translate them back slightly on the X axis. Tag only the bottom points of the second finger joints and move them up the Y axis approximately .25 units. Now, work on the sides of the hand and fingers. Tag the edge points along the thumb side of the hand (excluding the thumb) up to and including the index finger's first joint. Scale them on the Y axis, enough to take the edge off. Return to OBJ mode.

Add The Details

Copy palm_a8, and move the new object (palm_a9) forward on the X axis. Untag all points. Select **Effect|Rounding,** and set

Round to .5. If the model requires more points and a smoother contour, then repeat the rounding procedure. At this point, select **History|Undo**, and work the model further. Add the bends of the fingers, fatten the knuckles, and so on. Continue making adjustments until the hand looks anatomically correct, as in Figure 1.16.

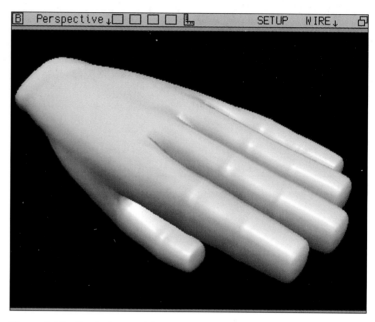

Figure 1.16 Shaded view of the completed hand model.

That's it for the hand. As you repeat the steps, you'll get faster at creating lifelike hands. Add some texture and fingernails, and you're on your way.

Wrap-Up

This chapter covered a wide variety of modeling tools and techniques. In the next chapter, we'll continue exploring Softimage's modeling features with more examples and samples. Everyone models in different ways. The tools are just a starting point for you to express yourself. As you become more comfortable with the tools, you'll start to use them in more creative ways and in different combinations. Most of the modeling tools perform one simple function. It's then up to you to combine these instruments to compose the forms you desire.

MODELING II

2

Key topics:

- **Skinning**

- **Meta-Clay**

- **Lattice**

- **Duplicator**

This chapter continues to examine the modeling tools available within Softimage. We will examine more of the surface tools, such as skin and four sided. Then, we'll look at meta-clay and lattices. The chapter wraps up with some hands-on Duplicator and Volume Duplicator projects.

The modeling process is very physical: You arrange objects, loft them through space, and pummel control points to form the shapes you desire. The tools in this chapter stress the generation of surfaces and techniques for manipulating and moving objects and surfaces around to create models. The methods suggested in the examples are by no means definitive or exhaustive procedures for creating models using Softimage. The power of the Softimage modeling tools lies in the fact that you can achieve modeling goals by using a multitude of tools, applying whichever method is most appropriate for a particular circumstance.

Select **Get|DB Manager**, and link up the Chapter2 database contained on the CD-ROM enclosed with this book. To get started, select **Delete|All**, and press F1 to enter the Model module. Make sure you still have **Preferences|Create Modelling Relation** set to on; it will be useful for adjusting surfaces throughout the chapter.

Surface Tools

One of the core tasks of modeling is the ability to sculpt free-form surfaces. Chapter 1 covered two tools for doing this: extrusion and revolution. In this section, we'll look at some of the remaining techniques for surface generation and manipulation.

Skin

Skin is a general-purpose tool for creating surface geometry. It takes a number of generation curves and stretches a membrane between each to create an entire surface. By developing intricate generation curves, you can create very complicated geometry.

The generator curves for skin must all have the same number of control points. One easy way to assure this is to make all the generation curves for a skin operation from duplicates of the same curve. First, determine how many control points will be sufficient to define the most complicated curve on the skin. Create an initial curve with that many control points, and duplicate that initial curve to make each of the generation curves for the skin. You can then edit the point on each generation curve to create the desired shape.

Here's a quick example. Select **Draw|Curve|B-Spline**, and in the Front window, draw a somewhat horizontal curve with six points. Now, select **Duplicate|Repetition**, and set occurrences to 3, make the Z translation 3, and click on OK. In the Schematic view, select one spline at a time, and use **Edit|Move Point** to adjust the control points of each curve. Build up some interesting peaks and troughs on each curve, and don't forget to edit the initial curve, which isn't part of the repetition group. (See Figure 2.1.)

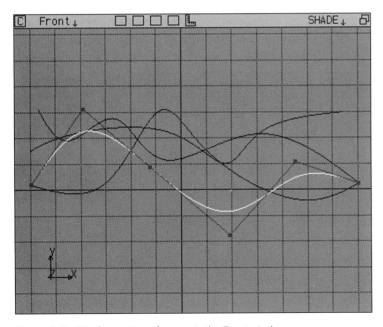

Figure 2.1   Wireframe view of curves in the Front window.

When you're done editing, select **Surface|Skin**. You will be placed in Skin mode, where you left-click on each element of the skin surface. Order is important, because you don't want to end up with some pathological surface that curves back in on itself.

In the Top window, left-click on each of the curves, going from bottom to top. As you select each curve, it is highlighted. When all the curves are chosen, select the skin operation by right-clicking. This opens the Skinning window. (See Figure 2.2.) Accept the default values, and click on OK.

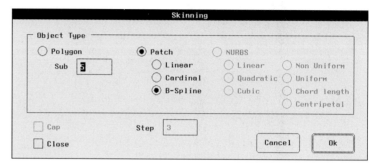

Figure 2.2   The Skinning dialog box.

Well, isn't that a fine surface? Okay, maybe it needs a little work, but, as you can see in the Schematic window, modeling relations exist between each curve and the skin surface. So, you can edit any of the generator curves, and your skin surface will be updated in a lively fashion.

As an example of a more complicated skinning operation, select **Get|Element**, and load skin_sample from the Chapter2 database. This will bring in a series of curves that you can skin to create the surface in Figure 2.3.

Four Sided

Four sided, another surface-generation tool, takes four curves and generates a surface between the curves. Unlike skin, the surface is not locked to the generation curves; it uses them only as control structures to build the geometry. Think of four sided as skinning between two pairs of curves. Each pair must have the same number of control points.

Select **Delete|All** to clear away any previous work. In the Top window, draw four B-Splines in a roughly square pattern; the ends don't need to match. Give the top and bottom curves six

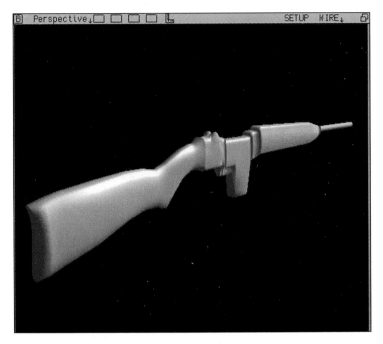

Figure 2.3 Shaded view of the skinned surface.

points and the side curves only four. Select **Edit|Move Point**, and adjust the curves in the Front and Right windows so that they undulate some. Now, select **Surface|Four Sided**, and left-click on each of the four curves in order clockwise in the Top view. After you have selected the fourth curve, the surface will be generated.

Edit the four generator curves to see better how they affect the resulting surface. Try rotating and scaling the curves, as well as moving their control points. You can create some interesting shapes but controlling where the edges of the surface lie is difficult. To gain control, use NURBS instead of B-Splines for your generation curves. With NURBS, four sided is much more useful for creating rich curved surfaces. The fact that you have four generation curves makes four sided less of a general-purpose tool. But, when you need it, you'll be glad it's there.

As one more quick example, load fourside_sample from the Chapter2 database, and create a surface using these four curves. Trying to create this surface with any tool other than four sided would be painful. (See Figure 2.4.)

STYLE LINES

Industrial designers refer to the main lines of a form as *style lines*. They define the shape of an object. If you find that a shape you are modeling can be defined with four style lines, then it's an obvious candidate for four sided. As an example, imagine the four lines that could define a car windshield.

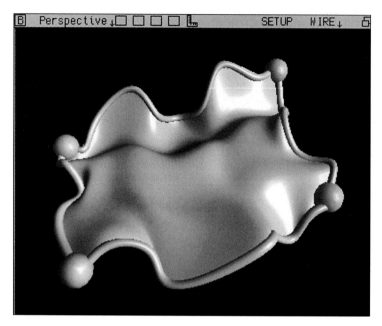

Figure 2.4 Shaded view of the four-sided surface.

Meta-Clay

Meta-clay is quite different from the other modeling tools we've examined. Instead of generating surfaces from curves, meta-clay combines volumes that influence one another to create surfaces. Think of meta-clay as balls of liquid mercury that you can scale and stretch. When two spheres of meta-clay interact, they create a fluid surface. (See Figure 2.5.)

To create a simple example, select **Meta-Clay|Add Element**. This places a default meta-clay element at the origin. Note how the icon is constructed in the Wireframe view. It is actually made of two spheres: The one in the center is solid, and the outer one is drawn with dashed lines. (See Figure 2.6.) The solid part is where surface is guaranteed; the dashed part shows the distance up to which this meta-clay element will influence other meta-clay elements.

Duplicate the element, and move it one unit along the X axis. Make shading in the Perspective view continuous, so you can see the surface that meta-clay generates. Drag the second sphere around the first, observing the final surface in the Perspective view. Scale up one element, and add some more into the scene.

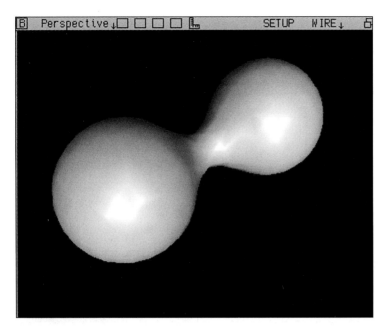

Figure 2.5 Shaded view of meta-clay objects.

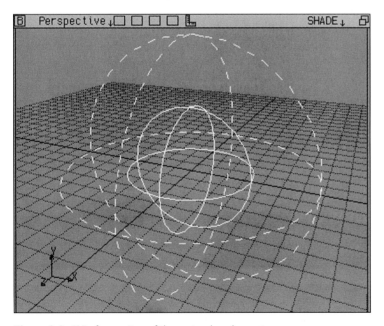

Figure 2.6 Wireframe view of the meta-clay element.

Note how each element tugs on the other until the surfaces combine to create a single fluid body. Stretch the sphere into ellipsoids, and combine them. See how adding a small element can subtly alter the shape of a larger meta-clay element. Create a leg or arm from a number of ellipsoids.

Select **Delete|All**, and load in the element metaclay_sample from the Chapter2 database. Rescale and rearrange some of the elements in this example to see how each element affects the overall shape of the resulting surface. (See Figure 2.7.)

Meta-clay can create some very organic forms but controlling its surface texture and animating meta-clay elements as part of a character can be somewhat tricky. One way around some of these difficulties is to generate a surface from meta-clay elements using **Meta-Clay|Convert to Polygon**. Unfortunately, these polygonal surfaces are rarely as cool-looking as the original meta-clay, and, of course, you can no longer dynamically change the shape of the form as a meta-clay element. All that aside, however, you can create some nice and useful polygon meshes with meta-clay. On their own, they look great.

Figure 2.7 Shaded view of the meta-clay model.

Lattice

Lattice is a tool for model manipulation. It creates a scaffolding around an object and allows you to modify this frame, which in turn deforms and stretches your object. You can apply a lattice to an entire object or just to single branches in your model hierarchy. This way, you can apply very localized control or pull on an entire model.

Load the element lattice_model from the Chapter2 database, and select **Lattice|Branch|Create**. Accept the default values in the Create Lattice window, and click on OK. (See Figure 2.8.) If you

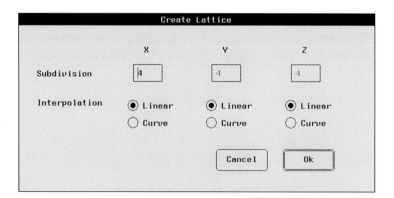

Figure 2.8 The Create Lattice dialog box.

have a complicated model and want a fine level of control, you can increase the Subdivision values to produce more edit points. The lattice surrounds your object, and by editing the points on the lattice, you can deform the underlying model without changing its geometry.

When you remove a lattice, its influence on the geometry disappears. If you want to remove the lattice and maintain its effect on the model, select **Lattice|Branch|Freeze**. This removes the lattice yet keeps the deformations. At any time, you can select **Lattice|Branch|Info** to get information about the lattice, including its number of subdivisions and interpolation methods. A checkbox in the Lattice Info window allows you to temporarily deactivate a lattice, while leaving it attached to the model.

The preceding examples all used **Lattice|Branch** operations. You can also apply a lattice to a single node. All the same tools are available under **Lattice|Node**. You'll find that lattices provide you a quick way to make global changes to an object's shape without having to worry about the construction properties of the underlying geometry. They also provide a handy framework for locally tweaking elements of a large structure.

Duplication Tools

Making copies of models can be a very powerful option. Many forms are symmetric or built up from repetitive patterns of geometry. The Softimage duplication tools allow you to make copies in some interesting ways. The following examples will show off some of the features of the duplicate and volume duplicate tools.

Volume Duplicate

Start out by selecting **Get|Primitive|Cone**. Enter 10 for Radius, and 15 for Height, and set the Longitude Step to 24. Press Shift+A to center the selected cone within the orthographic views, and press *a* in the Perspective view. The goal now is to fill the cone with little spheres.

STAR FIELD

Volume duplicate can be used to generate a star field very quickly. Use the same procedure as the numbered example, but instead of using two cones as a bounding volume, use two spheres. Make the spheres huge so that they surround your whole scene at a great distance. Merge them together, and volume duplicate some simple geometry, such as a triangle or cube, into the volume. Experiment with the number of stars, and try performing the duplicate twice with differing geometry or the same geometry scaled down. This will add some visual interest to your star field.

Select **Get|Primitive|Sphere**, and within the Create Sphere window, choose Polygon, and set Radius to 1, Longitude Step to 8, and Latitude Step to 8. With the new sphere highlighted, select **Duplicate|VolumeDuplicate.** When the VolumeDuplicator window opens, choose Random, and increase the Number of Duplicates to 250. Select Merged Mesh so the spheres are fused as one object, and leave all the Jittering boxes unchecked. (See Figure 2.9.) When asked to choose the enclosing mesh, left-click on the cone. When the status line changes to "select the object to duplicate," left-click on the sphere. Preview the selected mass of spheres (press F4, and select **Preview|Selection**). The resulting structure is quite organic looking.

Upon closer inspection of the sphere structure, you will see that the spheres are randomly constructed throughout the cone. This causes the majority of the spheres to overlap one another within the unseen center of the cone.

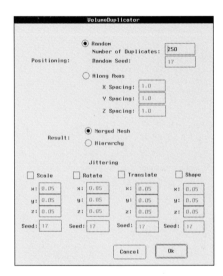

Figure 2.9   The VolumeDuplicator dialog box.

Try the following steps to minimize this object data and decrease rendering times. First, delete the complex sphere structure.

1. Select the cone and **Duplicate|Immediate**. Scale the new cone to about .7 in X, Y, and Z.

2. Merge the cones to form a new object by selecting both cones.

3. Press F1, select **Effect|Merge**, then click on OK.

4. With only the original sphere selected, middle-click on **Duplicate**, decrease the Number of Duplicates to 200, and click on OK.

5. Left-click on the merged cone and then on the original sphere.

A preview of the new object will show essentially the same random spherical mass but with fewer spheres squashed into the middle. (See Figure 2.10.) Use this type of setup whenever possible to decrease the amount of geometry generated by a volume duplicate operation.

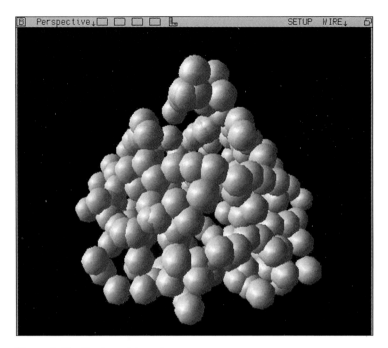

Figure 2.10 header: `[B] Perspective↓ ☐ ☐ ☐ ☐ [▪]                    SETUP   WIRE↓   [⊟]`

Figure 2.10 Preview of the sphere mass.

Necklace Project

Now for a specific project using the Duplicate function. This project works through an example similar to one of the SI_DEMO scenes, which uses Duplicate to create a repeated pattern along a spline.

Load the scene "necklace" from the Chapter2 database. Select the first object in the Schematic window, which is named "necklace-original B-spline." If this object is hidden, select **Display|Hide|Toggle & Keep Selected**. This is the original spline used to create the necklace. After examining this spline, middle-click on **Display**, and deselect the hidden object.

The original spline was duplicated and converted with different subdivisions. This created tagged areas on the bottom half of "spline-necklace-bottom" and on the top half of "spline-necklace-top." The reason for using two splines is that the pendants on the bottom half will be different from the pendants on the top half. (See Figure 2.11.)

Select the second object in the Schematic window (spline-necklace-bottom), and notice the tagged areas on the bottom half of the

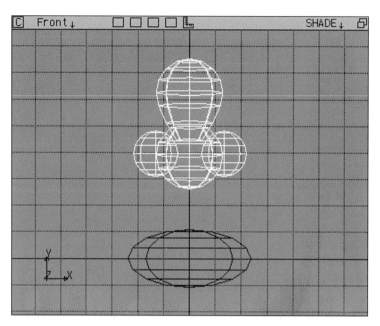

Figure 2.11 Wireframe view of the necklace elements.

object. Pendants will be attached to each of these tagged areas. Select the fourth object in the Schematic window to see the tagged areas on the top half of spline-necklace-top. Select the third object in the Schematic window ("pendant-bottom"), and view this object in the Front window. The positioning of pendant-bottom on the spline depends entirely on its relation to 0,0,0. It will always point toward 0,0,0 with the X axis replaced by the spline. It has nothing to do with where the center of the object is. The view in the Front window shows pendant-bottom as inverted (pointing up rather than hanging down). "Pendant-top," the fifth object in the Schematic window, is basically just a flattened sphere.

While in Single mode, highlight spline-necklace-bottom, and select **Duplicate|Duplicator**. In the Duplicator window, check Surface Vertices, Tagged Points Only, Y Axis, and Merged Mesh, then click on OK. When queried to select the surface, left-click on spline-necklace-bottom. Then, for the object to duplicate, left-click on pendant-bottom.

The pendants all seem to be oriented straight up and down on the Y axis. This is not the intended look, so delete the object. Once again, select spline-necklace-bottom, middle-click on **Duplicate**, and choose Surface Normal rather than Y Axis. Follow the Status line prompts to construct the new bottom necklace. Now, all the pendants are attempting to orientate toward 0,0,0, as desired.

Follow the same procedure for spline-necklace-top and pendant-top. Once the model is constructed, you can view it from all angles in the Perspective window in Shade mode. (See Figure 2.12.) If you encounter any problems, the finished necklace-bottom and -top are included in the database for reference.

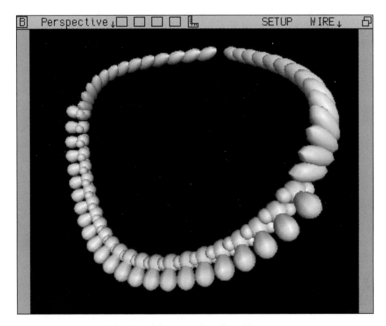

Figure 2.12   Shaded view of the completed necklace.

Cemetery Scene

This project also started as an SI_DEMO scene, but we've extended and enhanced it to create more drama and intrigue. The scene shows how you can quickly generate an interesting set by duplicating some elements across a landscape.

Construct The Landscape

Load in the scene "cemetery_begin." In the Model module, select **Polygon|Fractalize**; select Additive, Subdivide; set Seed to 12; Iterations to 6; Magnitude to 9; Jagginess to .4; and click on OK.

Left-click on the grid and you will have created rough terrain. Name the object "ground".

We want to pull up the ground in the distance to create a false horizon. Select the ground in the Top view, then rectangular tag two rows of vertices about 10 columns from the left edge and ending 10 rows from the top edge. Tag two rows of vertices in about 10 rows from the top edge and connecting with the left edge of tagged points. View the tagged rows in the Perspective window, and make sure they cover the visible horizon. Select **Edit|Proportional Setup**, set the Distance Limit to 15, check off Global, and click on OK. Using TAG mode, translate the tagged points up on the Y axis to a satisfactory height to give the sensation of a horizon. (See Figure 2.13.)

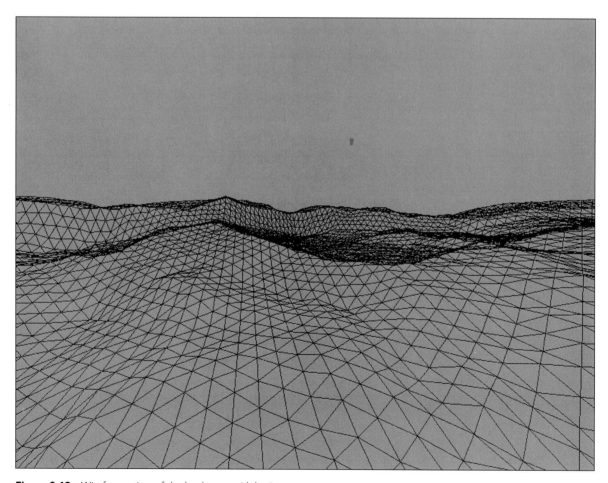

Figure 2.13   Wireframe view of the landscape with horizon.

Select the tree_tall model in the Front window. Notice where it is positioned in relation to 0 on both the X and Y axes. Whatever part of the tree is touching 0 on the X axis will be locked to any selected points on the ground. If the tree were located 10 units above 0, then all the duplicated trees would be located 10 units above their respective points on the ground mesh. By the same reasoning, if the tree were located 10 points to the left of 0 on the X axis, then all duplicated trees would be 10 points to the left of their respective ground points. Therefore, all trees, rocks, and crosses will start the project with their base centers located at 0,0. These starting objects are grouped as source_objects in the initial scene.

Duplicate Elements Of The Scene

The first objects to be placed will be duplicates of tree_tall. In the Top view, tag six random points. Then, select **Duplicate|Duplicator**, and choose Surface Vertices, Tagged Points Only, and Hierarchy. Under Jittering, check off Rotate, and set X to 0, Z to 0, and Y to .5. Select Shape, leave the X,Y,Z values at the default setting of .05, then click on OK. When queried, left-click on the ground and then on the tree_tall model. The six trees are then positioned on the ground mesh (note in the Schematic window a hierarchy of one parent and six trees has been created).

Follow the same procedure for positioning four tree_shorts and five rocks_b. Expand the Perspective window to full screen, and liberally tag numerous vertices. Scatter the points across both the foreground and background, being careful not to select points where trees or rocks have been placed. Select **Duplicate|Duplicator**, click on Merged Mesh, and click on OK. This time when

queried, left-click on the ground and then on the cross model. If you need to make changes, delete the mesh, change the tags, and use the Duplicator again. (See Figure 2.14.)

Set Up Textures

The source_objects already have both materials and textures assigned to them. Switch to **Multi** mode, deselect everything, press F4 to enter Matter mode, and rectangle-select the new tree_tall objects. Select **Txt_Oper|Copy All**, and left-click on tree_tall within the source_objects group. In the Schematic window (with Matter mode chosen), you can easily confirm the transfer of textures and materials. Preview the newly textured trees, and adjust texture settings as needed.

Deselect all (**Select|Clear**), and use the same procedure for tree_short, rocks_b, and cross (a merged object). Texturing the ground will require the use of two textures. Highlight only the ground, select **Texture|2D Global** to open the 2D Texture window, left-click on Select next to 2D Texture. Choose grass first, then left-click on the Next button, and select sand for the second texture. The sand texture is masked to allow random dirty patches to overlay the grass. This is a useful method for breaking up tiling of a texture. Make sure the repeats for the sand texture are set to 4 under both U and V, then click on OK. Preview the ground mesh with textures.

Create The Scene Background

Select **Get|Primitive|Sphere**, and in the Create Sphere window, select NURBS and Quadratic under both U and V. Uniformly scale up the sphere to include both the ground and the camera. Reverse the normals (**Effect|Inverse**) so that the sphere can

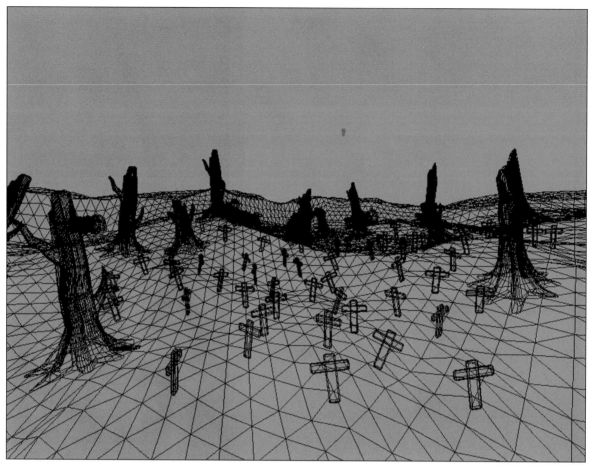

Figure 2.14 Wireframe view of the scene with duplicated elements.

be viewed from the inside. Press F4 to return to the Matter module, and select **Material**. Choose Constant (no need to worry about lighting), and under Mental Ray, check on Material Shader. Within the MR database, select the standard environmental atmosphere moon_1, which creates a dramatic nighttime moon scene on the inside of the sphere.

If you don't have Mental Ray, you can create a cloudy night sky texture in your favorite paint package and apply that as a 2D texture to the sphere.

Ambience And Layered Fog

Select **Atmosphere|Ambience**; set R to .042, G to .073, and B to 1.159; then click on OK. Select **Atmosphere|Layered Fog**, check off Layer Fog, and set Starting Distance to 20, Ending Distance to 150, Density to .04, Base to -1.0, and Thickness to 12.

The scene is now complete. As a final touch, you can unhide the distant model houses within the Schematic window. Make sure they are touching the ground of your scene. Render the final image. (See Figure 2.15.)

Wrap-Up

So ends our brief introduction to the mighty modeling tools of Softimage. Using the techniques of these first two chapters, you should be able to start churning out some great models.

Look at models for construction hints, and try to reverse engineer them so you understand how they were built. Through experi-

Figure 2.15 Final rendering of the cemetery scene.

mentation, you will come up with your own bag of tricks for constructing geometry. The more tools you have, the better prepared you'll be to handle any modeling situation. Be flexible, and try not to get trapped into modeling your objects with the same techniques over and over. A little time spent researching some of the more arcane modeling methods now could save you a lot of time in your day-to-day scene construction.

In the next chapters, we'll cover some of the application-specific tools and then move on to lights, materials, and textures.

3 MATERIALS

Key topics:

- **Shading models**

- **Local materials**

- **Material shaders**

Chapters 1 and 2 presented many tools for creating surfaces and geometry within Softimage. This chapter will examine how to apply material properties to those surfaces. Materials describe the basic physical nature of an object, such as how it reflects light and what color it is. We'll review the shading and color models provided by Softimage and quickly cover the optical properties of a material, such as transparency and refraction.

Learning about the various material properties is only part of using materials in Softimage. To deal with materials quickly and efficiently, you also need to understand how to copy materials from one object to another, how to save and restore material types, and how to apply materials to only part of an object. This chapter will cover these topics. Along the way, you'll build up some materials of your own; we'll also examine some of the materials in the Softimage material library. Finally, we'll introduce material shaders for Mental Ray.

To begin, set up the databases for this project. Press F1 to enter the Model module. Open the Database Manager by selecting **Get|DB Manager**, and move up the directory structure to the Database level. Create a new database called "chap3", and make it your default database. Link up the Chapter3 database on the CD-ROM enclosed with this book. You will load project elements from the CD-ROM and save your work to chap3.

Material Properties

All the parameters that define a material are accessed from a single dialog box called the *Material Editor*. To bring up the Material Editor, you first need an object to apply a material to. Select **Get|Primitive|Cube**, and create a cube with a side width of 1. Leave the cube highlighted, switch to the Matter module, then select **Material**. Figure 3.1 shows the dialog box for the Material Editor.

The Material Editor has a fair number of parameters, most of which should be familiar to you if you've worked with similar systems. This section is a quick review of these parameters.

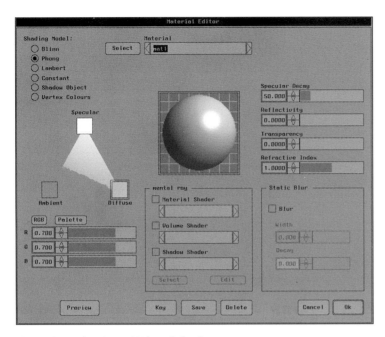

Figure 3.1 The Material Editor dialog box.

Shading Models

The shading models determine the basic look of a material. They define how a surface reacts to lights and, thereby, what the surface looks like. Is a material shiny or matte? Dull or sharp? These models aren't physically based on real-world materials, but they provide a stylistic range of appearance that allows you to create materials that look the way you want.

Softimage provides four shading models: Blinn, Phong, Lambert, and Constant. Figure 3.2 shows a model rendered with three different shading models. Selecting which is appropriate for a material you are constructing is rather simple. You need ask only two questions:

- Will the surface have specular reflections?

- Will it be shaded?

If the answer to the second question is no, you will apply the Constant shading model.

Constant surfaces don't care what direction light is coming from. Constant materials are flat and unshaded; they simply exhibit

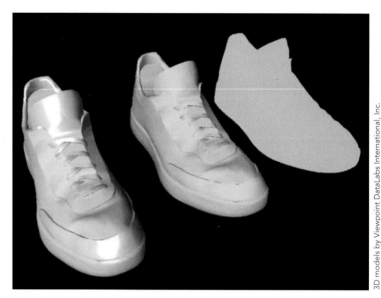

Figure 3.2 Model with Phong, Lambert, and Constant materials.

whatever color has been selected. They are not affected by lights in the scene and are rarely used in a standard scene. You can use Constant materials to create shadow maps and matte images. They are sometimes useful for creating strangely lighted or glowing-effects surfaces. Most of the materials you'll want to render, however, are shaded, meaning that their appearance is affected by the direction of the light that falls on them. Usually, you will answer yes to our second question.

The first question, however, is the main one. Do you want your material to have specular reflections? If not, Lambert is the shading model to apply. Lambert surfaces are pure diffuse reflectors. They create a perfectly matte surface, such as flat paint or a piece of dull paper. If a material doesn't have any gloss, gleam, or shininess to it, it's a Lambert material. When you start examining materials in the real world, you'll notice that very few are purely matte. So, most of the time, the answer to our first question is also yes.

That leaves two shading models to choose from: Blinn and Phong. These two shading models produce similar results. The general rule is: Always use Phong. Blinn materials produce more drastic specular highlights at grazing angles. But, the difference

SPECULARITY

A specular reflection is the glossy highlight seen on an object at the mirror angle between your line of view and a light source.

is rarely worth adding any calculations during render time. You may find Blinn shading more effective for creating metallic-looking materials. Experiment with your own models, but most of the time, you will be hard pressed to tell the difference between the two.

As mentioned previously, most materials have some specular component, so Phong becomes the shading model of choice. As you select shading models, some parameters will be grayed out. This is because a particular shading model has no need for that property. For example, if you choose Lambert, the Specular Decay parameter is no longer accessible, because the Lambert model doesn't have any specularity and won't need that parameter.

In addition to the four shading models covered here, you will see two other entries—Shadow Object and Vertex Colours—listed under shading models. These two aren't really shading models for creating material types. You can explore their use on your own.

Color Selection

The color properties of a material are crucial to defining a specific look. The color settings are a stylized representation of the spectral reflectance of a sample material. Three colors define a Phong or Blinn material: Diffuse, Specular, and Ambient. These color values are set in the Material Editor using sliders or the palette shown in Figure 3.3.

The most important term is the *Diffuse* color, which defines the actual color of the object. The second most important is the Specular color. It defines the color of the highlights on a surface. The Ambient color isn't very important as long as it is turned down toward black. High Ambient coloration will wash out a material. Start with an Ambient of black and then tune up until you get the effect you desire.

The Specular color should usually be set to match the color of the light source. For most materials, this is a good approximation. It

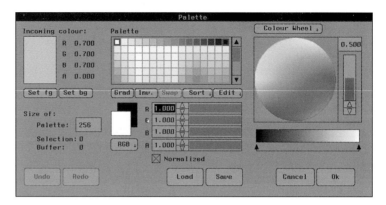

Figure 3.3 Palette dialog box.

simulates the light color bouncing off the object or being reflected off the glossy outer coating of a material. To create metallic materials, however, tune the Specular to be similar to the Diffuse color.

Optical Properties

On the upper-right side of the Material Editor dialog box, you will find four parameters: Specular Decay, Reflectivity, Transparency, and Refractive Index. These emulate some simple optical properties of the material being modeled.

Specular Decay defines how quickly a highlight on a surface will drop off. The higher the Decay, the sharper and smaller the highlight will appear on an object. Reflectivity is a measure of how mirror-like the material is. A Reflectivity of 1.0 is a perfect mirror, whereas a value of 0.0 shows no reflection.

Transparency is a measure of how "see-through" a material is. A material with Transparency of 0.0 is opaque, 0.2 somewhat translucent, 0.8 nearly see-through, and at 1.0 the object is actually invisible.

Light traveling through a semi-transparent object is bent depending on the physical nature of the medium it is passing through. This optical phenomenon is simulated with the Refractive Index. A material with a Refractive Index of 1.0 will not bend the light that passes through it; smaller or greater values will bend light. The Refractive Index of glass-like materials is around 1.2. To see through multiple layers of transparent and refractive surfaces, you

COPYING COLOR VALUES

The Diffuse, Specular, and Ambient colors can be copied from one to the other. Highlight the color to copy to, then middle-click on the color you wish to copy from. This is a quick way, for example, to make the Specular the same as the Diffuse color.

will need to increase the Ray Traced Depth. You can set this value under **Preview|Setup**; or for rendering, select **Render**, then click on the Options button to bring up the dialog box shown in Figure 3.4.

Static Blur

Static Blur is an effect that creates a glowing halo around an object. It isn't actually part of any standard model of materials, but in Softimage, it's lumped into the Material Editor, so we'll discuss it here. To turn the effect on, activate the Blur checkbox. You can then set the Width and Decay parameters. Width defines how far the effect extends from the object, and Decay sets up how quickly the effect fades away.

This effect works best with rounded objects, where the normals on a surface don't change very quickly. So, if you need a fuzzy sphere, this is your tool. Other than that, it doesn't have much utility. Figure 3.5 shows Static Blur being used to simulate a glow around the headlights of a car.

Material Operations

Building materials is one thing, using them is another. In this section, we'll examine the tools to save and reload the materials

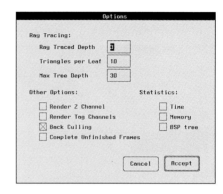

Figure 3.4 Render Setup Options dialog box.

3D models by Viewpoint DataLabs International, Inc.

Figure 3.5 Static Blur used to create glowing headlights.

GLOW

Static Blur can create some simple glowing effects. Flatten a sphere, apply a Constant color, and set the Transparency to a high value, such as 0.8. Don't let the glow sphere intersect with any other geometry.

you've created, we'll present methods for exchanging materials between objects, and we'll briefly explain how you can animate material properties.

Loading And Saving Materials

You call file operations for materials from the Material Editor. To load a material, click on the Select button. This brings up a file browser that allows you to navigate to any saved materials. Navigate to SI_material_lib and its METALS directory. Click on the Options button, and activate the Use Icons feature, if you haven't done so already. This will display thumbnail images of material samples, as shown in Figure 3.6. Highlight the copper material, and select Load. The copper material properties are loaded into the editor. You can select Preview to see how the material looks on your object.

Saving your own materials to a file is just as easy. From the Material Editor, click on the Save button. This brings up a dialog box that allows you to set the file name for the material and to select the database into which it is stored. When you select Save, the material properties are written to a file in the MATERIALS directory of the chosen database.

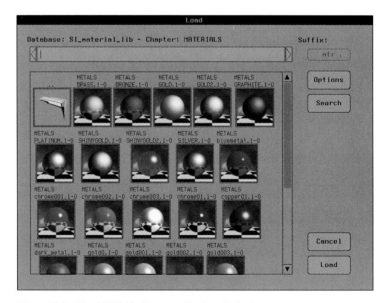

Figure 3.6 The METALS directory displayed with icons.

Copying Materials

Often, you'll want to copy the material properties of one object to another. This can be especially useful if you need to copy one material onto a number of objects at the same time.

Copying materials is a simple process, but to make it even easier, set your Schematic view to Matter mode so you can see material nodes. To copy a material, highlight the object or objects you want the material copied to, and then select **Mat_Oper|Copy Mat**. Click on the object that has the material you want to copy. That's all there is to it.

Associating Materials

Copying materials is useful, but after copying your favorite slime-green material to a dozen frog models, what if you decide the Specular Decay needs to be decreased? Because each frog has its own copy of the material, you would have to open the Material Editor for every object. Wouldn't life be better if you could somehow associate a single material with a number of objects?

To associate materials, highlight the object or objects you want to attach materials to, then select **Mat_Oper|Associate**. When prompted, click on the material you wish to associate in the Schematic view. A link will be added from the objects to the original material. You can now edit the one material, and all the objects associated with it will be affected. Likewise, you can use **Mat_Oper|Disassociate** to sever a connection between an object and an associated material. Figure 3.7 shows three objects that are associated with the same material.

If you'd like to merge a number of similar materials into one, highlight them in the Schematic view, and select **Mat_Oper|Optimize Selected**. A single material will be left associated with all the parent objects. If you don't want any redundant materials, select **Mat_Oper|Optimize All**.

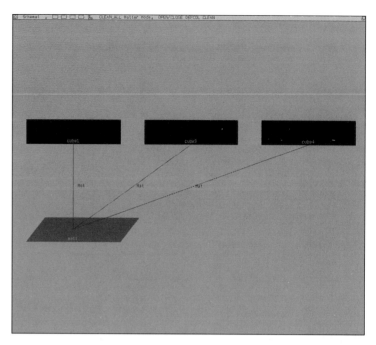

Figure 3.7 Schematic view showing material associations.

Keyframing Material Properties

Softimage is about animating, so changing materials across time is no problem. This, too, can be accomplished in the Material Editor. Move the timeline to indicate where you want to set your material keyframe. Adjust the material properties to the desired settings, and then click on the Key button.

The Key button creates a keyframe with the current material values. Continue to move the timeline, and set keyframes to animate changes in material properties. You can also press the Playback button and watch the material sliders shift from one keyframed value to the next. These keyframes actually set up function curves that can be edited with more control in the Motion module.

Local Materials

Up to this point, all the materials we have examined have been applied to an entire object. This section looks at how to use separate materials for different parts of a polygonal model. These polygon-specific materials are referred to as *local materials*.

As an example, we'll apply some local materials to a polygonal torus. Select **Get|Primitive|Torus**, and accept the default values, as shown in Figure 3.8. The torus is made up of eight segments, each with eight quadrilaterals. We will apply local materials to these polygons.

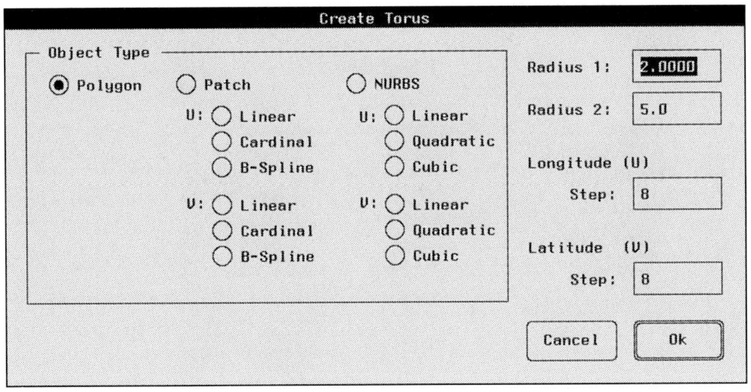

Figure 3.8   Create Torus dialog box.

Applying Local Materials

Before you can apply a local material to a polygonal model, you must assign a global material for that object. Begin by assigning a global material to the torus. Highlight the torus, select **Material**, and accept the default white; this will be the global material for the object. Now, use polygon selection tools to highlight the polygons you want to apply local materials to. (If you've never tried it, use the *g* key to raycast selected polygons.) Now with the polygons highlighted in pink, select **Polygon|Assign New Material**.

This brings up the Material Editor, where you can change the material properties of the selected polygons. Using this technique, you can create as many local materials for an object as you like. In the Schematic view, if you still have Matter mode on, you'll see that each new local material creates another material node under the parent object.

Selecting And Editing Local Materials

Now that you have applied local materials, you'll probably want to edit them. You can use a few **Polygon** commands for accessing the local materials; again, the Schematic window is very useful.

In the Schematic view, when an object is highlighted, the links to its children materials are color coded. The current material link is in red. Select **Polygon|Assign New Material** to bring up the Material Editor to make changes to the current material. To adjust which material is current, use **Polygon|Previous Material** and **Polygon|Next Material** to navigate through the available materials.

As you select various materials, the polygons associated with those materials become highlighted. This is a powerful way for quickly selecting all the polygons that are set to a particular material. You can delete materials just as you would delete regular nodes. Highlight the material, and select **Delete|Selection**; or hold down the Backspace key, and click on a material in the Schematic view. This will remove the material node, and the associated polygons will revert to the global material for that object. Figure 3.9 shows the torus with a series of local materials applied.

Material Shaders

Material shaders are functions called by Mental Ray, which apply materials to an object at render time. The material shaders provide tools for creating procedural materials in which you control the generation parameters of the material. Mental Ray will be covered more thoroughly in Chapter 7. This section covers only those features that are specific to materials.

Before starting work, you will need to set up **Preview** so that it uses Mental Ray instead of the Softimage renderer. Select **Preview|Setup**, and switch the Preview Renderer from SOFTIMAGE to Mental Ray. Then, exit Preview Setup.

OPTIMIZATION

The Mat_Oper|Optimize commands do not work when shaders are applied. So, lay out associations beforehand, or you'll have to optimize by hand.

Applying A Material Shader

You'll begin back in the Material Editor. Highlight an object you want to place a material shader on, and then select **Material**. Just below the preview area is a Mental Ray section with three

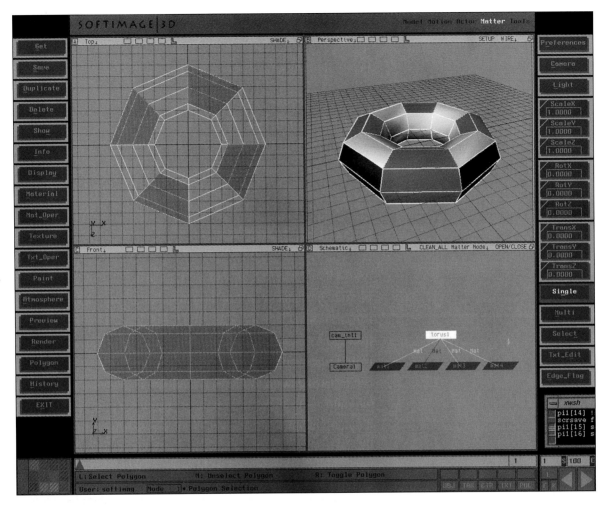

Figure 3.9 Torus with local materials.

checkboxes and type-in fields. For now, you are interested in only the Material Shader pair. Activate the Material Shader checkbox. This will bring up a file browser for you to select a shader. Navigate to the Shader_Gifts database, where you will find a number of material shaders to choose from. Load the JB_cptn_nemo shader.

The material shader is now applied to the object. Clicking on **Preview** will show you its effect. These are the default settings for the Captain Nemo shader. This particular shader creates ripple-like patterns that look like the caustics caused by light shining through a water surface. Figure 3.10 shows the Captain Nemo shader applied. The next section will examine how to modify the material shader parameters.

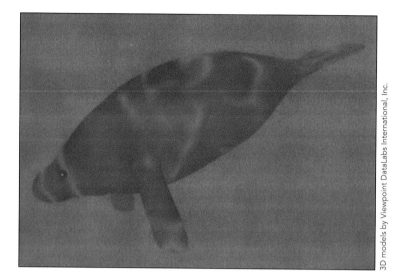

3D models by Viewpoint DataLabs International, Inc.

Figure 3.10 Character with Nemo shader applied.

Editing Shader Parameters

To change shaders or to edit a shader's parameter, click on the name of the material shader. This makes the Select and Edit buttons active. Click on the Edit button to bring up the interface for the Captain Nemo shader, as shown in Figure 3.11. These are the parameters that control the various features of the shader. Each shader will have its own interface. To get some help on what all the parameters do, click on the Info button. This will open a scrolling text window that describes the purpose and range of the shader variables. Click on OK to exit the Nemo shader parameters.

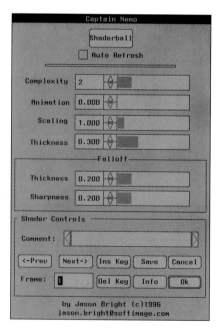

Figure 3.11 Material shader dialog box.

Shaders can provide extremely powerful functionality for creating interesting and useful materials. To explore other material shaders, click again on the file name, and then choose Select to open the file browser. Under Options in the file browser, you can turn on Use Icons to display thumbnail images of each shader. Material shaders that don't have icons will be displayed with a question-mark image. Load some of the other shaders, and play with their parameters. You will find more material shaders under the MR_Effects and Shader_Lib databases.

Wrap-Up

Materials are the foundation for creating the look of an object. The coloration and reflectance properties of a material are the key ingredients to its overall appearance. Don't settle for default material settings; hand-tune your materials to give them a distinctive appeal.

The next two chapters will deal with the other components that define the appearance of an object: texture and lighting. But remember, you can't rescue a bad material with good lighting. Spend the time it takes to get your materials looking good first.

TEXTURES 4

Key topics:

- **Local and global textures**

- **Animated textures**

- **UV mapping vs. projection**

- **Reflection maps**

Texture mapping is one of the most important components of creating synthetic imagery with Softimage. Mapping, in its simplest form, is the process of assigning a 2D image to a 3D object. The objective is to create a realistic-looking surface for the object. The correct combination of texture mapping and efficient modeling provides the most valuable use of storage, improves interactivity, and enhances the visual quality of the final rendering.

For example, if you need to create a brick wall, you can proceed in one of two ways:

- Model it from scratch, which is a substantial and time-consuming undertaking. This method requires a large amount of geometry and negatively impacts model size and interactivity.

- Use texture mapping. Often, it is this mapping that separates a great scene from a satisfactory one. Remember, just because a brick wall has a million polygons, took three days to model, and has no maps, does not mean it looks any better than a brick wall that was modeled in a few hours, using 300 or 400 polygons and a few texture maps.

Local And Global Textures

Both 2D and 3D textures support global and local mapping. Global mapping allows maps to be applied without restriction at the object level. Local mapping allows textures to be applied only to a selected group of polygons on an object. This local mapping is accomplished by linking a texture to a given material that has been applied to an object. Hence, the map becomes localized/linked to the polygons assigned to that material.

The following example shows the differences and values of a local texture mapping method. The creation of three 3D bevelled letters is the first step. Once the bevelled letters are created, you will apply a material on the bevel only. Next, you will attach a local texture map to the bevel material. The map will then be animated to produce a traveling glint effect.

Bevelled Text Construction

The Model module (F1) should be active. Select **Get|Text** to open the Text dialog box. Within the window, choose Arial Bold as the font, leave "abc" as the text, and click on OK. The 2D faces are generated in the scene. Press Shift+A to center the objects in all viewports.

Open the Schematic view, and select the hierarchy by holding down the Space bar and right-clicking on the hierarchy. Now that the text is selected, choose **Surface|Extrusion** to open the Extrusion dialog box, shown in Figure 4.1. In the open window, make sure the Object Type is set to Polygon, extrude Depth is set to 5 units, and the Axis of Extrusion is Z. Click on **Active** to turn on bevelling, set Radius to .75, and check only Top Bevelling. Close the Extrusion dialog box by clicking on OK. This will generate the new 3D objects.

Now, place the 3D text in its own hierarchy. First, deselect everything by holding down the Space bar and pressing *c*. Select the menu cell **Parent**; the cell is highlighted in purple. In the Schematic viewport, click on the three isolated (extrusion) icons, one at a time. As you select the icons, they are each placed into a hierarchy. After the last icon is added to the hierarchy, right-click to end the Parent mode. This should leave two hierarchies in the Schematic viewport. Before continuing, hide the original 2D faces by selecting them and holding down the *h* key while pressing *u*. Next, choose each letter, and name it by selecting **Info|Selection** and typing in the new name: "a" for *a*, "b" for *b*, and "c" for *c*. In the Schematic viewport, click on **Clean all**, and press *a* to center the icons.

Within the Schematic view, turn on Matter mode so you can visualize the upcoming material and texture changes. The objective is to produce three chrome letters with a different texture on the bevels than on the main body of the letter. The next step is to assign a material to each letter. You cannot assign a local material without first assigning a global material to the whole object. Therefore, before assigning a material to the bevels, you must assign a global material to the entire letter.

Make sure the Matter module (F4) is active, and toggle the Perspective view to Shading mode (open the pull-down menu at the

USE FACES FOR TEXT EXTRUDES

When extruding text, leave the default Faces selected. You should use faces for normal text extrudes, because the individual letters are treated as solids and, if necessary, solids with a hole cut out of it. For example, the letter *b* is treated as a solid with a cut-out hole; during the extrusion, the shape of the hole is maintained. In contrast, an extruded spline font would result in two objects: a *b* with no hole and an object that is shaped like the hole. This spline font would be unusable for text. You can use a spline as a path to animate a camera, light, or object around a font.

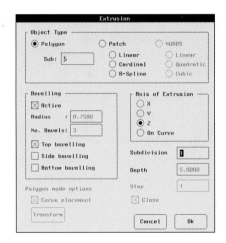

Figure 4.1 Extrusion dialog box.

top of the frame, and select Shade). Position the camera at a 45-degree viewing angle by using the *o* (orbit) and *z* (zoom/pan) supra keys. Select the letter *a* by holding down the Space bar and clicking on the letter in one of the views or the letter's icon in the Schematic view. When selected, the letter *a* turns white.

Next, choose **Material** to open the Material Editor window, and click on **Select** at the top of the window. This opens the Load window, which lists the material databases. Locate and open the SI_material_lib database. Once inside, click on **Options**, and make sure **Use icons** is checked. Once the screen is full of icons, find and select one of the chrome materials. This loads that material into the Material Editor. Click on OK to select the default settings. This should bring the user back to the main screen with a chrome assigned to *a*. Note the blue icon is attached to the *a* icon in the Schematic view.

Now, you can transfer the material to the other letters. Select **Multi** from the menu. Once in **Multi** mode, make sure that only *b* and *c* are selected. Select **Mat_Oper|Copy Mat**, then select either the object *a* or its icon, and the material will be copied from *a* onto both *b* and *c*. Right-click to end **Material Copy** mode, and select **Single** to return to **Single** mode. **Mat_Oper** is not highlighted when **Copy Mat** is active, which is somewhat confusing, but **Copy Material** is displayed next to **Mode** (on the bottom command line), indicating that the **Copy Mat** mode is active.

The next step is to assign a second local material to the bevels, using polygon tools in the Matter module. To start, select only the letter *a*. In the top viewport, press the *f* key to center the letter within the viewport. Choose **Polygon|Select by Rectangle** (or use the *y* supra key), and drag a bounding box over the front of the letter, turning the bevel and front face pink (Softimage depicts selected polygons as pink). For this part of the project, only the bevels need to be selected. You should work in the top viewport to change the selection status of the front face. This face can be deselected by pressing the *y* supra key and dragging a box over the front face, while holding down the middle mouse button (see Figure 4.2).

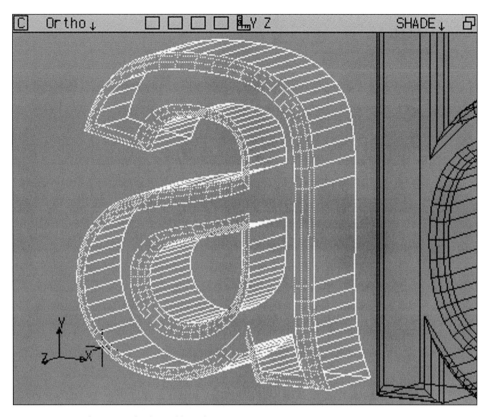

Figure 4.2 Ortho view of selected bevels.

As usual, Softimage provides an alternative mechanism for accomplishing this deselecting task—Raycasting. You may find this method easier to use when deselecting the front face of the letter *a*. Choose **Polygon|Select by Raycasting**, or hold down the *g* supra key. In the Front viewport, middle-click on the face of *a* (remember, middle-clicking deselects). This should deselect the front face, leaving only the bevels selected.

With the bevels selected, choose **Polygon|Assign New Material** to open the Material Editor. Once again, click on **Select** to open the materials library and the Metals directory. Choose a material that is slightly different from that on the body of the letter. Once you have selected the material, you are returned to the Material Editor. To make sure all is well, press the **Preview** button. This opens a quick render, which should show a slightly different bevel than the main part of the object. Click on OK to accept the settings, then repeat the procedure for letters *b* and *c*.

At this point, each letter has been assigned two different materials. The objective is to find a way to work on each material selectively, independent of the other. You can do this in a few different ways. One way is to toggle the open/close icon in the upper right of the Schematic viewport to on (red). This means any selected icon will have its Info dialog box opened (bypassing the **Info|Selection** step). In the present case, clicking on a Material icon will open the Material Editor. The problem with this method is the confusion involved in deciding which polygons go with which material. Opening the Material or Texture dialog boxes in this manner also does not allow for previewing from within the main dialog box.

Softimage handles this problem by allowing the user to toggle or step through all the materials or textures assigned to a given object. First, select the whole hierarchy by holding down the Space bar and right-clicking on any of the children of the hierarchy. This action will highlight the icons in the Schematic viewport. Upon closer examination of the hierarchy, you will notice that the links connecting the object icons to the material and texture icons are different colors. These colors represent the current (red) versus noncurrent (yellow) material or texture. The difference between these two is that the current (red) is the material or texture that actively opens in the Material Editor dialog box, within the Matter module (allowing for full editing capability). Another way to think of the current material (or the current texture) is as a marker or pointer in the string of materials. This also fits with the way Softimage uses the **Polygon|Next Material** and **Polygon|Previous Material** stepping or toggling functions.

Animated Textures

The next step in the project is to put an animated texture on the bevelled part of the text. Therefore, you need to select the material that will be the parent to the local texture via the **Polygon|Next|Previous** menus.

While in **Single** mode, select the letter *a*. Alternate between **Polygon|Next Material** and **Polygon|Previous Material**. When the bevels turn pink and the materials link is red, then the bevels material is current. At this point, you're ready to add a local texture that will affect only the bevels. Select **Texture|2D Local** to open the 2D Texture File window.

The Glint Map

The next objective is to add movement in your text bevels via a glint passing across the front of the text. You will use a white picture with a vertical black bar running down the middle of the image. Under Picture Filename, select the picture named "glint.pic," located in the abc database under the Picture directory. This loads glint.pic into the Texture Editor.

Now, you want to set up the picture to pass across the front of the letter *a*. This requires the map to travel along the object's local X axis. Under Mapping method, select XY coordinates, and enter 2 under U in both the Repeats and Scale fields. This sets up the projected map to run parallel to the front of the object on its local XY axis (see Figure 4.3). More specifically, these values will repeat the picture twice along the X axis, and the new scale will enlarge the projector by a factor of 2, also along its X axis. The effect will appear to be two pictures sitting side by side in front of the object,

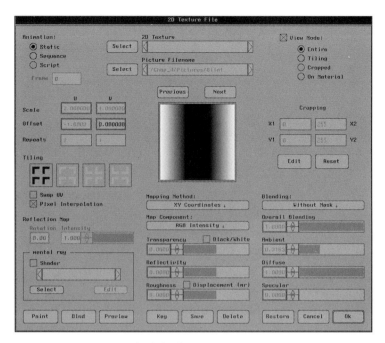

Figure 4.3   2D Texture File dialog box.

the letter *a*. To view the settings graphically, click on OK to get out of the dialog box and return to the main screen.

At the main screen, click on TXT to put Softimage into Texture mode. Select **Texture|2D Local** to inform Softimage that the local rather than global textures will be edited. The **Previous** and **Next** buttons serve the same function as the **Previous** and **Next** buttons in the Material Editor discussed in Chapter 3. These functions, however, act on textures.

In the Front viewport, two red squares should appear in front of the letter *a*. This is the way Softimage represents the applied map to that object. Each square is a copy of glint.pic. Normally, both squares would fit within the extent of the selection it was applied to. In this case, however, the image was scaled by a factor of 2 along the X axis, prior to exiting the Texture dialog box (see Figure 4.4). You can confirm this by looking at the **ScaleX** menu cell in the upper right of the screen. The scaling could also have been performed in the **ScaleX** cell with the benefit of visual feedback. Try changing the **ScaleX** value, and notice how the map-projecting icon changes in size. In fact, all the XY transformation tools

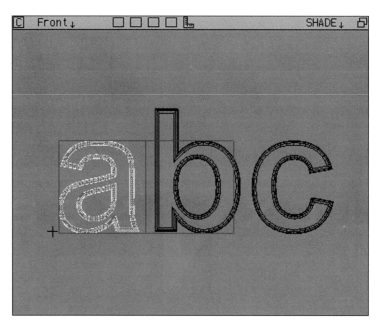

Figure 4.4 TXT Mode and Scaled Mapping icons.

work on the icon as if it were any other object. One point to remember, however, is that **History|Undo** does not function with these transformations.

UV Coordinates

The U and V coordinates in the Texture dialog box are variables representing the 2D horizontal and vertical orientation of the map. Generally, U is horizontal, and V represents the vertical axis. For example, in our project, we selected the map to be projected on the XY projection plane of the object. In this case, the U coordinate represents the X axis. If you projected on the side of the object, mapping coordinates would have to be assigned to the YZ projection plane. In this case, the U coordinate would represent the Z axis, and the V coordinate would handle the Y axis. Also, in certain procedural shaders, a W is sometimes used to refer to the far/near axis. You often see this in shaders using 3D or volumetric effects.

Animating The Glint Map

The desired effect requires an animation of the glint map moving across the object. The map already appears to have moved to the right, across the face of the object, to the end position. Therefore,

---

ANIMATION AND THE RIGHT MOUSE BUTTON

Using the right mouse button freezes everything as it is prior to dragging the pointer. For example, suppose the pointer was at Frame 70, with an attached animation. Subsequently, dragging the pointer to Frame 100 (while depressing the right mouse button) would cause the object to have the same attitude found at Frame 70. Essentially, this function allows you to copy whatever is happening at Frame 70 to Frame 100, or any other frame for that matter. This is a useful and easily overlooked feature.

placing a keyframe on the last frame of the animation makes this the position for the map at the end of the animated sequence. Accept the default of 100 frames, and drag the frame pointer to the last frame while holding the right mouse button.

At this point, you have to set the keyframe to instruct the software that the object assumes this attitude at Frame 100. Select **Texture|2D Local** to open the 2D Texture File dialog box. The dialog box should open on the current local texture. If this is not the case, toggle between the materials, until the material with the attached local texture is the current (red link) material. Press the *k* key, and click OK to return to the main screen.

Depress the right mouse button, and drag the frame pointer to Frame 1. Within the **TransX** menu cell, enter the value -1.0. This should move the icon 1 repeat to the -X (see Figure 4.5). You could also drag the icon there using the left mouse button.

At this time, the right square (repeat of the icon) should cover the *a* at Frame 1. It is time to set another keyframe. Once again, select **Texture|2D Local**, and press the *k* key to set the keys at Frame 1. The basic animation should now be complete. Confirm

> ## MOUSE CONTROL IN TXT MODE
>
> When in TXT mode, all Scales, Rotations, and Transformations are performed in local space. Therefore, the left mouse button controls the X axis, and the middle mouse button controls the Y axis.

Figure 4.5 Mapping icon movement via TransX.

this while still in the 2D Texture File dialog box. Left-click on the frame pointer, and slowly drag the pointer between Frame 1 and Frame 100. Notice the U value of the offset changes as the pointer is moved. These offset values represent the projecting icons being dragged across the front of the letter *a*. For the skeptics in the audience, confirm by clicking on OK to return to the main screen. Left-click on the frame pointer, and drag the pointer. Notice the icon moving along the X axis.

Copying Maps And Animations

The final steps for this project are to copy the map and animations to the other letters. Select each letter, one at a time, and, by using **Polygon|Next Material** or **Polygon|Previous Material**, make sure the bevelled polygons are highlighted and materials are current (red link). The object is to copy current to current. Therefore, make sure the same polygon sets and materials are current on both objects. Now, select *b* (make sure the bevelled polygons are pink), choose **Txt_Oper|Copy_all**, and click on the letter *a* at the prompt. In the Schematic window, a small *a* should appear next to the blue texture icon under the *b* bevelled material icon. This indicates that the texture represented by this icon is, in fact, animated. Repeat the same copy procedure for the letter *c*.

To check that the setup is correct, you must first select the whole hierarchy (Space bar and right-click on hierarchy). Because you are in TXT mode, you should see all the relevant projection icons. Once again, left-click on the frame pointer, and drag the pointer. All the icons should be translating along the X axis in response to the pointer movement.

Render A FlipBook

To render a low-resolution version and a flipbook, select **Render** to open the Render Setup dialog box, and set a resolution of 200 by 169. Choose the renderer to use in the Rendering Type field, select the database to store the pictures in by clicking on **Db List**, and give the frames a name under Filename. You can also set antialiasing, motion blur, and other render options at this stage. Once all is set, click on **Render sequence** to begin the render. After the renderer is finished, enter the Tools module (F5), and select **FlipBook** to open the FlipBook dialog box. Once in the FlipBook dialog box, enter the values of 1 to 100 for the number of frames, and set the step value to 1. The frames per second should be set to 10 or 15 for a slow playback speed. Now, navigate to the picture location, and click on one of the pictures. Set the X and Y zoom values to 2, which will enlarge the playback by a factor of 2. Click on OK to exit the window, and wait as the frames are loaded into memory. Once loaded, they will play back at the rate of 10 or 15 frames per second.

You should see a classic animation of chrome text with subtle movement occurring in the bevels of the letters. There are countless variations on this theme, but this is the foundation of 90 percent of all shiny metal logos broadcast in the past 10 years. Add a few moving colored lights and a lens flare, and you'll have a decent, semi-professional-looking logo in no time.

Global Texturing

Now, let's examine some of the features of global texturing. Switch to the Matter module (F4), and activate **Single** mode. Choose **Get|Scene**, and select "pic_frame" from the abc database. The scene contains a hierarchy called "curves", which contains the frame X-section (source curve) and the path (frame_path) that was used as the extrusion path. The other hierarchy contains a grid (your canvas) and two frames (one hidden and one visible), a cube on the center surrounded by a sphere, and a few more hidden elements.

The Perspective viewport should be in Shading mode. At the top of the Perspective window, click on **Setup** to open the Shade View Setup window. In the dialog box, check off Enable Hardware Texture and Affected Models/All. Accept the default values for the rest of the options in the setup dialog box, and click on OK to return to the main menu. Select the grid by holding down the Space bar and left-clicking on the grid. Select **Texture|2D Global** to open the 2D Texture File window. Click on the **Select** box under Picture Filename, and choose abc/pictures/CITIES. Select the black-and-white picture of London, which should now be visible in the dialog box. Select **Preview** to make sure the grid with the attached London image renders.

Cropping

Softimage allows a certain amount of cropping at application time, an extremely useful feature. The Texture Editor has two methods of cropping maps. The first method requires nothing more than dragging the borders of the View window to isolate the section of the map to be placed on the model. For example, too much water and sky is showing on the canvas. Normally, this would require a trip to a paint program for a cropping session. In Softimage, the cropping feature allows you to adjust the image frame and crop off any desired section. Pull the top frame down about a quarter of the way. Grab the bottom frame, and pull it up over the water to crop off this section. Select **Preview**. With the new orientation, the image is stretched vertically to compensate for the cropped sections of the image. Middle-click to cancel the preview.

Now, try cropping out everything but the tower on the left. Again, push and pull the bounding frame in the center viewport to frame the tower. Select **Preview**, and notice how the tower is full frame.

For finer control over your cropping process, use the second cropping method, and click on the **Edit** pad just to the right of the Texture Editor viewport. This function creates a full-size viewport (Cropping Utilities window) for performing the cropping, as shown in Figure 4.6. Within the Cropping Utilities window, you have three view modes to choose from:

- *Unscaled*—You will need to pan around if the image is too large or squint if the image is too small.

- *Entire*—The image is scaled to fill the Cropping Utilities viewport.

- *Cropped*—This fills the viewport with the cropped portion of the image.

Another interesting function is the ability to save the cropped map as a picture by clicking on **Save Pic**. Also, selecting **Accept** transfers any crop information from the Cropping Utilities window back to the center viewport of the 2D Texture File window. For now, set the bounding frame back to accept the full picture.

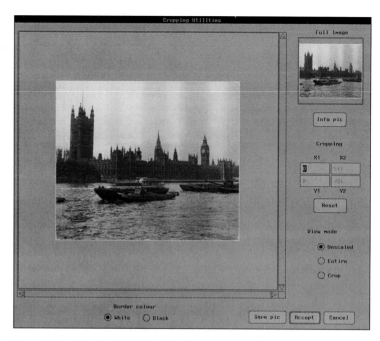

Figure 4.6   Cropping Utilities dialog box.

Blending

Blending determines how the current map will composite over the preceding map. If the current map is the first map, then blending determines how the map will composite over the material. To help visualize this process, check out how the current map is interacting with the material (it blends with the material because there is only one map). Select **On Material** under View mode, which is the way Softimage allows the user to view texture compositing on material. The grid material has green assigned to its Ambient component, blue to its Diffuse component, and red to its Specular component. This color scheme should help to explain how components are interacting.

Blending Without A Mask

The default for **Blending** is **Without Mask**. This setting simply means that the whole RGB part of the map/image is applied to the object. Notice how the whole image is visible. The same is true if you preview the grid as well.

CROPPING AND MULTIPLE MAP STORAGE

The main advantage of this feature is the ability to try different crops without committing to one in particular—the original image is left untouched. You could store multiple maps on one pic. Although this makes things tidy, it's not advised. Softimage still needs to load the whole pic for each map, and duplicates can use a lot of memory.

Blending With RGB Intensity Mask

When used as a compositing filter, a mask (a gray-scale image) determines which parts of the RGB portion of the image will be opaque or transparent. The opaque areas (usually represented by the white areas of the mask) block the underlying RGB values. The transparent sections (represented by the dark areas of the mask) allow whatever is under the current image to show though.

Click on the **Blending** pull-down menu, and select **RGB Intensity Mask**. Note that some portions of the image become more transparent to the preceding map, or in this case, to the material, because this map is first. Under these settings, a mask is being created from the RGB values of the image. In other words, the darker the given pixel is, the more the transparency increases. The brighter the pixels, the more opaque that section of the image becomes.

Blending With Alpha Channel Mask

Click on **Blending**, and select **Alpha Channel Mask**. An alpha channel is simply a gray-scale mask attached to an image file. This mask is usually represented as an *A* residing next to the RGB channel description, producing the RGBA channel description. In this case, notice that the sky is no longer visible, allowing the first layer—the material—to show through.

Overall Blending

Overall Blending is a slider that controls the total amount of opacity of the current map. In our example, try bringing down the Overall Blending to .5, and note the effect with the different Mask options. The total opacity is reduced by 50 percent. In other words, the parts of the image that used to render 100 percent opaque are now rendering 50 percent opaque.

Under Overall Blending are the sliders controlling the visibility level of the current map, as applied to the Ambient, Diffuse, and Specular (ADS) components of the selected object. You can see

BLENDING WITH ALPHA MASKS VS. TRANSPARENCY

Do not confuse blending and alpha masks with a transparency map. A transparency map controls the opacity of the object it is applied to. Blending controls only the current map's visibility in relation to previously applied maps or materials on an object. Overall Blending serves the same purpose as the Opacity slider in the Layers dialog box in Photoshop 4. It controls the visibility of the layer it is attached to, relative to the other layers in the sandwich, or stack.

this with the tricolor ball: green (Ambient) reflects the ambient light in the scene; blue (Diffuse) reflects direct light; and red (Specular) reflects the highlights or specular components.

Specular

For our example, set the three sliders to 0. Starting with the Specular slider (because it is the most obvious), bring it up to 1. The area of the object where the specular highlight is being generated is now using the map to generate the highlight. The map is replacing the red values set in the Material Editor. The values of the map directly under the Specular can also determine the shape of the highlight. This can be demonstrated by selecting **Alpha Channel Mask** under **Blending**. Notice how the building tops are cutting into the red highlight.

Next, choose **Without Mask**, and bring the Specular slider down to a value of .01. The highlight is pretty much cut out where the map is. This occurs because the map value of .01 determines the amount of specular highlight on the object. Now, set the slider to 0, and the Specular slider returns to the original settings of the Material Editor. This happens because Softimage completely removes a component of the map when faced with a value of zero.

Diffuse

Try moving around the Diffuse slider. At zero, despite Blending being at 1, no map components show on the preview ball. Also, as soon as the slider is not 0 (.0001), the map is present but reflects a value of only .0001 and, therefore, is very dark. Finally, the Specular component (on the preview ball) is taken from the preceding layer.

Because this is the first layer, it is taken from the material. To sum up, the Specular and Ambient components of the preview ball are coming from the RGB material, while the map is supplying the Diffuse components to the ball.

Ambient

Return Diffuse to zero to examine the Ambient slider. As the slider value increases, the image produced on the preview ball acquires a flat, bluish tint. Remember, the Ambient component of light is nondirectional. More specifically, it hits all parts of the object with equal intensity. This will produce a flat, evenly lit image. The blue tint is a result of Diffuse being set to zero, which means that the preceding layer or material is supplying the Diffuse component of the preview ball. Return Ambient to zero.

This idea of zero meaning pass-through is often overlooked, confused, or just ignored. The concept is the basis of having multiple maps serving different functions. For example, suppose you want to use a checkered map for specular highlights on the rendered object, as well as the current city image. Remember, the city map would act as Ambient and Diffuse. To accomplish this, increase the Diffuse and Ambient sliders in the city map, and set Specular to zero. These actions produce the red specular from the material. Layer another map (checkered) on top of this one. In the new Texture dialog box, set Diffuse and Ambient to zero, which allows the city layer to pass through. Set Specular to 1, which inserts the Specular component of the current (checker) map into the mix. The result is not pretty, but once you get used to it, it's workable.

Transparency, Reflectivity, And Roughness

The maps used in these components—transparency, reflectivity, and roughness (TRR)—are never actually seen. They act as a kind of mask to control some of the basic surface functions. Full white in an alpha channel means full Transparency, Reflectivity, and Roughness under that area of the map, while full black alpha means zero Transparency, Reflectivity, and Roughness under that area of the map. Before that can happen, however, these maps/images must be converted into something Softimage can understand.

The controls for this are under Mapping Component. RGB Intensity, the default, simply takes the current map and internally converts it to a gray scale (without some planning here, you could end up with unexpected results). The second and preferred type is alpha channel. As previously discussed, this ignores the RGB components of your map and uses the alpha channel information, if present. All images do not contain alpha information, so be wary of the types of images you use.

Another more obvious difference between the middle column of Transparency, Reflectivity, Roughness and the right column of Ambient, Diffuse, Specular in the Texture dialog box is that the middle column (TRR) sliders allow for negative as well as positive values to be entered.

One area of similarity is that Blend Control has control over the TRR as well as the ADS functions. Reducing the Blend Control value will reduce the effect of the Transparency, Reflectivity, and Roughness sliders. Dragging any of the Transparency, Reflectivity, and Roughness sliders to the left of zero simply inverts the map. From that point, it simply behaves as normal, though inverted. Dragging these sliders off zero and to the right causes them to behave in the same manner as the ADS sliders.

Transparency

A setting of zero causes the map to have no effect at all on the object. If the current texture is the first texture in the stack, the transparency of the object will be determined by the transparency settings of the material. If the current texture is farther up the layer stack, transparency will be determined by the first non-zero texture or the material transparency setting.

A 1 setting takes the brightest values of an RGB map or the white of an alpha channel and renders the parts of the object under these areas of the map transparent. As before, the settings of the preceding layer or material are lost as soon as the slider is moved off zero. A -1 setting takes everything under the darkest values of an RGB intensity map or the black of an alpha map and renders them transparent.

When checked, the Black/White checkbox above the slider treats everything on the map as if it were either black or white—in other words, no grays. Hence, the rendered object is either full transparent or full opaque.

Try setting the Ambient, Diffuse, and Specular values to zero to take them out of the equation. This leaves your texture acting as a solo transparency map. Now, set the Map Component to alpha. Because this map has an alpha channel, the alpha channel option is active in the pull-down menu. Without an alpha channel in the current map, the alpha channel option would be grayed out and unavailable to select. Just experiment with different settings of the Transparency slider, and try to get a feel for how things change. Then, try the following example:

Set Blending to RGB Intensity; Overall Blending to 1; Ambient, Diffuse, and Specular values to 0; Map Component to alpha channel; and the Transparency slider to 1. Select **Preview**. Try loading multi_pict from the abc database as an example of multicomposite mapping.

Reflectivity

Reflectivity works the same as Transparency, in that a setting of zero removes the slider from the whole mix. A 1 setting takes the brightest values of an RGB map or the white of an alpha channel and renders the parts of the object under these areas of the map to allow full reflectivity. As noted before, the settings of the preceding layer or material are lost as soon as the slider is moved off zero.

A -1 setting takes everything under the darkest values of an RGB Intensity map or the black of an alpha map and renders them transparent. Try experimenting with this slider as well.

Roughness

Once again, a setting of 0 removes the whole slider from the mix. A 20 setting takes the brightest values of an RGB Intensity map or the white of an alpha channel and renders the parts of the object under these areas of the map to allow full deflection into the object. The shape of the image appears to be carved or gouged out of the object it is applied to.

A -20 setting takes everything under the darkest values of an RGB Intensity map or the black of an alpha map and renders the image on the map to appear as if it is set in relief on the object.

Roughness has another unique feature: For some reason, this is the only slider in the group that is *not* controlled by the Blend slider. Try it.

2D Texture File Animation

Another aspect of the Texture Editor is the Animation section in the upper-left corner of the 2D Texture File dialog box. These simple controls are:

- *Static*—The default, used whenever the user has a single, nonanimated map to use.

- *Sequence*—Allows you to use an animated sequence for a map.

- *Script*—Gives you complete control in a totally noninteractive way. You simply write a list of the frames you want to play in sequential order.

Reflection Maps

The last part of the interface is the Reflection map area (right above the Mental Ray box). Reflection maps are normally used when there is no real background to reflect onto the object. You can also use these maps when you want more control over what is reflected or want to avoid the speed hit of raytracing. In general, the software calculates a spherical projection of the map onto the object that is supposed to be reflecting its surroundings.

Objects with slowly changing normals are better candidates for reflection mapping. To see an example, exit the Texture dialog box, and choose **Delete All**. Load the scene "Ref_map," and select the **Preview** button. Both objects have the same map applied to it. Notice the difference between the top and bottom objects.

One extremely cool feature of Softimage is the Raytraced Reflection Map. This allows you to mix a raytraced reflection with a reflection map. To see an example, make sure both objects are selected, and open the 2D_Global Texture Editor. Under Mapping Method, change to Raytraced Reflection Map. Now, render the scene again, only this time note the reflection of the cube on top of the sphere. At times, it allows you to avoid placing a centerpiece inside an environment, to get real-looking reflections. With this feature, you can sometimes have just a few recognizable objects reflecting off

the main object, while an indistinct reflection map fills in the blanks.

UV Vs. Projection

Clear everything, and reload the scene "Pic_Frame." Select the frame and choose **Matter|Texture|2D_Global**. Select **Preview**, and note that the wooden texture gives the appearance of an unbroken wooden map traveling around the frame. A UV is the reason for this unbroken appearance. UVs are the glue that attaches a map to an object. A UV mapping method is the only way you can get a map to deform with an object. For example, say you have a carpet or blanket and you want it to be asymmetrical, showing a little deformation. You'll quickly find that when you start deforming the carpet, the map remains rectilinear. In other words, it does not deform with the object it is assigned to. This is obviously a problem with projecting maps onto objects.

What if the software could remember which area of the map is over a given vertex or face, and maintain that relationship at all times? Then as a vertex is moved, it would drag that portion of the map along with it. That would solve the problem. Let's take a look at that very situation and how to solve it.

Load "Carpet" from the abc database. Both these models, Carpet_Left and Carpet_Rt, have a map of a carpet applied to them with an XY projection. Enter the Matter module (F4), and click on **Preview** to see a correct rendering. Now, hold down the *m* supra key, and round the edges of the carpet on the left side by pushing points around in the front viewport. Try to deform Carpet_Lf to see the effect.

If you run into problems, you will find another object hidden under the left grid called "Carpet_Lf_Deformed" that is already deformed. With the left grid (Carpet_Lf_Clean) selected, hold the *h* key down while pressing the *u* key. This will hide the currently selected object, Carpet_Lf_Clean. Open the Schematic viewport, select the icon named "Carpet_Lf_Deformed," hold down *h*, and press *u* to unhide it, as shown in Figure 4.7. At this point, you should have a distorted grid on the left and a clean grid on the right (Carpet_Rt_Clean). Go ahead and preview. Notice that the grid is deformed, but the map is not. In fact, when the grid is pulled outward, in some places you have no map at all. This demonstrates the problem with projected maps not using UV coordinates.

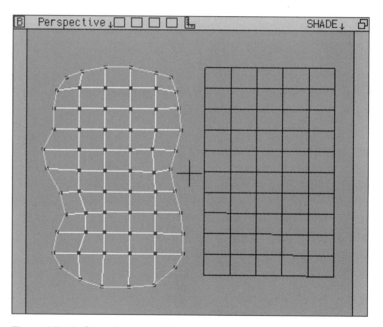

Figure 4.7 Deformed carpet grid.

The objective now is to stick the map to the vertices of the clean grid, with the carpet texture on it. This will allow us to deform the grid and have the map deform as well. Select the grid on the right side (Carpet_Rt_Clean). Make sure **Single** mode is active, and select **Textures|2D_Global** to open the 2D Texture File window. Under Mapping Methods, notice that it reads "XY Coordinates", and click on OK to exit the Texture dialog editor. Now, choose

Txt_OperInfo UV Coord (2D Global). This is how Softimage converts projected non-UV maps to projected ones. Note the blue text at the bottom of the screen, stating "Projection Method will be converted to UV (nonwrapped)". Click on OK to exit. This completes the conversion and sticks the map to the object. Click on **Texture|2D_Global** to open the Texture dialog box, and, note under Mapping Methods, it now shows "UV Coordinates". At this point, click on OK to return to the main screen.

To prove the map is actually stuck to the object, start deforming the object. Hold down the *m* (move point) supra key and round the edges of the carpet on the left by pushing points around in the front viewport. Once again, significantly deform Carpet_Rt_Clean to see the effect. A deformed object is hidden under Carpet_Rt_Clean, called "Carpet_Rt_Deformed." Use the same procedure, as stated earlier, to swap Carpet_Rt_Clean with Carpet_Rt_Deformed via the hide/unhide command. At this point, you should have distorted grids on both sides, showing the differences when rendered. Choose **Preview**, and notice how the grid on the right is deformed and the applied map is deformed in the same manner.

Spline/NURBS And UV Coordinates

As previously stated, users can convert a projected XY or cylindrical map into a UV map. That will not help, however, with objects that are already deformed prior to the map application. For example, examine the previous picture frame. The objective is to have the wood texture wrap around the frame in one continuous map. Accomplishing this on a polygon (no UVs) would be difficult. You

would have to start out with a straight plank, assign the XY map, convert to UVs, and, finally, bend the plank into a square.

An easier way would be to take advantage of the Spline/NURBS UV coordinates. Most NURBS and spline surfaces have UVs applied at the time they are created. Take the previously mentioned picture frame as an example. To create the frame, you could extrude a square around a larger, square curve. Rather than selecting polygons (objects that do not remember how they were made) as the output from the extruder, select linear NURBS or splines, as shown in Figure 4.8. This would give the same look as polygons and already contain the UV information needed for the map to follow the contours. When the map is assigned, therefore, the wood will appear to bend around the corners of the frame.

This effect can be exploited in ways that allow you to create animations that otherwise could not be done. By animating the U, V, or W, you can force maps to travel down an object, as if the maps were tracking the contours exactly. How about milk traveling up a looping straw or a signature being created out of thin air? The signature could be created by a blue UV map scaling along the V of an object. This object would be extruded along a curve that resembles a signature. The pen would then use that same curve as an animation path. The only tricky part is timing the pen to track in front of the expanding map.

With some transparency maps, you can get all kinds of things flying around in a way that otherwise would be very difficult to do. You could produce animations with hundreds of little glass tubes, each with a burst of fire traveling down its length in cycling patterns. You could create blue

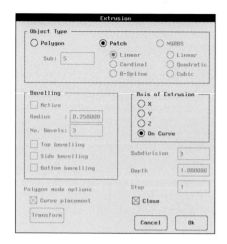

Figure 4.8 Extrusion dialog box.

glows traveling around the base of a spacecraft or disembodied bursts of plasma flying down a cyberspace tunnel. There are endless uses for this type of animation.

Examples Of Multiple Map Layers

In this section, we'll run through some samples of using layered textures. Once you get used to mixing textures, you'll rarely find yourself using only one.

Shadow Box

Retrieve the scene "Shadow_Box" from the abc database. The object of this exercise is to apply three maps globally to the center cube. Make sure the cube is selected, and choose **Textures|2D_Global** to open the 2D Texture File window. Click on **Select**, click on the image "stainglas4," and set the Mapping Method to XY coordinates. Because the material is 100 percent transparent, if you leave the Transparency slider set to 0, the texture will inherit characteristics from the previous layer or material, which in this case, is 100 percent transparent. Therefore, move the slider .001 to the right. This will make the map pretty much opaque. Click on OK to exit the dialog box, and return to the main screen.

Enter TXT mode by clicking on the **TXT** pad on the bottom-right section of the screen. A square red icon should become visible in front of the cube, representing the current map. Press the x key to enter Scale mode. While depressing the left and middle mouse buttons, move the mouse until the icon scales down to fit over the inner box (somewhere around .8, .8, 0), as shown in Figure 4.9.

The next step is to position the cube for better viewing. Return to Object mode by clicking on the OBJ pad on the mode selection panel. Notice that the map icon disappears. Press the c key to enter Rotate mode, and rotate 45 degrees on the Y axis. This is accomplished by holding down the middle mouse button and moving the mouse until 45 is showing in the RotY box (it doesn't need to be exact).

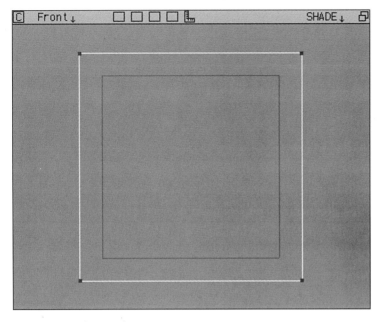

Figure 4.9 Adjusting the TXT mapping icon.

Choose **Texture|2D_Global**, and click on the **Next** pad. Now, select the picture "stainglas3," and make sure the XZ mapping coordinates are active. Using XZ will put this map at a 90-degree angle to the first map. The new map will be positioned on top of the cube.

This second map also has an alpha channel. You can use the channel to make the white borders disappear. Under **Blending**, select **Alpha Channel Mask** from the pull-down menu. As with the last texture, make sure to nudge the Transparency slider off of 0. Select **Preview** to check that the circle map is on top and the white borders are gone. Click on OK to exit to the main screen and go into TXT mode. Use the same procedure on the second texture as was used on the first, to scale the icon down to .8, .8, 0.

One more time, select **Texture|2D_Global**, and click on **Next**. This action adds a third texture to the stack. Now, select the pic "stainglas2," and make sure the YZ mapping coordinates are active. Using YZ will put this map at a 90-degree angle to the first map and place it on the side of the cube.

Once again, move the Transparency slider off zero to .001 to make the map solid. Also, position the face standing upright by swapping the U and V. Perform this function by clicking on **Swap UV** to swap the horizontal with the vertical of the map. Note that the map is now right-side-up. Before exiting to the main screen to scale the map icon down, do a quick preview.

The new map overlaps the other textures. Local textures are not being used, so nothing is keeping the applied textures from overlapping. This is why scaling the icons down in size is important. Because there is no limit to the number of textures you can place on one surface, you need to preview the project repeatedly.

Click on OK, and exit to the main screen. Make sure that TXT mode is still active. The map you want to scale was the current texture in the editor prior to the exit. Therefore, that map is active and current, or, phrased differently, the mapping icon belongs to that texture. Enter Scale mode, scale down the texture icon to .8, .8, 0, and select **Preview**.

Animating The Shadow Box

The next task is to attach an animation to the cube that causes it to rotate around the Y axis. Enter the Motion module (F2), select OBJ mode, and set the frame pointer at Frame 1. Select **SaveKey|Object|Rotation|Y** to set an animation key. This key says that whenever Frame 1 appears, the cube is in its current Y-axis position. Middle-click on the Frame End Field (E), and enter a value of 300. Slide the pointer to Frame 300, and type 720 into the **RotY** field. Middle-click on **SaveKey** to create another key. Remember, middle-clicking on a menu cell repeats the last entered command. In this case, the command was **Object|Rotation|Y**. Click on the Play arrow to make sure the cube

spins around the Y axis and returns to the Matter module (F4).

Txt_Edit Previous And Next

Open the Schematic viewport, and examine the material/texture links to the cube. Recall that the red link signifies an active or current texture or material. Choose **Txt_Edit**, and notice that **Previous** and **Next** are options in the pull-down menu. These functions act the same on textures as **Polygon|Previous Material** and **Polygon|Next Material** act on materials.

Remember, the last texture added was "staingls2", and "staingls3" was the name of the picture used in that particular texture. Because no name was given to the texture, Softimage named it—in this case, "t2d8" (which means texture, 2D, number 8). Select **Txt_Edit|Previous**, and notice that the mapping icon has changed to the XZ (top) icon. Click on **Txt_Edit|Previous** again to see the mapping icon cycle to the XY (front) icon. Within the Schematic viewport, the red link connecting the current texture to the cube is also cycling through the various textures. Remember, whichever texture is current/active determines which one will be loaded in the 2D Texture File dialog box. Select **Texture|2D_Global**, and the first texture in the stack is loaded and ready to edit. While the Texture Dialog Editor is open, click on **Next**. Note the capability of stepping through the stack to the second texture.

Return to the first texture by clicking on the **Previous** button. At the top of the 2D Texture File Editor, change the name from "t2d?" to "cube_txt_a". Once this is completed, click on **Next**, and rename this texture "cube_txt_b". Finally, click on **Next** again, and name the last texture "cube_txt_c", as shown in Figure 4.10. Click on OK to return to the main screen. Note that the original texture is once again current.

Info Textures Window

Select **Info|Textures** to open the Scene Information-Textures window, shown in Figure 4.11. This dialog box lists all the maps used

NAMING TEXTURES TO SIMPLIFY SEARCHES

Softimage will name any unnamed texture. This naming convention is fairly nondescriptive, using a combination of letters and numbers to describe the type of texture and creation sequence. Naming your textures and objects is good practice. This will make life a lot easier when scrolling down a list of 100 similarly named textures.

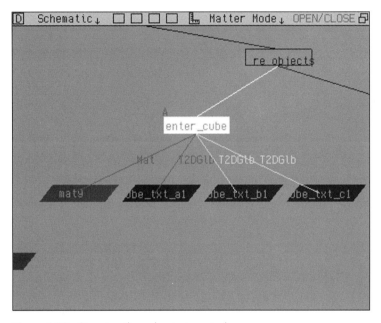

Figure 4.10   Stepping through a texture stack.

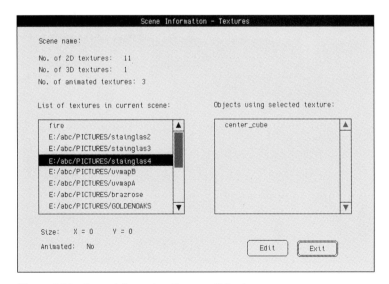

Figure 4.11   Scene Information-Textures dialog box.

in the scene. Left-click on one of the maps to highlight it. Softimage lists the objects that currently have that map applied to it. At the bottom of the dialog box, the software provides information about the size of the map and whether it is animated. Now, highlight an object in the right side of the dialog box. Selecting the Edit button at the bottom of the window returns the user to the 2D Texture File window, where texture editing may commence.

The Amorphous Sphere

This texture project involves placing an amorphous, churning sphere around the cube. While in **Single** mode, select the hidden object icon (sphere) next to the selected cube. Unhide the sphere, which should remain selected. Make sure the sphere is visible in all the viewports by pressing Shift+F. Select **Texture|3D Global** to open the 3D Solid Texture (global) window, shown in Figure 4.12. Press **Select** at the top of the 3D Texture dialog box. In the abc database, choose "fire". This is a free Softimage shader using a fractal algorithm to create some deformations of a color gradient. It also supports alpha channels, which in this case are used

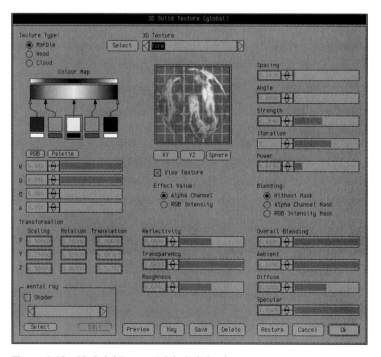

Figure 4.12   3D Solid Texture (global) dialog box.

for transparency. Click on the **Preview** button, and check that all is well.

Animating The Amorphous Sphere

Now, let's add a small amount of animation into the mix. In the End box at the bottom right of the screen, enter 300. Within the 3D Solid Texture window, enter 0 in the Z field under Translation in the Transformation Group. Make sure the frame counter is reading frame1, and click on the **Key** pad next to **Preview** in the 3D Texture dialog box. This sets a key for every parameter in the dialog box at Frame 1 of the animation. Drag the frame pointer to 300. Enter 20 in the Z field under Translation in the Transformation Group, and click on **Key** again. This just set up an animation to drag the shader 20 units in the Z direction through the sphere.

UV Traveling Textures

The last demonstration will include examples of translating and scaling textures along the UV axis of extruded NURBS objects. These examples will create the feeling of objects flying around. Within the project are some tubes that circle around the sphere/cube objects in the center of the shadow box. The idea is to attach some green fireballs going one way and yellow fireballs traveling in the opposite direction.

Find the hidden object inner1 in the Schematic viewport, then unhide and select this object. Press Shift+F to frame everything. Select **Texture|2D_Global** to open the 2D_Texture File window. Within this window, click on **Select** under 2D Texture. Go into the abc database, select "uv_sparks," then enter a value of .005 for Scale in the V direction. Click on **Preview** to check out

what is happening. Notice that because the V scale is .005, the map covers only the top of the tube. Make sure the frame pointer is at Frame 1 (the end frame should still be set to 300). Within the open window, click on **Key** to set a keyframe locking the map's position at the top of the tube, and click on OK to exit the window.

At the main screen, click on TXT to go into Texture mode, and notice the icon at the top of the tube representing the map, as shown in Figure 4.13. The objective is to get the map traveling down the length of the tube every 15 frames. Therefore, drag the pointer to Frame 15, and click on **TransY** to enter the Translate mode. Hold down the middle mouse button, and drag the mouse around, causing the map icon to travel down the tube. Drag the mouse until **TransY** reads 1 (this is the other end of the tube).

Now, middle-click on **Textures** to open the 2D Texture File window. Once in the window, click on **Key** to set the key at Frame 15. This function has set up the animation between Frames 1 and 15. You need to repeat this cycle through the full 300 frames. To do this, click on OK to return to the main screen, and make the Motion module (F2) the active module. Select **FcrvSelect|2D Texture Global|V offset** to open the Fcurve window. Select **FcrvEdit|Extrap Mode|Cycle** to repeat this 15-frame cycle throughout the animation. The Fcurve should change to represent the cycling. Middle-click on the Fcurve window name next to the *c* to return to the Front viewport. Click on the Play arrow, and note that the map icon is tracking down the tube.

Next, select the outer tube, called "outer1", and unhide it. The objective is to have the same

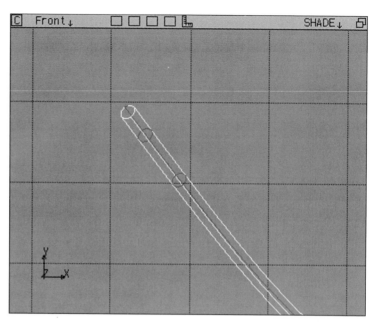

Figure 4.13 TXT icon at top of inner1.

animation as the inner tube, except traveling in the opposite direction. Within the Matter module (F4), start by copying the material from the finished tube (use **Mat_Oper|Copy Mat**). Copy the textures from the first tube by using **Texture_Opt|copy_all**. Go to Frame 1, and select **Texture|2D_Global** to open the 2D Texture File window. Replace the orange map with a green one named "uvmapB" in the abc database. With the frame pointer set at Frame 1, change the 0.000 value under the V offset to 1, and click on **Key**. A warning should appear stating old keys at the bottom of the screen are being replaced. Go to Frame 15, change the 1 in the V Offset to 0 and click on **Key** again (the same warning should appear).

At this point, you have reversed that animation for the first 15 frames or the first and only two keyframes. The extrapolate function added on the first tube should still work. It doesn't really care what it is repeating; it just repeats whatever is before the last set keyframe. Click on the Playback arrow to confirm that the map icons are traveling in opposite directions. The last step is to unhide the remaining straws—inner and outer. Copy material and textures—from inner1 to inner and outer1 to outer—following the same steps.

Place the camera, and render a low-resolution FlipBook. Try different textures throughout, perhaps adding some small point lights with a falloff of 2 or 3 units to give some scale. Experiment by turning the spots into volume lights, for example.

Wrap-Up

The variety of effects you can create with texturing is staggering. We've covered the essentials but barely scratched 3D textures, skipped 3Dpaint, and didn't mention the SpreadSheet texture tools. Successfully applying textures is arguably the most important element to creating effective synthetic imagery. Animating textures creates limitless possibilities.

Explore the texturing abilities Softimage offers. These tools will distinguish your work and provide a source of constant imagination expansion.

LIGHTS 5

Key topics:

- **Light types**

- **Selective lights**

- **Shadows**

This chapter is about lights, not lighting. We'll look at the various lighting tools available from within Softimage and explore what they can do and how they are applied. We'll also explore properties of the lighting tools, using quick samples of how to set up and edit lights. Lights can be assigned to affect only specific objects, called *selective lighting* in Softimage. You will set up a simple scene that associates and disassociates a set of lights with some geometry. Finally, we'll examine the properties of shadows and work through some samples of different types of shadows.

Types Of Lights

The following sections will cover each of the light types available from within Softimage. Because each light can be used in a variety of circumstances, we'll stress the differences and create some examples of how to use each. Although each light is a tool unto itself, you'll find that many of the settings or parameters for the lights are similar. Once you understand the parameters for one light, you'll know most of the settings for all the lights.

Point Lights

A point light radiates equally in all directions. It is represented in the scene by a light-bulb icon. To create a point light, select **Light|Define**. This will bring up the Create Light dialog, which you will use to create all the various lights. (See Figure 5.1.) The Point radio button is selected by default. Left-clicking the OK button will create a default point light that will be placed at the origin.

Let's examine all the attributes of the point light. Select **Light|Edit** to bring up the Edit Light dialog box, which has all the properties of a light and allows you to change their values. At the top of the box is the name of the light. The program automatically names it—something like light1. If you desire a more meaningful name for your light, this is a convenient place to assign it. Meaningful names for lights can be helpful, especially when navigating through a crowded Schematic window.

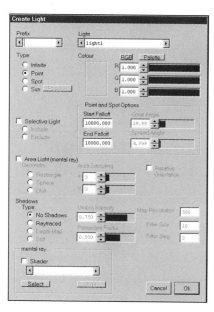

Figure 5.1   The Create Light dialog box.

The next control is a color selector, which controls the color emitted by the selected light. It defaults to a stark and saturated full white. As with all color selectors in Softimage, you can edit the color values in a variety of forms. The HSV color model lends itself well to selecting lighting color values.

The last parameters to examine for the point source for now (we'll cover shadows and the other parameters in later sections) are the falloff values. The Start and End Falloff values express the distances in your scene at which the light begins to fade away and at which all the light has been attenuated. In other words, from the position of your point light to the Start Falloff distance, your light will cast the color it is set to. From Start Falloff to End Falloff, the light will shift from the set color to a total lack of light.

In the real world, light is attenuated by the square of the distance between the source and where the light hits. By creatively setting your falloff values, you can approximate this natural-looking falloff. Setting the Start Falloff value to 0 is a good place to start, because this assures that you get a continual gradation of light. You can then set the End Falloff to the distance at which you don't want the light to affect the scene or the distance at which the light should naturally fade away.

Falloff allows you to control the size of your lights. The default Falloff values will cast light equally out to a distance of 10,000 units. This isn't practical if you want to create a dimly lit scene in a small area. If you are modeling in a real-world coordinate space where one unit equals one meter, determining your Falloff values is much easier. You don't want a streetlight to shine for 10 kilometers, so set your falloff values to match the scale of your scene and lights.

Exit the Edit Light dialog and select **Get|Primitive|Grid** to add a simple polygonal plane to the scene. Drag the light up vertically a bit so it shines onto the grid and turn shading on to see how the light affects the grid. Set the material of the grid to Lambert and preview the grid. The resulting lighting distribution is due solely to

OUT OF RANGE COLORS

Note that color values range from 0.0 to 1.0, but don't let that hamper your artistic style. The values *can* be set outside that range. So, if you want to crank up a light to get an unnatural burning glow, try setting the RGB values to 5,5,5. Color is your only knob to control light intensity. Experiment with negative values and radical combinations, such as RGB -3,0,3

the angle at which the light strikes the grid. To gain some control over your light, highlight it and select **Light|Edit**. Change the Color to RGB 2,2,2, the Start Falloff to 0.0, and the End Falloff to 5.0. From the Matter module, select **Atmosphere|Ambience** and set the Global Ambience to RGB 0.05,0.05,0.05. Then preview the results. (See Figure 5.2.) Now you are controlling the light rather than letting the defaults control you.

Figure 5.2   A point light distribution on a grid.

Spotlights

A spotlight simulates a perfect cone of light. The position of the source is the tip of the cone, and the beam of the spot points down the cone toward the spotlight's interest. The interest is a null object that the spotlight is constrained to point toward. To see the cone of light cast by a spotlight in wireframe, select **Show|Cone** or **Show|Cone (Unselected)**.

Delete the point light from the scene you created and select **Light|Create**. Set the Type of the light to Spot and accept all the other default values. Drag the spotlight up and to the left. Notice how its beam stays fixated on the interest, which is currently at the origin. Open a Schematic view and see that the spotlight is both the light itself and its interest. The spotlight is portrayed in wireframe as a theatrical spot. (See Figure 5.3.)

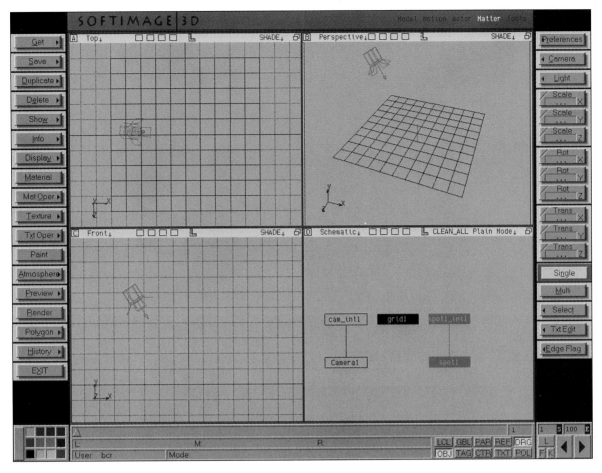

Figure 5.3 Scene with a spotlight.

Highlight the spotlight and select **Light|Edit** to examine its prop-
erties. All the properties of the point light are still in play, but
now you have two new variables: Cone Angle and Spread Angle.
Both are expressed in degrees. The Cone Angle defines how wide
open the cone of the spotlight is, and the Spread Angle defines
over how many degrees the light fades from its color value to no
light at all.

If you set the Cone Angle to 90 degrees, you would have a hemi-
spherical light source or half a point light. More likely, you'll be
using Cone Angles of fewer than 45 degrees to create very di-
rected light sources where you have a lot of control over the
direction and shape of the light.

Spread Angle allows you to adjust how quickly the spotlight fades out. By setting a wider Spread Angle, you can create softer roll-offs. If you want a sharp dramatic spot or a hard-defined edge to the scallop of your light, use a small Spread Angle.

Adjust the angle values of your spotlight and preview the changes. Reposition the spotlight and see how the angle of the light hitting the grid changes the distribution. (See Figure 5.4.) Try some grazing angles and adjust the spot's Falloff values as well.

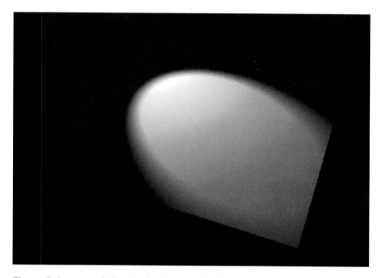

Figure 5.4 A spotlight distribution on a grid.

Infinite Lights

An infinite light casts light in a single direction. It gets its name from the fact that light from an infinitely distant source would arrive in parallel beams. The most common analogy is that light from the sun arrives on the earth's surface in nearly parallel rays. Light bathes an entire scene from one direction when using an infinite light.

Imagine a scene where you rotate the view in one of the orthographic windows. The visible surfaces are those that would receive light from an infinite light pointing down that axis. Direction is the primary component of the infinite light.

Delete the spotlight from your working scene and add an infinite light. The infinite light is represented in wireframe views as a sphere with an arrow that points at the origin. Direction is the only property that matters with an infinite light. Varying the incident angle of the light is the only adjustment you can make.

Infinite lights are stark and globally affect the scene in one direction. Using them too liberally can quickly saturate all the detail out of a scene. They are best used to create a wash of light from a specific direction; whether that is the light from a distant sun or light bouncing off a nearby wall is up to you.

The Sun

The Sun light type has limited utility. It is basically an infinite light whose direction is determined by assigning a time and geographic location. Solar geometry is used to calculate the angle of the light at that location at that time. This angle is assigned as the direction for the Sun light.

Delete the infinite light from your scene and select **Light|Define**. Select Sun for the type of light, then left-click the Position button to assign the time and location of your scene. (See Figure 5.5.) You may either input longitude and latitude values or choose from a database of selected city locations. Assign a time (preferably during daylight hours) and create the Sun light.

The Sun is shown as a ball with lines through it in the Wireframe views. It hovers above your scene and lights it as an infinite light would.

Mental Ray Lights

The Extreme version of Softimage includes a ray tracer called Mental Ray, which provides a host of other lighting abilities and tools beyond those already covered. Some of these, such as Area lights, are available from the standard Lights dialog box. Others, such as Volumetric lights, are available as plug-ins to Mental Ray. For further specifics on Mental Ray and how to apply shaders and plug-ins, refer to Chapter 7.

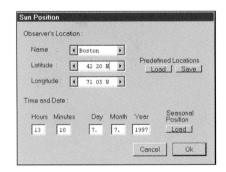

Figure 5.5   The Sun Position dialog box.

Selective Lights

In many situations, you want one light to affect only a single object or a group of objects. Softimage calls this ability selective lighting. It allows you to assign lights with great control and is an essential tool for adding localized lighting effects. Selective lights are also useful for creating dramatic washes of color or gentle bounce light, only where you want it.

Associating Selective Lights With Objects

When you first create a selective light, it is not associated with any objects and its light doesn't affect the scene. You can choose from two types of selective lights: Include and Exclude. Include selective lights shine on objects they have been associated with, whereas Exclude selective lights shine on everything except the objects they have been associated with. Use the **Light|Associate** command to assign selective lights to a particular object. This relationship can be revoked by applying the **Light|Disassociate** command.

Select **Delete|All** to clear everything for a new scene. Create a primitive cube with a length of 2.0, duplicate it twice, and move the duplicates to the left and right of the original. Now create a point light. Drag it up in the Y axis about four to five units, duplicate it twice, and move the duplicates so that a point light is above each cube. (See Figure 5.6.) Open up a Schematic view of your scene and in the upper-right corner, switch the Schematic to Light mode.

Highlight the leftmost light and select **Light|Edit**. Make the light selective by choosing the Selective check box. Selective lights default to the Include type, which is fine for this example. Change the color of the light to full-on red and rename the light Rlight. Accept this light and then edit the other two, making them both Include types. Make the center light green and name it Glight, and the right-most light blue and called Blight.

If you have Shade mode turned on in the Perspective view, you'll notice that as you switch each light to Selective, it no longer

SELECTIVE LIGHTS

The colors in Shade mode won't match the actual colors of your objects under selective lighting. Switch to the Matter module and Preview|All to see the correct colors.

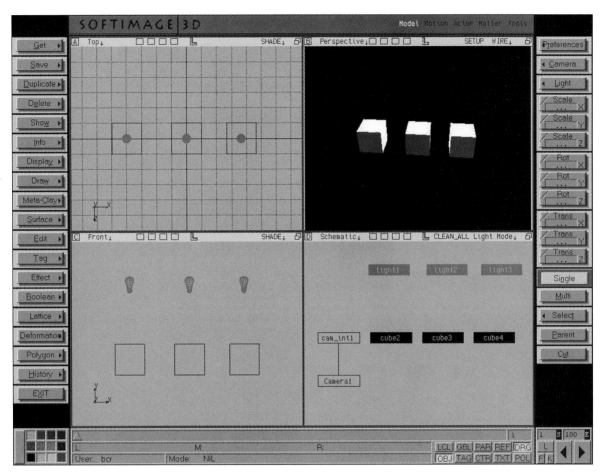

Figure 5.6 A simple scene to test selective lights.

shines onto your cubes. This is because the lights have not yet
been associated with any objects. Use **Multi** to highlight the
three cubes and then select **Light|Associate**. Left-click on all
three lights to associate them with the three cubes and right-click
the mouse to end the Associate mode. The associations between
the lights and cubes are shown as labeled links in the Schematic
view. (See Figure 5.7.)

As expected, all three objects receive some contribution of light
from each of the sources. This is how three normal point lights
would act. In the next section, we'll disassociate some of the
lights and objects to make each light affect only a single cube.
Before moving on, though, highlight each cube and select
Info|Selection to change the names of the cubes to leftcube,

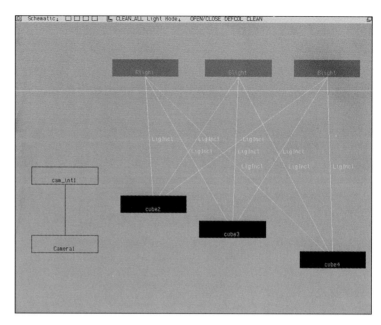

Figure 5.7 The Schematic view showing associations.

midcube, and rightcube. This will simplify making the selections in the next section.

Disassociating A Selective Light

To make the red light shine only on the leftmost cube, you must disassociate the middle and right lights from leftcube. Highlight leftcube, then select **Light|Disassociate**. Now, in Disassociate mode, left-click on the middle and right lights. This leaves leftcube lighted only with red from the left light.

Now perform the operations to make Glight shine only on midcube and Blight only on rightcube. Highlight midcube, select **Light|Disassociate**, then left-click Rlight and Blight. Highlight rightcube and left-click Rlight and Glight. Right-click to exit Disassociate mode.

This leaves the three cubes selectively lighted by only the one colored light above each. It's this kind of control that makes selective lights a powerful tool. If you want to add a dramatic specular reflection to an object, assign a selective light to affect only that one object, then safely manipulate the light to

SELECTING LINKED LIGHTS

Sometimes, the Schematic view can get a little crowded in Light mode. For a quick way to see which lights are affecting an object, go into Multi selection mode. Just above an object node, hold down the space bar and highlight across the association links. Selecting a link highlights the light connected to that link. By multiselecting all the links, you will highlight all the lights associated with that object.

get just the right highlight without affecting any other objects in the scene.

Shadows

Shadows are an integral part of how a light affects your scene. Shadows, in fact, are as important as the light that comes from the light source. Shadows lock objects in place, so they aren't floating over a surface. They provide cues of light directions, brightness, color, and a host of perceptual spatial cues that help us to interpret three-dimensional scenes.

Turning On Shadows

Shadows are turned on or off within the **Light|Define** or **Light|Edit** commands. All the shadow parameters for a particular light are available from the now-familiar Define/Edit Light dialog boxes. The parameters available vary from light to light, but they all have an option to set the Shadows type to No Shadows or Raytraced.

No Shadows, as the name implies, means that a light source will not cast a shadow. That particular light will not be checked by the renderer to see if its light is blocked by any objects in your scene. It's as if all the light from your source passes right through the objects.

Shadows don't come without some cost. If you have a lot of lights in your scene, you may want to analyze how important the shadows from each light are to the overall appearance of the scene. You can gain substantial speedups in render times by turning shadows off on lights whose inclusion won't add a lot. So, as you create lights, ask yourself: Do I really need shadows for this light? Usually, the answer will be yes, but not always.

Raytraced shadows are generated in roughly the following manner: When a pixel is being rendered for your final image, Softimage figures out on which object or objects that pixel resides. The renderer then traces a geometric ray up toward your light source. If the ray reaches the light, your final pixel receives the full contribution of light energy from that source. On the other hand, if an object is in the way of the ray, then this pixel is in shadow and the light from that light source does not reach this place and is not added to the final pixel's value, making it a darker shadowed pixel.

Delete|All and set up a simple scene of primitives sitting on a grid, as in Figure 5.8. You'll use this scene as a test bed for trying out some shadowing parameters. Add a point light, turning Raytraced shadows on. Drag the light above and to the northeast of the scene. Select **Preview|All** from the Matter module to view the shadowed scene.

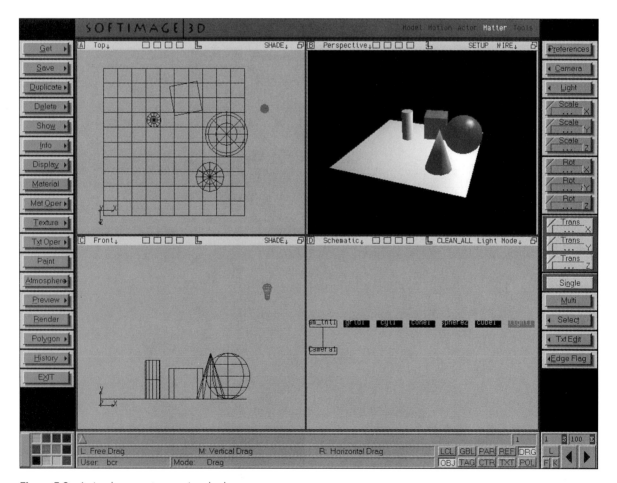

Figure 5.8 A simple scene to examine shadows.

Shadow Parameters

Highlight the point light source and select **Light|Edit**. The only shadow parameter available for the point source is Umbra Intensity. The Umbra Intensity, which ranges from 0.0 to 1.0, defines how dark the cast shadow is. Values approaching 1.0 create very transparent shadows, while smaller values create darker, starker shadows. Preview the scene with Umbra intensities of 0.1 and of 0.95 to see the difference firsthand.

Delete the point light from the scene and add a spotlight. Drag the spotlight over to the front right of the scene and place it low enough and far enough back so that the beam covers most of the scene. Leave the interest at the center of the grid and preview the scene. (See Figure 5.9.)

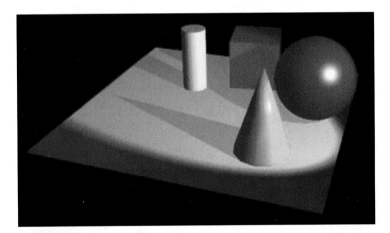

Figure 5.9 Scene with a spotlight and Raytraced shadows.

Highlight the spotlight and select **Light|Edit**. Notice that a spotlight has two new shadow types available: Depth Map and Soft. Depth Map is another technique for creating shadows, and Soft shadows simulate shadows with blurry edges.

A Depth Map generates shadows by creating a depth image of the scene from the vantage point of the camera. The resolution of this image is the Map Resolution parameter that activates when Depth Map is selected. At render time, instead of tracing rays back to the light, a quick depth check is performed against the depth image. If the point being lit lies deeper than the depth value in the image, it must lie in shadow. This type of test is, in many simple cases, faster than using Raytraced shadows. For detailed shadows, however, you must bump up the Map Resolution to capture the complexity of your geometry. If the Map Resolution is too low, you will start to see artifacts. Preview the scene with the shadow type set to Depth Map. The result is similar to Raytraced shadows. Turn the Map Resolution down to 100 to see how a small Depth Map will degrade shadow quality.

Now, switch the shadow type to Soft. Soft shadows are the same as Depth-Mapped shadows, although they perform a filtering on the depth image so that the shadow edges are blurred, or soft. The amount of blurring is controlled by the Penumbra factor, which ranges from 0.0 to 1.0, where high numbers are softer.

The other two parameters for soft shadows are Filter Size and Filter Step. The Filter is a blurring filter and the Size and Step parameters are in pixels on the depth image. Set the Penumbra to 0.7, the Map Resolution to 800, Filter Size to 80, and Filter Step to 1. Your results should look as they do in Figure 5.10. Notice that the shadows, although somewhat softened, have lost accuracy. Soft shadows are best used when combined with an area light source and rendered with Mental Ray, but they still have application even with the standard Softimage renderer.

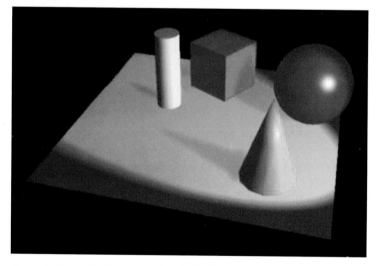

Figure 5.10   A simple scene with soft shadows.

Wrap-Up

This chapter introduced Softimage's lighting tools from a functional point of view. It covered the basics and explained the parameters, but the art of rendering is not about lights, it's about lighting. If you understand what types of light and shadow you need in your scene, you'll be able to achieve that look with these tools. We'll touch on lighting issues throughout the later project chapters.

PART 2

TOOLS
AND
TECH-
NIQUES

TO6OLS

Key topics:

- **Bevels**

- **Proportional editing**

- **Jitter**

- **Magnet**

- **ShrinkWrap**

One reason Softimage is such an attractive system is the large number of tools it includes. These tools allow the user numerous methods of attacking the same problem. In a production environment, this can mean the difference between finishing a job on schedule and not getting paid. On the downside, some of these tools address only a narrow range of object types or have arcane input parameters. This makes some of the tools a challenge to learn and use effectively. The intent of this chapter is to illustrate how multiple tools give you a choice in how best to work through a design problem, and also to make you aware of some of the lesser-used tools.

A Bevel Is A Bevel Is A Bevel?

Say you need a bevelled cube. Most software packages perform a bevelling operation when the object is created. Softimage, too, allows for bevelling during the object's creation via the **Surfaces|Extrusion** command, but it also provides a variety of ways to bevel *after* an object's creation. It is this freedom to create an effect with the best tool available that we will explore in the following sections.

Let's begin by creating a cube to bevel. Make sure the Model module is active, select **Get|Primitive|Cube**, enter 3.0 as the Length value, and click on OK to exit the window. In the Perspective window, turn on Shading mode. Press Shift+F to frame the cube in all viewports. Hide the selected cube by holding down the *h* and *u* keys (hot-key combo for hide) or choose **Display|Hide|Toggle & Desel.Hidden**. In the Schematic window, highlight the hidden cube1. Choose **Duplicate|Immediate** to create a visible copy (cube2) to work on. Now, let's see how many different ways you can bevel your object.

Effect|Bevel

First, let's apply a straightforward bevelling effect. This function allows the user to define global and local bevelled edges for polygon meshes. The amount of bevelling is measured in Softimage reference grid units.

In the Model module, select **Effect|Bevel** to open the Bevel window. Accept the default 0.1 Bevel value, and click on OK to close the window. The bevels are created, but they are hard to see in the shaded perspective view. To correct this, choose **Info|Selection** (press and hold *s* then *q*) to open the Polygon Info window seen in Figure 6.1, and select Faceted to eliminate the smooth shading in the Perspective window. Now, the bevelled edges are plainly visible.

Polygon|Coplanar

The next bevelling tool is Coplanar, which adds polygons around the edges of an object. Delete cube2 (**Delete|Selection**), select hidden cube1, and copy cube1 (**Duplicate|Immediate**) to create cube3.

Select **Polygon|Coplanar** to open the Coplanar window, as seen in Figure 6.2. Set Inset and Height to 0.1, and click on OK. When asked to select a mesh, click on cube3. A new bevelled cube has been created. This time, Softimage made a copy of cube3 (cube3_cplnr1) and performed the bevel on this copy. If you want to bevel only part of the cube, the Coplanar tool allows you to work specifically on tagged polygons.

Effect|Rounding

Strictly speaking, the Rounding tool is not a true bevel, although it is in the same family and can function as a bevelling operation. This effect allows you to define global and local rounded edges on an object.

Delete cube3 and cube3_cplnr1, highlight hidden cube1, and select **Duplicate|Immediate** to create cube4. Select **Effect|Rounding** to open the Round window, change the default Round value from 0.5 to 0.1, and click on OK to exit. Cube4 now has a decent bevel.

The 0.1 rounding value of this example does not refer to a division of the reference grid. This procedure simply measures the distance from the center of the object to the bevelling point and

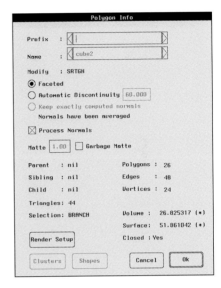

Figure 6.1 Polygon Info dialog box.

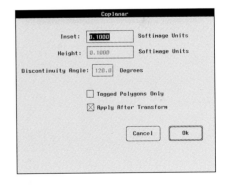

Figure 6.2 Coplanar dialog box.

takes a percentage of that distance. By setting 0.1 as a round value, the software creates a bevel with a depth of 10 percent of the distance from the center of the object to that face. To make this clear, select **History|Undo** to remove the effect, then repeat **Effect|Rounding**, but change the Round value to 0.5. The depth of the bevel will equal half the distance from the center of the cube to any edge, as shown in Figure 6.3.

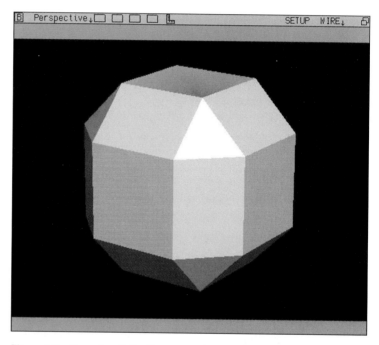

Figure 6.3   Rounding (0.5) effect on a cube.

Draw|Polyskin

This fourth example of creating bevels takes the long way around. This procedure is a little tricky, and there are easier ways to create bevels on cubes. However, on larger objects, such as a sphere, you can achieve some interesting effects. (Following this exercise, try repeating these steps by replacing the cube with a 16-by-16 sphere.)

Delete cube4 to get started. Copy the hidden cube again, and scale the resulting cube5 to 0.9, 0.9, 0.9. Select **Polygon|Breakup**, accept the default values, click on OK, then click on cube5 to create cube5_brk1. Rename this cube break1. This newly formed

cube has been split into six faces. To verify the breakup, select
Info|Selection, and notice that the vertices have increased from
8 to 24. This breakup allows each polygon to move independently of the others.

You don't need cube5 anymore, so delete it. At this point, make
sure that break1 is the only visible object. Now, make a copy of
the hidden cube1, which should be a little larger than break1.
Select **Polygon|Breakup**, and click on the larger highlighted
cube. Once again, the software has performed the function on a
new cube (cube6_brk1). Rename this cube break2, and delete the
template (cube6).

Only break1 and break2 should be visible. Select **Effect|Push** to
open the Push window, set the Push Points value to 0.25, click on
OK, and click on the smaller cube (break_1). In the resulting
object, the polygon faces are pushed (translated) 25 percent of a
Softimage reference unit along their normals. Because the cube
has been broken up, the polygons are all visible, as you can see
in Figure 6.4.

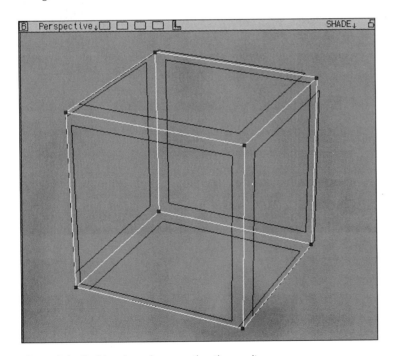

Figure 6.4 Pushing the polygons rather than scaling.

PUSH

Push is similar to scale with one important difference. Like the scale operation, polygons move out from the center in the direction of the normals. Unlike scale, however, the polygons do not increase in size. For example, if you scale a hand model x2, the only element that changes is the size of the hand in relation to other objects in the scene. If you use Effect|Push on a hand model—depending on whether you use a positive or negative number—you would end up with either a fatter hand or a thinner hand, but the overall size would remain basically the same.

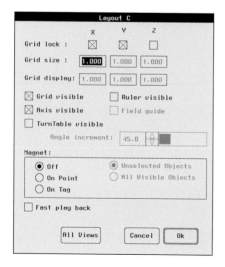

Figure 6.5 Front view Layout C dialog box.

Now, use Polyskin to connect the outer polygons to the inner polygons. Select **Draw|Polyskin**, click on the inner cube when asked for the Starting mesh, and click on the outer cube when asked for the Ending mesh. This creates the new object, poly_skin1. Delete break1 and break2. Choose **Info|Selection** (press and hold s then q) to open the Polygon Info window, and select Faceted to eliminate the smooth shading in the Perspective window. Now, the bevelled edges are plainly visible.

Surface Bevel

This next group of bevel tools allows for some cool animation. Unlike the tools just discussed, these are used during the creation of the object and can be used on branches, splines, animations, etc.

Start with a fresh screen by selecting **Delete|All**. Select **Get|Primitive|Square**, set the Length to 10, and click on OK to create square1. Hide square1 (**Display|Hide|Toggle & Desel.Hidden**), highlight the hidden square1, and select **Duplicate|Immediate** to produce square2. Select **Camera|Frame All** (Shift+A) to frame the square fully in the Front view. Select **Draw|Curve|Linear**. To create spline2, place points in the Front view at the following coordinates: -6,0 -5,1 5,1 6,0. (See the Grid Lock tip and Figure 6.5.) Select **Surface|Bevel**, accept the defaults, and close the window. Follow the prompts, select square2 when prompted to select the spline or face to bevel, then select the bevel guide (spline2). Once again, a bevelled cube is produced.

This operation is similar to a guided extrude. Spline2 was dragged around the defining square to create the bevelled cube. The front and back faces cap the object. At this point, delete spline3; the work will require only spline2.

Hierarchy Bevel

This is a handy tool for working with text. To start, you will create a hierarchy of squares to work with. Delete all visible objects with the exception of spline2 (the bevel guide). The

Schematic window should contain only the camera, square1 (hidden), and spline2. Highlight only the hidden square1, and select **Duplicate|Repetition**. Set Number of Occurrences to 4 and Translation X to 14. Frame the square by pressing *a*. At this point, make sure nothing is selected (**Select|Clear**).

Now, to make bevelled cubes out of those squares, choose **Surfaces|HrcBevel** to open the HrcBevel window, accept the defaults, and click on OK. When prompted to select the hierarchy of splines and/or faces to bevel, click on the top node (null1) of the square hierarchy, and when prompted to select the bevel guide (spline2), click on spline2. The new bevelled hierarchy with the parent null2 is created. Every square within the hierarchy has been bevelled. If the squares are replaced with a text hierarchy, the HrcBevel function can be useful for quickly creating bevelled text elements.

Animated Bevels

Softimage provides animation capabilities for some of the bevelling tools we've just covered. Make the Motion (F2) module active, and click on **Path**. Notice that both AnimatedBevel and HrcAnimatedBevel are available. These functions are the same as their "Model" counterparts, with the exception of being able to animate the generation curves.

HrcAnimatedBevel

Delete any leftover items so that the Schematic window contains only the camera, null1 hierarchy, square1 (hidden), and spline2 (bevel guide). Make sure the Motion (F2) module is active, select **Path|HrcAnimatedBevel** to open the HrcAnimatedBevel window, and click on OK to accept the default values. When prompted to select the hierarchy of splines and/or faces to bevel, click on the top node (null1) of the square hierarchy, and when prompted to select the bevel guide (spline2), click on spline2. Once again, a hierarchy of bevelled cubes has been created. Now, you will animate the bevel guide.

The object of this animation is to have the size of the bevel, on all of the cubes, change over time. Position the timeline to Frame 1 of the animation. Select only spline2 (the bevel guide), and choose **SaveKey|Object|Scaling|All**. This action creates a keyframe, setting the scale size of spline2 for Frame 1 of the animation. Now, slide the frame pointer on the timeline to Frame 100, and middle-click on **SaveKey**. Middle-click on **SaveKey** again to create a keyframe. Move the frame pointer to Frame 50, scale spline2 down to 25 percent of its original size (on the X and Y axes), and middle-click on **SaveKey**. Slide the frame pointer from 1 to 100 and back again. Notice that the shape of all bevels changes as the scale of the bevel guide changes. Only a simple scale operation was used in this example, but you can, of course, animate the generation curve in any way you like to create rich and dynamic animated bevels.

Proportional Editing

While transforming vertices, proportional editing influences other nearby points. As you pull on a single point, the points surrounding it are pulled as well. You can define the distance to which other points are affected and to what degree they are influenced.

In the Model module, select **Get|Primitive|Grid**, and accept the defaults. This places a 2D 10-by-10 grid on the XZ axis. Tag a point in the middle of the grid by holding down the *t* supra key and drawing a rectangle around the point you want. The point will turn red, indicating that it is tagged.

Press Shift+F to center the GRID in all views and turn Shading mode on in the Perspective view.

Now, press *v* (Translate supra key) to enter Drag mode. This will set up the mouse buttons so that the left one is free to translate, the middle one is constrained to vertical motion, and the right one allows only horizontal movement. Now, click on the TAG pad, located at the bottom-right corner of the screen, to the right of OBJ. This will make only tagged points affected by your translations.

Using the middle mouse button in the Front view, translate the tagged point up 3 or 4 units. Notice that only the tagged point moves. This creates sharp angles on the affected polygons. Hold down the *u* supra key (undo), and left-click to return the grid to normal.

Select **Edit|Proportional Setup** to open the dialog box shown in Figure 6.6. Set the Distance Limit field to 4, and click on OK. This value sets up the sphere of influence around the tagged point—in this case, 4 Softimage units. Exiting from this dialog box automatically turns on Proportional editing. You can check this by selecting Edit and noting that Proportional is now checked.

Go to the Front view, and translate the point up 4 units, as you did before. More than just the tagged point moves. An area of influence was set up around the tagged point, which responded proportionately to the motion of the tag. In fact, in the Front view, the edge that is formed by the moved points matches the graph displayed in the Proportional setup dialog box.

Hold down the *u* key while left-clicking to undo the last process, returning the grid to flat. Select **Edit|Proportional Setup**. Click on the Exponential1 and Exponential2 buttons, and see how the proportion curve changes. Linear is the default shape; it sets up a falloff so that the amount of action applied to points is full on at the tagged points and then drops linearly until there is no influence beyond the distance limit.

Click on Exponential1, then click on OK to return to the main screen. At this point, you should have a flat grid on the screen. Make sure you are still in Translate mode by looking at the right menu cells—the three TransXYZ cells should be purple, indicating they are still active. If not, just press *v* (the translate supra key). Go ahead and repeat the previous moves by, once again, holding down the middle mouse button, and, in the Front view, moving the tagged point up 4 units. Another way is to simply enter the value 4 in the TransY text field. This is an additive field; it simply adds whatever value you place in it to the current value.

The tagged point rises 4 units now with a sharper, more pronounced curvature, which again matches the graph in the Setup dialog box. If you like, you can undo this last move and try out Exponential2. This gives a slightly different curve, which isn't as drastic as Exponential1. Try inputting different distance limits and denser grids to get a feel for the way neighboring points are affected by the various parameters.

Now, let's examine some of the other features in the Proportional setup dialog box. The Surface option is for use with NURBS and spline surfaces only—this is a 2D effect, not a 3D effect. Instead of a sphere of influence, it has an elliptical or rectangular influence across the surface of an object. Rather than a distance limit, it has a UV limit. Experiment on a NURBS grid to see how this works. In general, instead of distance measured in units, it is counting points in the U and V directions. For example, a setup with U=4 and V=4 will affect a NURBS object only by influencing points within four U or V ISO lines. Instead of acting over a specified distance, actions are now constrained by how many points "away" they are.

The Affect Tag Only checkbox works with the *m* (move point) supra key. Delete the grid you've been working on, and select

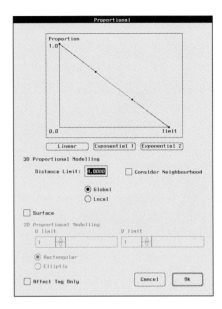

Figure 6.6 Proportional setup dialog box.

Get|Primitive|Sphere to create a polygon sphere with 20-by-20 UV and a radius of 4. Now, tag the lower half of the sphere. Open the Proportional setup dialog box, activate Affect Tag Only, and click on OK to exit. Hold down the *m* key, and place the cursor over one of the tagged points. Use the left mouse button to move the point around. Only tagged points inside the distance limits are affected. This is a great way to get localized control.

The Consider Neighbourhood option is somewhat of a hidden usage item. The manual says something like: If selected, a point within the area of influence does not move if all of the neighboring points are outside the limit. Don't be ashamed if you had to read that three or four times to get only a fuzzy idea of what the feature does. This feature is useful when dealing with merged polygon objects. For example, select **Get|Primitive|Sphere** again, and this time, create a polygonal sphere with a radius of 1 and UV set to 20. Make a copy of it using **Duplicate|Immediate**, and place the two spheres side by side. Now, make another copy, and scale it up 300 percent. Position the two smaller spheres as if they were eyes on the face of the larger sphere.

Select **Multi** mode, and highlight all three spheres. Then, select **Effect|Merge**, accept the defaults, and click on OK. This merges the three spheres into one object. Open the Schematic view, and select the three original spheres only. Now, hold down *h* while pushing *u* to hide the selected three original spheres. This should leave you with only the merged spheres on screen, as in Figure 6.7.

Here is the interesting part. Say you have a dense polygon model of a head and you want to move just the eyes. Because you can't select them as objects, the only ways to move them would be to tag just the eyes and detach them. You could also create a cluster, or—if you're lucky—the eyes have a separate material, so you can use **Next|Previous Material** to select them. If all this fails, you can turn on Proportional and use Consider Neighbourhood.

Select **Edit|Proportional Setup**, and set the distance limit to 15. Make sure Consider Neighbourhood is on and Linear is selected. Now, you want to set your curve to produce as little difference from the selected point as possible. To do that, click on the handle 3/4 down the line, and move it up and to the right, so the handle is straight up and about level with the top of the box. Now, move the handle on the upper-left part of the curve over to the right until it intersects with the other handle you just moved. The curve now looks like Figure 6.8.

Because the curve is flat most of the way across, your points will move with the selected point through most of the sphere of influence. That's why we set the distance limit fairly high. In essence, because your curve is flat two-thirds of the way across to Limit, any point inside a 10-unit radius should respond exactly the same as your selected point. Make sure Affect Tag Only is *not* activated, and click on OK to exit the Proportional dialog box.

Make sure the object is selected, Proportional is turned on, and you are in TAG mode. Tag a point in the left eye—any point somewhere near the middle of the eyeball will do. Now, press the *v* key, and start dragging the point around— wow, *only* the left eye is moving. Try untagging

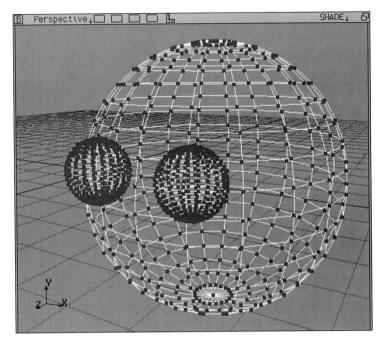

Figure 6.7 Merged polygon spheres.

everything and just using the *m* (move point) supra key. Try moving your cursor over different elements, hold down the *m* key, and use the left mouse button to drag points. All the elements move in solo.

This is happening because all the points on the little spheres are within the flat range of our curve and, hence, respond the same as the tagged points. The Consider Neighbourhood operation recognizes that points on the other objects are in a different neighborhood.

This tool has a lot of uses in this mode. Suppose you had a head of hair and needed to move a few hairs at a time. You could have a nasty object hierarchy, or you could do a merge. Then, just tag a point or two on the hairs you want to move. Or, say you have a wall full of rivets. Merge the rivets with the wall to create a single object. Then, to move a single rivet, hold down the *m* key, and click and drag. Only the rivet under the mouse moves. You can quickly rearrange the whole wall of rivets. I'm sure you'll come up with other interesting ideas for this use of proportional editing.

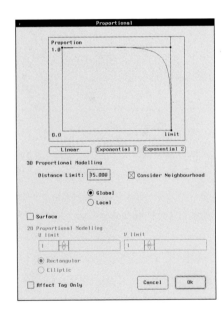

Figure 6.8 Consider Neighbourhood adjustments.

Jitter

Jitter is one of the most often-used animation tools. One way to think of Jitter is as a random noise generator that produces random values of xyz SRT (for Scale, Rotate, and Translate) and can be plugged in anyplace that will accept animated xyz values of SRT. Applying Jitter to nulls and then using the result in a part of an expression increases its functionality even further. Its main function, however, is taking an animated object and applying some discontinuity to it.

For our first example, load in the scene "top" from the chap6 database. Make sure the Perspective view is in Shading mode, and click on the Play arrow at the bottom right of the screen. You should be seeing an animation of a spinning top, balancing itself on top of a pyramid. By applying a little random jitter to the top's rotation transform, this simple little animation takes on a much more realistic quality.

Before you do anything else, make sure you are in the Animation module by pressing F2. Select **Effects|Jitter** to open the Jitter dialog box. Note that the top part of the dialog box deals with the extent of the animation. These should be set to show a Start frame of 1, an End frame of 300, and a frame rate of 30 frames per second with a tension of .5. The next section deals with the amount of jitter applied to the three transforms: Scale, Rotate, and Translate, or SRT.

The first checkbox determines if the transform is applied to the object. You want to apply only some rotation jitter so make sure that Rotate is the only box checked. Next is the seed, which gives you a way to reproduce—or make sure you

don't reproduce—the same Jitter on an object. Basically, it is a number that all the random data to come is based on. Hence, by changing this number, all the Jitter-generated values that come after it will change as well.

The XYZ value is the level of magnitude applied to the object and to the XYZ components of the object's animation. Frequency determines the rate, or speed, of change. Cumulative determines if the effect keeps getting larger over time or if the total amount remains the same. Fcurve Present is asking if the component of the animation SRT you are applying Jitter to already has animation applied to it—in other words, is jitter creating the animation, or is it deforming an animation that is already present? Next, Previous, Delete, Key, and Frame are the controls that allow you to animate the values applied in the Jitter dialog box and are the same functions used through Softimage's custom effects.

In this case, you want to apply Jitter only to the Rotate components of the top to give the impression it is balancing itself precariously on the pyramid. Because the Y axis is already animated as the spin, you can leave that alone. This leaves only the X and Z axes to work with. So, make sure the Rotate checkbox is the only one checked. Set the Y value under Rotate to 0, because you should leave the spin alone.

In the remaining X and Z Rotate fields, try the default values of 0.5. Normally, start with Cumulative off, and see if it is enough. The last item to check is the Fcurve Present checkbox.

At this point, click on OK to get out of there. You will be prompted to click on the model you want to apply Jitter to. Select the top; you'll see the five-ball Jitter icon appear in the viewports. Click on the Play arrow, and you should see the top wobbling around trying to stay on the point of the pyramid. This is a vast improvement over the first animation of the spinning top.

Now, how do you make changes once Jitter is applied? Softimage uses an icon-based system to control its *persistent effects*, which are effects that remain active and adjustable until they are deleted. These effects are usually known by their viewport icons, which appear to be models. Jitter is one such effect. Any time you see an effect with icons that appear as geometry in viewports, the only way to adjust their settings is by selecting the icon of the effect in question and selecting **Effect|Custom|Edit**. This will open the dialog box first used to apply the effect and allow adjustments to the values contained therein.

Also under **Effect|Custom** is the Freeze effect. This allows you to stop at any point in the animation and freeze the object/effect by removing the effect and leaving the object in the state it was in while under the care of the effect.

Another effect is Detach and Re-Attach, which allows you to remove an effect, such as Jitter, causing the object to react as if no effect were ever applied. Once ready, the effect can be Re-Attached, picking up right where it left off. Also, note that you can simply delete the icon to return an object back to its pre-effect state.

The chap6 database has another example of Jitter worth looking at, called "top_hand." It takes the same scene with the top a little further, balancing the top on a hand's extended index finger instead of the pyramid. The hand has Translate Jitter as well as a small amount of Rotate Jitter, making it move around the screen in a random manner. Because the top is grouped as a child of the hand, it is perched on the index finger in sync with the hand. Once again, the top has a lot of Y Rotate applied to give the appearance of it spinning. In addition to the Translate Jitter on

Note: Because individual XYZ Fcurves don't have a checkbox, you need to keep an eye out for situations like the one this scene is setting up—that is, the only Fcurves present on the top is the Y Rotate. This begs the question: What if some components have and some have not? What do you do? In that case, set keys on the X and Z components of the top at Frame 1, then go ahead and check off the FCurve Present checkbox, as shown in Figure 6.9.

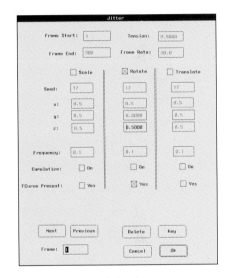

Figure 6.9 Jitter dialog box.

the hand, the top has the same Rotate Jitter as the previous example, giving the appearance that it is wobbling around trying to stay upright.

Look at both these scenes, and try entering different values throughout the Jitter dialog box. Note the effects on the object it is applied to. Two other Jitter tools are ShapeJitter and HRCShapeJitter; instead of working on the whole object, they work at the vertice level.

Magnet

The Magnet effect allows the user to deform points of one model by using another model as a magnet. The parameters control which points of the object are moved, how far, and in which direction. Magnitude controls the strength of the magnetic force, where each point of the magnet pushes or pulls nearby points of the object. The distribution of this magnetic force can be either Proportional to Area or Located at Vertices. In Proportional to Area, the force assigned to each polygon of the mesh object being used as a magnet is proportional to its area. In other words, the larger the polygon the more force is applied. In contrast, an equal amount of force is applied from each vertex of the magnet in Located at Vertices. This is also used if the magnet is a spline or NURBS surface.

Snake Face

This example scene is based on a shot from a popular sci-fi television series. In the scene, black worms crawl around an actor's face, popping in and out of his skin. First, load the scene "snake_face." To recreate the effect, start with a head model. Trace around the face with the Curve tool, creating a NURBS curve that runs around the face.

Once that is done, select **Deformation|by Curve** to have a simple cylinder ride down the curve while deforming to its bends and turns. Run the animation and notice how the cylinder slithers along the spline over the face of your model. This was done by selecting a cylinder and using **Deformation|by Curve**. The curve running over the face of the model was selected at the prompt. This takes the cylinder and bends it to fit over the curve.

Remember the way **Deformation|by Curve** works is to replace the selected object's local Y axis with the curve/path. Then, to get the cylinder to travel down the path, you set the Translate mode to local. Y=0 would be the beginning of the path, and in this case, Y=15 is the end of the path; hence, at Frame 1, you want to translate the cylinder to read Y=0. Once done, you set a keyframe under **Motion|Object|Node Curve Deformation|translation** at Frame 1. The next step is to set the current frame to 100, then repeat the last move, translate the cylinder to Y=15, and set a keyframe here as well, using the same **Motion|Object|Node Curve Deformation|translation**.

The object here is to make the cylinder slither over and under the mesh, while deforming the mesh using **Motion|Effect|Magnet**, so the snake appears to be under the skin.

Select **Effect|Magnet** to open the Magnet window, and change the value of End to .15 and the Magnitude value to .5. Accept the rest as defaults, as shown in Figure 6.10. (The Start and End values define the area of the object where the magnet exerts its force. Points closer than the Start distance receive the full force, while points farther than the

End distance receive none; in between Start and End, the force gradually diminishes.) This is the most difficult part of setting up Magnet. Often, when you first apply it, either the object shoots off the screen or nothing happens. You need a bit of fine-tuning to dial in decent parameters, but it can be done with a little perseverance.

Now, move out of the Magnet dialog box back to the main screen. You are prompted to choose Magnet, so left-click on the control object (the cylinder), and then select the model (the head). "Custom effect complete" is displayed at the status bar. Once again, play back the animation, and experiment with the settings until you are comfortable with the effects of all the parameters. Remember, to modify parameters within Magnet or any of the other persistent custom effects, you'll need to select **Effect|Custom|Edit**.

Also, check out HrcMagnet. By convention, this is the same as Magnet, except it works on hierarchies.

ShrinkWrap

ShrinkWrap is an incredibly useful tool. You'll often find yourself an hour or two into a NURBS modeling session and decide you have to try something else before it turns into a four-hour NURBS session. You may be able to find what you are looking for by using a few primitives and shrinkwrapping them.

A minimum of three components is required:

- The mesh or curve that is going to be the wrapper

- The object or Hrc that is going to be wrapped

- A copy of the wrapper placed either within or on the other side of the object to be wrapped

Once everything is selected, Softimage tries to transform the outer wrapper so that it fits perfectly over the inner wrapper. Because the target—or object to be wrapped—is between the outer and inner wrappers, the outer wrapper cannot reach the

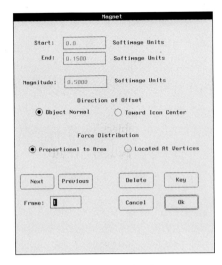

Figure 6.10 Magnet dialog box.

inner wrapper. The result is that every vertex goes as far as it can toward the inner wrapper without hitting the target. Once it intersects the target, it stops. The result of having all the vertices on the outer wrapper behaving in this manner is the appearance of the outer wrapper vacuum-sealing itself to the target.

In short, think of it as the inner wrapper sucking the outer wrapper onto it. One example is shrink-wrapping a curve onto a polygon mesh. This would be no big deal if your target object was a NURBS surface: You would simply perform a **CurveOnSurface**. Projecting a curve onto a surface (and everything you can do with that curve) is one of the best reasons to use NURBS. ShrinkWrap can, in fact, provide that same functionality with polygonal objects.

Let's take a polygonal head model and perform a few operations that would normally be difficult. Start with a simple task, such as projecting a curve onto the head that you can use as a path or as a curve in a skinning operation.

Load the scene "shrink_head" from the chap6 database. Three objects are in the scene: the head/target, the outer spline wrapper, and the inner spline wrapper. You are going to project the outer spline onto the head. The shortest point between the outer and inner wrappers will be the projection vector.

To perform the wrap, select **Deformation| ShrinkWrap**. This will open the ShrinkWrap dialog box.

The first field, Shrink Wrap Factor, determines how close to the target the wrap is placed. A

value of 1 means it is laid on the object. A value of .5 means it will travel halfway between the outer wrapper and the target. Emboss Factor controls the amount the model will be indented. The ShrinkWrap Tagged Points Only checkbox determines whether tagged points *only* are wrapped on to the target. The remaining fields determine the number of subdivisions made while calculating the effect, as you can see in Figure 6.11.

Click on OK to exit the dialog box. You should be prompted to select the Target Mesh or patch. This is the object being wrapped, so click on the head. The prompt now asks you to select the outer wrapper model, so select the outer spline. This may be easier in the Schematic view. After the outer wrapper spline turns red for a second, you'll be prompted to select the inner wrapper. This is easier in the Schematic view. Again, after a brief color change of the inner wrapper, a new spline will appear on the head and shoulders.

At this point, you could do many things with the curve shrunk onto the surface. For example, you could animate a point light down the path, or you could have a snake trace around the path. This would be done by selecting the cylinder (the snake), selecting **Deformation|by Curve|Node|Create**, and choosing the shrink-wrapped curve. The cylinder should jump to the start point of the curve. To animate it, go into "Motion" by pressing F2. Make sure you are in Local Object mode, and enter a value of -3 in the TransY field. This should move the cylinder back a bit off the path. Make sure you are at Frame 1, and set a key by selecting **Savekey|Object|Node Curve Deformation|Translation**.

Drag the frame pointer to Frame 100, and enter a value of 30 in the TransY field. This should position the cylinder off the nose of the face. Set a key here by middle-clicking on the Savekey menu cell. Remember, a middle-click on a menu cell will repeat the last command—in this case, **Savekey|Object|Node Curve Deformation|Translation**. Hit the Play button, and you should have your cylinder snake traveling over your head and shoulders.

Another example of shrink wrapping is a unique way to do the now-common face-in-the-wall effect. Made popular in a variety of horror and special-effects films, a floor or wall appears to flex as a rubber sheet, conforming to a character's face or body. To create a similar effect, try Shrink Wrap, Animated Shrink Wrap, or the Hrc versions of the same tools.

Load "wall_face" from the chap6 database. You will see the model with two grids arranged over its head. Because of the way ShrinkWrap handles vertices that do not intersect the target— that is, they don't do anything—you're going to need to reverse the procedure. Instead of having the outer wrapper shrink in toward the inner grid, the inner wrapper should project out to the outer wrapper. This will give us a flat grid with the face protruding from it. Feel free to experiment using the opposite approach.

Click on **Deformation|ShrinkWrap**, and accept the defaults. At the prompt, click on the head. After the red flash, click on the grid behind the model's face. Again, after the red flash, click on the outer grid. After a brief wait, the new object—a flat grid with a face protruding from it—should appear.

Hide everything except the new object, called "Result." This is easily done by selecting **Display|Hide|Unselected**. This gives you a good view of the new object. The resolution of the face depends on the density of the grid. If you want more detail, perform this example with denser grids.

Go into the Motion module by pressing F2. Select one of the hidden grids, and click on **Duplicate|Immediate**. When the

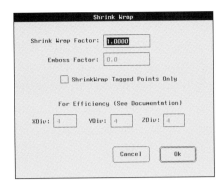

Figure 6.11 Shrink Wrap dialog box.

duplicate is selected, place it at 0,0,0, and freeze everything. Now, select Result, translate it to sit on top of the duplicate, and freeze that as well. Hide the Result object, so the only object visible is the new grid you just copied. Set the frame pointer to Frame 1, and select **Savekey|Object|Shape**. This sets a shape (or morph) key on this object at Frame 1. Now, drag the frame pointer to Frame 50. Select **Shape|Select key shape**, and at the prompt, click on Result. The new object should change shape—depending on whether the centers were at the same places and all concerned were frozen at 0,0,0. You should see a face appear in the clear grid. If the centers were not the same, the face will still appear, but the whole object may translate or scale down.

Included in the database is a working scene called "wall_face_morph." You can load this scene to see a more complete example. This is just the basic concept of how to re-create this effect. You would need to use Animated_ShrinkWrap and many more shapes to merge the wrappers into a wall.

Wrap-Up

Softimage is packed full of useful tools. This chapter has covered some of the highlights and shown you enough so that you can explore the others on your own. This variety of tools can at first seem overwhelming or disconcerting. Start slowly, and add one new tool at a time to your repetoire. Soon, you'll find yourself exploring strange new uses for tools, and what once looked like a crazy mix of functions will become a trusted tool belt for your creative problem solving.

MENTAL RAY
7

Key topics:

- **Render options**

- **Shaders**

- **Command-line rendering**

Mental Ray is a ray-tracing renderer that is tightly integrated with the Extreme version of Softimage|3D. It provides a high level of image fidelity and quality, while offering an open architecture for extension through plug-ins. Renderings with area light sources, volumetric effects, and displacement mapping can all be achieved with Mental Ray, and rendering can be distributed over a number of processors or across a network of systems.

This chapter will cover the rendering features specific to Mental Ray and explore some of the shaders that ship with Softimage Extreme. We will also introduce the text files that Mental Ray produces (.mi files) and examine how you can use them to speed up your rendering workflow and help create or debug complicated scenes.

Rendering With Mental Ray

The process of rendering imagery using Mental Ray is identical to rendering with the Softimage renderer, but Mental Ray has a host of added capabilities. You will still use **Preview** and **Render** from the Matter module, but you will need to set up the program to use Mental Ray rather than the default renderer. The next few sections will cover how to set up and render with Mental Ray, highlight the differences between roughness and displacement mapping, examine some of the lighting essentials unique to Mental Ray, and look at how multiprocessor rendering is handled.

Mental Ray Setup

To render or preview with Mental Ray, you must first select it as your renderer. Otherwise, the Softimage renderer is selected by default. To set up for previewing with Mental Ray, switch to the Matter module, and select **Preview|Setup**. This opens the Preview Setup window, as in Figure 7.1. Halfway down the Setup window is the Preview Renderer section, with two radio buttons: one for the Softimage renderer, and the other for Mental Ray. Activate the Mental Ray radio box, and exit the Setup window. Now, any previews you perform will be rendered to the screen with Mental Ray.

LOW-RESOLUTION PREVIEWS

Previewing should be a nearly interactive process. Depending on your processing power and the complexity of your scene, previewing with Mental Ray at full resolution may be less than interactive. Turn down the resolution of your preview images to speed up the tune-preview-retune cycle.

As a quick test, add a few primitive objects into your current scene, and select **Preview|All**. A brief message will appear at the bottom of the screen, stating "Translating frame 1." This is Softimage sending your scene data to Mental Ray. Next, the screen will go black, and your preview image will start to render. Rather than rendering one scan line at a time, Mental Ray displays small chunks of the image. The image is broken into quarters, and each of these pieces is split into quarters, until small granular image segments are calculated and displayed. When the preview is completed, you can exit as normal by middle-clicking on the mouse.

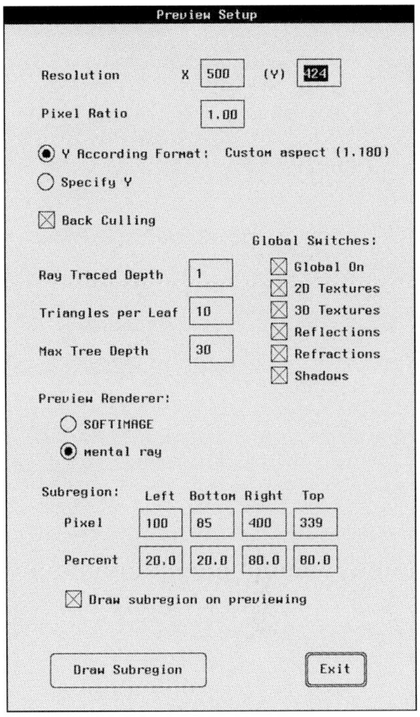

Setting up Mental Ray as your default renderer is similar to selecting it as your current renderer. Select **Render**, which opens the Render Setup window. At the top of the window is a pull-down menu titled "Rendering Type." Left-click on the default type Softimage Renderer. This opens the pull-down menu, allowing you to select an alternative renderer. Select Mental Ray, so that it is now the displayed Rendering Type. Set Sequence Start, End, and Step to 1. This will render a single image to your current database with the name that is in the Filename field. This defaults to "default". Left-click on the Render Sequence button to render the frame. The image is rendered on screen and written to your database. To view the image, switch to the Tools module, and use **Picture** to display it.

Roughness Vs. Displacement

Mental Ray has the ability to render displacement maps. This section will examine the differences between roughness and displacement, and render a simple example to show the benefits of displacement mapping.

Roughness, as previously discussed, is the ability to perturb the normals of a surface to simulate a higher level of detail than is actually modeled. It can be used to create bumps, divots, scratches, and many other useful effects. Unfortunately, roughness has some limitations. Roughness features are rendered only

Figure 7.1   Preview Setup dialog box.

ROUGHNESS VARIES

Be careful when switching scenes from the Softimage renderer to Mental Ray, because roughness is not calculated the same and will produce different results. Tune your textures for the renderer you will use.

on the surface of the object. So, bumps that look as if they protrude from an object are actually only painted onto the object. This can be convincing under many circumstances, but it doesn't hold up under a few conditions.

Roughness has two main shortcomings:

• Roughness features don't cast shadows onto themselves or the surface they protrude from.

• The features are only on the surface, so when you map, say, bumps onto a sphere, the bumps don't push off the edge of the sphere. Instead of seeing a bumpy surface at the edge of the sphere, you see the perfect circle of the underlying geometry.

Both of these shortcomings are alleviated through the use of displacement maps.

Let's make a sample image that shows how a displacement map pushes up off of a surface. Delete any objects in your current scene, and then create two identical B-Spline spheres with Radius 3 and Steps of 20. Place them side by side in your Perspective view. Highlight the one on the left, and select **Texture|2D Global**. Click on the top Select button to set the 2D Texture field. Navigate to the SI_material_lib database, load the "bump medium" texture, and exit the Texture dialog box. Note that this texture has a roughness of 5.0.

Now, select the sphere on the right, and apply the same texture. This time, activate the Displacement checkbox, and set the roughness down to 2.0. Exit the Texture dialog box. If you get a warning about having identical names, just let the program rename the texture for you.

As you can see in Figure 7.2, there is quite a difference between the two. Particularly notice how roughness, when using displacement, actually becomes a measure of the physical distance in world space that the surface is displaced. The Step setting on the displaced sphere must be high enough to allow for any complex mapping to be transferred to the geometry of the object. Using displacement maps is a much more physical process than just using image textures, in that the actual structure of the model is being affected by the map. Unfortunately, the only way to see the effect of the displacement is to preview the scene.

Area Lights

Another distinguishing feature that Mental Ray has is the ability to create light sources that have shape. These area lights can be rectangular, spherical, or disc-shaped. All real-light sources subtend some area, and this is what causes the penumbra around shadows. Therefore, by using area lights, you can create some convincing soft-shadow distributions and can more easily create natural-looking lighting distributions.

Figure 7.3 shows a simple area light scene. Notice how the shadows are sharp near the objects and get softer farther away, and how the specular highlight on the floor has been diffused. This image was created with a single rectangular area light. Place the primitive objects on a grid, and then select **Light|Define** to open the Create Light window. Activate the Area Light checkbox, and change the Area Samplings from 3 to 4. Accept the default shape of rectangular. Add some bounce lights, so the scene is not too stark. Experiment with varying the Area Sampling rates. Sampling at

Figure 7.2 Spheres showing roughness and displacement mapping.

Figure 7.3 Area light rendering.

a rate of 3 or lower may leave noise artifacts in your imagery, but sampling at higher rates can be memory-intensive. You must balance visual quality against render times.

WARNING: TIME WARP AHEAD

Area lights can be very expensive. Use them sparingly. The shadow calculations for area lights can eat up a lot of render time.

Rendering On Multiple Processors

On a machine that has more than one processor, Mental Ray will run multithreaded. The rendering task will be distributed among the available processors without you having to direct or control how the rendering proceeds. The results will be displayed in the usual manner. Two- and four-processor machines have become economical, and you will find Mental Ray makes good use of that extra processing power.

Rendering across a network of machines is nearly as simple as rendering on a single machine. After you have set up to perform network rendering, it becomes nearly automatic. A local file maintains a list of client rendering machines, and at render time, Mental Ray dices up your scene and splits it off to the available machines.

Distributed rendering does not come without a price. In addition to the LAN management and licensing issues, you must realize that a certain amount of overhead is involved in preparing and distributing a rendering job across the network. This said, you will have to tune your network configuration to find the correct blend of quick rendering, best use of network bandwidth, and optimal use of computing resources. Throwing more processors at a rendering problem is not always the best solution. Once you've invested the time to understand what elements are lengthening your render times, you'll be in a much better position to design a rendering configuration that meets your specific needs.

Mental Ray Shaders

Mental Ray is a powerful tool for rendering. Much of its strength comes from add-on utilities called *shaders*. Shaders provide a plug-in architecture that allows third-party developers to extend Mental Ray's functionality. A variety of shaders comes bundled with Softimage. In the next sections, we'll examine the different types of shaders and run through some examples of using them.

Material Shaders

A material shader defines how the common material parameters
for an object are interpreted. A material shader can change the
way an object reflects light in a scene or any other part of the
shading information associated with an object. All the parameters you assign in the Material Editor can be functionally
changed with a material shader to create effects that modify the
appearance of an object.

To apply a material shader, highlight the object to apply the
shader to, and select **Material** to open the Material Editor. In the
Mental Ray section, activate the checkbox for Material Shader,
and navigate to a database containing material shaders to apply.
Use the Select button to choose from the shaders, and use the Edit
button to open the parameters for a particular shader. Softimage
provides a variety of Mental Ray material shaders in the
Shader_Gifts and Shader_Lib databases, as shown in Figure 7.4.

Volume Shaders

A volume shader changes the way light travels through space. It
can create fog and atmospheric phenomena or show the effects

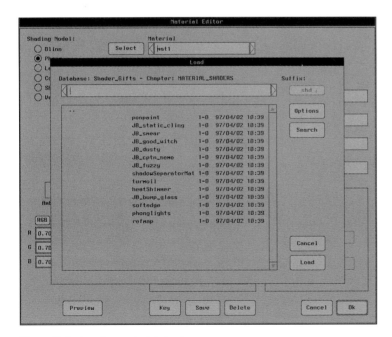

Figure 7.4 Loading material shaders.

of smoke, haze, clouds, or any other semitransparent occurrences in the air. Volume shaders can also make light visible as it passes through space, perhaps bouncing off dust or steam.

You can apply volume shaders from different places, depending on how you will use the volume effect. To change how light passes through an object, use the Volume Shader settings in the Material Editor, just as you did for material shaders. To create light effects, such as in Figure 7.5, you can apply the volume shader under **Atmoshphere|Depth-Fading**. Figure 7.5 was created using the VolumicLights Jr. volume shader.

Figure 7.5 Volume shader rendering.

Texture Shaders

A texture shader modifies the color across the surface of an object. It can reference imagery from files as well as procedurally produce patterns. Fractal noise routines are commonly used in both 2D and 3D to create interesting and useful texture shaders.

You apply texture shaders from the Mental Ray section of the Texture Editor. Figure 7.6 shows a single plane textured with the

Figure 7.6 Texture shader used to create a water look.

"water" texture shader. A variety of texture shaders is provided in the TEXTURE2D_SHADERS chapter of the Shader_Lib database.

Lens Shaders

A lens shader modifies rays as they are cast from the film plane. This allows a lens shader to simulate optical elements in front of the camera, such as lenses and distorting optics. Additionally, you can use a lens shader to add visual effects to incoming light just before it reaches the film back. Effects of this type include lens flares, highlights, glints, and lens scratches.

Figure 7.7 is an image with garish lens-shader effects applied. It uses both a lens flare and a star lens effect. Lens shaders are applied from the **Camera|Settings** dialog box.

Output Shaders

An output shader is called after a rendering is completed. At this point, the output shader can directly manipulate the pixels of the final image and perform a variety of imaging and compositing operations.

Figure 7.7 Image with lens shader effects.

To apply an output shader, open the Render Setup window, and press the Options button in the lower-left corner of the dialog. In the middle of the Mental Ray Options window that opens is an Output Shaders section. Select and apply output shaders here. Any output shaders you select will also be applied when previewing with Mental Ray. Figure 7.8 was created with the "fur grass" output shader. It composites the grasslike structure over the top of a standard grid.

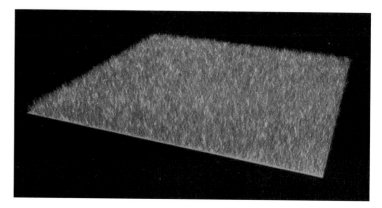

Figure 7.8 Grass effect created with an output shader.

Other Shader Types

Other shader types include light, shadow, and environment.
These are not as commonly used as the standard shaders just
presented. As you become more familiar with shaders and they
become a standard part of your work flow, we urge you to explore some of the more esoteric and niche-use shaders that are
available. You can create many funky effects by combining
shaders and using them in unique and unexpected ways.

POST PROCESS

An output shader is a process that happens after the render. The scene will render and then pause to calculate the output shader effects before delivering the final result.

Mental Ray In Standalone Mode

Mental Ray is tightly integrated with Softimage—the two applications communicate seamlessly as your imagery is rendered.
Sometimes, however, you may want to run Mental Ray all by
itself. In this section, we'll look at how Softimage talks to Mental
Ray and how you can, too.

Generating Scene Files

Mental Ray has a scene file format that contains all the object,
material, lighting, and texture information needed to create an
image. Softimage sends all this information directly to Mental
Ray and then receives the finished image in response. The scene
file itself, however, can be stored, viewed, modified, and rendered
outside of Softimage.

A scene file is often referred to as an .mi file, because .mi is the
suffix used for the files that Mental Ray saves. (Mental Ray was
developed by a German company called *Mental Images*; hence,
the *mi*.)

Delete the contents of your current scene, and add in a single
primitive cube. Now, to create a file for this scene, open the Render Setup window, and click on the Options button in the
lower-left corner of the dialog, the same place you applied output
shaders. In the Image Options section, activate the checkbox for
Output to File. The default file name is out.mi. This is fine for
now. Click on Accept to exit from the Options window and return

to Render Setup. Click the Render sequence button. The window exits, but instead of rendering your scene, the out.mi file is saved to disk.

Here are the slightly edited contents of out.mi (some non-ASCII data has been removed for readability):

```
#
# generated from Softimage file no_name.1-0
# Mon Sep 29 16:14:20 1997
#
verbose off

#-- Generation of 'CODE' statements

#-- Generation of 'LINK' statements

#-- Generation of 'DECLARE' statements
$include "/usr/softimage/3D/rsrc/
softimage.mi"

frame 1 0.033333

light "default" "soft_point" (
   "color"   1.0 1.0 1.0,
   "factor"  1.0
   )
   origin    100.000000 89.553352 89.354340
end light

view
   output "pic" "/usr/people/softimage/
book_database/
   RENDER_PICTURES/default.1.pic"
   focal 50.000000
   aperture 44.724029
   aspect 1.179245
   resolution 500 424
   acceleration spatial subdivision
   max size 6
   max depth 40
   recursive on
   adaptive on
   min samples -1
   max samples 1
   samples 1
   gamma 1.000000
   contrast 0.100000 0.100000 0.100000
```

```
   trace depth 1 2
   clip 0.100000 32768.000000
   face both
   shadow on
   trace on
   desaturate off
   dither off
   transform 1.000000 0.000000 0.000000 0.0
       0.000000 0.995037 -0.099504 0.0
       0.000000 0.099504 0.995037 0.0
       0.000000 2.000000 20.000000 1.0
end view

material "DEFAULT1"  opaque
"soft_material" (
   "mode"     2,
   "ior"          1.000000,
   "shiny"    50.000000,
   "transp"  0.000000,
   "reflect"  0.000000,
   "ambient"  0.500000 0.500000 0.500000,
   "diffuse"  0.700000 0.700000 0.700000,
   "specular"  1.000000 1.000000 1.000000,
   "ambience"  0.300000 0.300000 0.300000,
   "lights" ["default"]
   )
end material

object "_cube1" visible shadow trace tag 1
   transform   1.000000e+00 -0.000000e+00
0.000000e+00 0.0
       0.000000e+00 9.950372e-01 -
9.950373e-02 0.0
       -0.000000e+00 9.950373e-02
9.950372e-01 0.0
       -0.000000e+00 2.000000e+00
2.000000e+01 1.0
   group _mesh
# 0
     v 0   n 8
     v 1   n 9
     v 3   n 10
     v 2   n 11
# 4
     v 1   n 12
     v 5   n 13
     v 7   n 14
     v 3   n 15
# 8
     v 5   n 16
     v 4   n 17
```

```
     v  6    n  18
     v  7    n  19
#  12
     v  4    n  20
     v  0    n  21
     v  2    n  22
     v  6    n  23
#  16
     v  4    n  24
     v  5    n  25
     v  1    n  26
     v  0    n  27
#  20
     v  2    n  28
     v  3    n  29
     v  7    n  30
     v  6    n  31

     p  "DEFAULT1"      0  1  2  3
     p  "DEFAULT1"      4  5  6  7
     p  "DEFAULT1"      8  9  10  11
     p  "DEFAULT1"      12  13  14  15
     p  "DEFAULT1"      16  17  18  19
     p  "DEFAULT1"      20  21  22  23
   end group
end object

end frame

#  The end...
```

This code is very readable. There's nothing magic about a scene file; it just contains everything that Mental Ray needs to render a scene. As you can see, there is a light source, a camera view (including the file name of where the rendered image will be deposited), a material, and the object itself. In this example, the vertices are used to create the six polygonal faces of the cube.

At this point, you can make any modifications you desire to the .mi file. Be careful, of course, to maintain the syntax of the scene file. You can quickly change values and easily modify file names, etc. As an example, go to the section of the file where the soft_material, is held and modify the diffuse color values. It is currently set to 0.700000, 0.700000, 0.700000, the default RGB gray. Change the value to 1.0 0.0 0.0 to make your cube red. If you are handy at editing scripts, you should find working with .mi files a breeze. It gives you a powerful way of controlling exactly what parameters get passed to Mental Ray and how this can be especially useful when working with shaders.

Rendering A Scene File

To render a scene file, you need to pass the contents of the .mi file to Mental Ray. This is a simple process of calling Mental Ray from the command line.

Start up a command prompt window, and from the directory that contains your file, run the command **ray.exe out.mi**. This calls ray, which is the core ray tracer of Mental Ray, and uses out.mi as the scene to render. All the information needed to create the final image is in the .mi file. The image of a red cube is placed directly into the RENDERED_PICTURES directory of your default database. You can now use the **imgshow** command to view the image, or reopen Softimage and use the **Tools|Picture** browser to display the rendered image.

You may have noticed that the image rendered quite quickly. This is because all the overhead of generating the scene file occurred when the file was created. The scene file doesn't need to be transferred at all because Mental Ray is working with it directly. This can save some substantial time when you are fine-tuning shader variables. Just write the scene out once, and then edit it in one window, while rendering and displaying it in another. Also, if your machine can't spare the memory, rendering with only Mental Ray saves you the memory that Softimage was using.

Wrap-Up

This has been a brief introduction to the capabilities of Mental Ray. As you become more comfortable with this renderer and begin to explore its potential, you'll start to use the default renderer less and less. You'll find yourself becoming dependent on cool shaders, area lights, displacement mapping, and, in general, superior image quality.

PARTICLE 8

Key topics:

- **Particle parameters**

- **Forces**

- **Obstacles**

- **Command-line rendering**

Particle is a pixel-based application used for creating and animating particle systems. A particle system creates imagery by drawing large numbers of pixel primitives, such as points, lines, and small sprites or images. The system enables you to set particles into motion and build up rules for how particles generate, evolve, and interact. Particle runs as a separate application from Softimage. You create imagery and animations inside Particle and then import that imagery back to Softimage or composite it into another application.

In this chapter, we'll introduce the basics of Particle, including the Particle interface, sources, parameters, forces, obstacles, collisions, and the Particle file format.

Introduction

Particle's base element is the individual *particle*. Particle types define the properties of a specific particle. *Sources* emit particles of a specific type and have their own parameters, which define their shape and how they emit particles. To design a particle system, you place sources into an environment and animate all the parameters that control the system over time. Additionally, you can apply *forces* that influence particles and place in the environment *obstacles* that affect the particles.

Interface

To begin, start up the Particle application, and click on the **New** button under Source. This places a particle-emitting source at the origin of your scene, as shown in Figure 8.1.

At the bottom of the screen are the timeline controls. The start and end frame numbers are in text fields to the right of the timeline. There, you can set up the length of your particle animation. In the lower right of the screen are some simple transport controls for playing back animations, single stepping through time, and jumping to the beginning and end of your animation. As in Softimage|3D, you can drag a triangular time pointer along the timeline, updating the current frame to the right of the timeline.

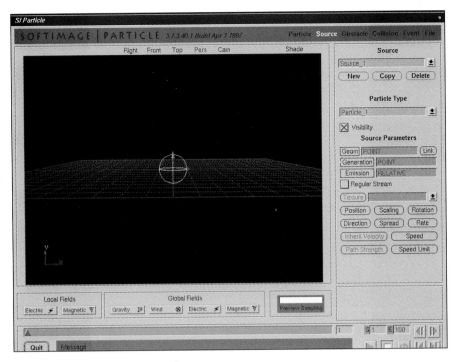

Figure 8.1 The Particle user interface.

Above the display window are some view controls that allow you to change how you view your scene. The default is a perspective camera view, but by clicking on the words (Right, Front, and so on), you can switch to orthographic camera views that give planar projections of your scene.

Below the display window are six buttons that toggle on and off a variety of forces that can be applied to particles. These simulate gravity, wind, and some force-field type effects that will be covered in detail later. Next to the force buttons is a slider labeled "Preview Sampling." This slider allows you to tune the percentage of the particles in the scene that will be displayed during previewing. By moving the slider to its half-way point, you can cut the number of particles in half. This can greatly reduce the number of calculations needed during previewing and is especially useful for scenes with large numbers of particles.

The right side of the screen is where the bulk of the controls lies. In Figure 8.1, you can see the Source tools. All the buttons and

PREVIEW SAMPLING

Tune the Preview Sampling slider to match the complexity of your scene. As you add multiple sources, turn the sampling rate down to maintain interactivity during previewing.

widgets for creating sources and editing their properties are on the right of the screen. In the upper right, where the word *Source* is highlighted, you can select from the other tools (Particle, Obstacle, Collision, Event, and File). Left-click on each of these words to see its tools on the right side of the screen. After you've looked around, finish by left-clicking back on **Source** so you can examine its parameters.

Sources

A source is a particle emitter. The current scene has only one source, Source_1, as displayed in the upper text window of the Source section. The next text window is labeled "Particle Type." This defines the type of particle that is currently assigned to the source. In this example, the source is set to emit particles of type Particle_1.

Below this is a checkbox labeled "Visibility." It is a toggle to switch off the display of the particles emitted by this source. When you are creating scenes with many sources, you may want to switch off all the others while you are tuning one up. This leaves the scene less cluttered and also speeds up playback while you get one source at a time just right.

The Source Parameters section is just below the Visibility checkbox. These values—Geom, Generation, Emission, Position, Scaling, Rotation, Direction, Spread, Rate, Speed, Speed Limit, Inherit Velocity, and Path Strength—define all the characteristics of a source.

The Geom section defines the shape of the source. Left-click on the **Geom** button to see the variety of shapes you can use. There are six shapes (Point, Line, Square, Disk, Cube, and Sphere) that emit particles, and the Scene Object option, which allows you to use objects from one of your Softimage scenes as source geometry. As you change between **Geom** types, you will see that shape highlighted in green in the center of your source.

Generation defines where particles are emitted from your selected geometry. The choices are:

* *Point*—from the center of the source
* *Linear*—along the X axis
* *Surface*—on the surface of your source geometry
* *Volume*—within the enclosed volume of your source

Emission controls the direction the emitted particles take from the source. A source has a white vector, which points away from itself. **Emission** can be set to act **Relative** to this vector or to emit along a global direction—this is the **Absolute** mode. In addition to the directional emission controls, a **Path** option allows you to define a curve in Softimage to use as an emission path from the source.

The remaining buttons bring up a parameter type in values. The three transformation buttons—**Position, Scaling,** and **Rotation**—allow you to set values for X, Y, and Z. You can also control these parameters directly by manipulating the source in the display window. These parameters change the position, shape, and orientation of your source element.

Direction sets the orientation of the white vector, which defines the direction of source emission. It is defined by two angles: the Inclination and

Azimuth of the direction vector. These angles are measured in degrees. The **Spread** parameter defines how many degrees from **Direction** particles will be emitted. It is a major parameter, because it defines the width of the stream of particles being emitted. You usually need to set **Spread**; otherwise, it defaults to 0, which emits all the particles in a straight line. Set **Spread** to 10, and press **Play** to preview the results, shown in Figure 8.2.

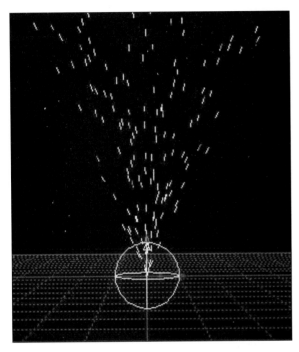

Figure 8.2 Source with Spread set to 10.

Rate defines how many particles are emitted per second. **Speed** defines how fast they are going, and **Speed Limit** allows you to constrain speed to a certain range. **Inherit Velocity** is used only with moving objects. Velocity is calculated in relation to the speed of the object.

The final parameter, **Path Strength**, is applied only when you emit along a path. It defines how tightly the particles cling to the original path.

Now that you've looked at all the source parameters, let's move on to the types of particles that you can generate. In the upper

Figure 8.3 The Particle parameters.

right of the screen, click on **Particle** or press F1 to open up the parameters for the particle types.

Types

The text box at the top of the parameters reads "Particle_1," the name of the particle type that is currently being edited. To create new particle types, click on the **New** button. You can select from any current particle types by clicking on the arrow to the right of the text box. Leave Particle_1 selected.

A series of nine buttons is labeled "Particle Parameters," shown in Figure 8.3. These are the traits that define how a particle will behave when emitted into a scene. The first three parameters—**Friction**, **Electric**, and **Magnetic**—relate to how the particle is acted on by external forces. By left-clicking on the buttons, you open their parameters to be modified. **Friction** acts as a dissipating force, as if the particle is being slowed down by passing through a medium. The global force **Wind** makes the medium move, so **Friction** and **Wind** are interrelated. Likewise, the other two force parameters define how global forces affect the particle. **Electric** sets how much electrical fields act on the particle. **Magnetic** defines the effects of magnetic fields. Forces will be covered later in the chapter.

When particles collide, **Mass** determines how they interact—heavy particles have more push. **Life Time** defines how long a particle is alive. **Trail Life** sets (in seconds) how long a path is left behind a traveling particle. Trails can enhance the look of motion among your particles. **Noise** randomly tweaks particles to modify their position, velocity, or acceleration values. **Sigma** is another collision parameter, which defines the percentage chance that like particles will collide.

Clicking on the last parameter, **Decay**, opens a dialog box used to set **Decay** attributes. When a particle reaches the end of its **Life Time**, it can decay into another type of particle. The Particle Decay dialog box allows you to set the type, number, and emission attributes of the new particles. By chaining **Decay**s, you can have one particle type decay into a second, which decays into a third, and so on to create complex effects.

The final parameters for particle types are the Rendering Attributes. These effects are seen only at render time and do not show up when you preview your particle system. **Size** is in Softimage units. **Color** opens a color editor. **Blur** allows you to define motion blur-type effects for each particle. **Multiplication** creates multiple instances of the original particle.

Obstacles

Press F3 to bring up the Obstacle parameters, as in Figure 8.4. Obstacles are objects in your scene that particles interact with (bounce off, stick to, and so on). After creating a new obstacle, you set up which particle types are affected by the obstacle by adding them to the Absorb list.

Geom sets the shape of the obstacle (Square, Disc, Cube, or Sphere). **Type** defines what particles do when they strike the obstacle (bounce off, stick to it, disappear, decay, or emit a new particle). The transformation parameters—**Position, Scaling**, and **Rotation**—let you move, stretch, and spin the obstacle.

The **Resilience** and **Friction** parameters affect obstacles that bounce or emit particles. **Resilience** changes the speed of particles that hit the obstacle, and **Friction** makes particles stick to it. If the obstacle is of type Emit, you must define which types of particles are emitted, how many, and what their emission parameters are (**Direction, Speed, Spread**, and so on).

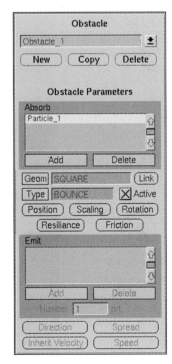

Figure 8.4 The Obstacle parameters.

Collisions And Events

Collisions set up the odds that two particle types passing through the same space will interact with each other. Press F4 to bring up the Collision parameters, shown in Figure 8.5. Define the two particle types that will collide by filling in the Particle 1 and 2 fields. Then, set the **Probability** that these two types will collide.

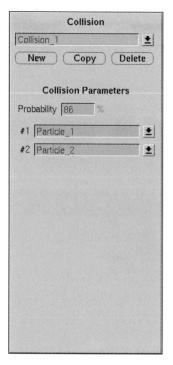

Figure 8.5 The Collision parameters.

A **Probability** of 100 means they will always hit each other, while 0 means they will never interact.

Events are collisions that cause particles to be generated at the point of the collision. Press the F5 key to see the Event parameters, as shown in Figure 8.6. Particle types that will cause events when they collide are **Added** to the Absorb list. The particle types they emit are **Added** to the Emit box. **Probability** defines the likelihood the Absorb particle types will collide, while the **Number** parameters define how many particles are absorbed or emitted when they do. The **Direction**, **Spread**, and **Speed** parameters define how the new particles are emitted.

Forces

Forces are fields of influence that affect particles. You can apply forces globally to affect all the particles in a scene, or you can position local fields at certain points in space. Forces allow you to create stunning dynamic simulations quickly and easily.

Gravity

Gravity is a global field that pulls according to the **Strength** parameter on all the particles in the scene. You can modify the **Direction** angles—Inclination and Azimuth—to redirect the pull of gravity. It starts out pulling directly down the Y axis.

Set **Strength** to 5, and see how that affects your current scene. You can also modify **Direction** by directly manipulating the white gravity vector in the display window. By moving the arrow next to the capital G, you can steer the direction of gravity.

Wind

Wind is also a global effect. It acts as a moving medium that particles must pass through. By setting the **Strength** and **Direction** of the wind, you define how the particles are affected. As with gravity, you can directly manipulate the Wind icon in the display window to update **Direction**.

The Turbulence section of the Wind dialog box has two other terms available for the wind force: **Correlation** measures how much turbulence is applied to a particle, and **Amplitude** turns up the power of the turbulence. Both these parameters refer to the **Friction** value that is set for a particle. Particles with a **Friction** of 0 are not affected by turbulence.

Magnetic

Magnetic forces can be applied globally or locally. A magnetic field asserts a rotational influence on the particles, creating a swirling pattern. The **Strength** parameter again defines how much of an influence the force has, while the **Direction** angles define how the force is oriented.

Additionally, a local magnetic field has a **Position**, where the force emanates from, and a **Droprate**, which defines how far the force influences particles from its **Position**. You can create a multitude of local forces, but you can have only a single global force of any one kind.

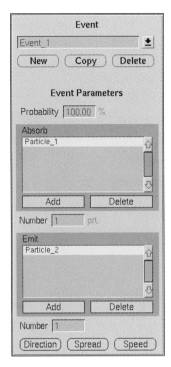

Figure 8.6 The Event parameters.

Electric

The electric force is similar to the magnetic, in that it can be global or local. An electric field attracts or repulses particles based on its **Strength**. Positive values attract particles, while negative values push them away. You must have the Electric parameter of your particles set to nonzero for multiple electric forces to have an effect.

You can create multiple electric forces by making local forces. As with local magnetic forces, you must supply the **Position** and **Droprate** for the force. Experiment with local electric forces. Try to get particles to orbit around multiple locally positioned fields.

Sample Particle Scenes

To examine a number of different particle systems, switch to the File parameters page. From here, you can load in some of the sample particle systems that Softimage delivers with Particle. Click on the arrow to the right of the Database field. From the databases that are displayed, select EXAMPLES_DB.

Press the **Load** button, and from the systems shown, select "Friction_final." This particle system has a linear source with two obstacles below it. The particle colors shift from white to green-blue as they travel. This creates a simple waterfall effect, as seen in Figure 8.7.

Figure 8.7 Rendered image of a waterfall.

Load the system called "flame." This uses a disc source and then some fields to perturb the particle flow, thus creating the look of a licking flame. The colors of the particles shift from yellow to red as they go up the flame, and they have a slight trail effect, which heightens the sense of motion. Figure 8.8 shows a sample image of the rendered result.

No examination of particle systems would be complete without a fireworks example. Load the system titled "FireWorks" as a

DO IT IN COLOR!

Do you dream in black and white, or in color? In this section, we'll present a variety of images that highlight the projects from the book, and also showcase other real-world Softimage work. For some of the animation projects, we display multiple small images to give you a feel for the motion, while reserving full pages for the glamour shots, so you can see all the detail. All imagery created by Gene Bodio and/or Phil LeMarbre for PCA Graphics Inc. unless otherwise stated.

If you don't find a specific image from the book here in color, you'll have to just complete that project and render it for yourself!

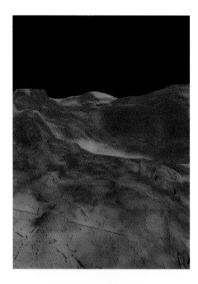

Alien City Project

This Alien City project will build directly upon the work you completed for the city project in Chapter 14. The city project constructed a low polygon count grouping of buildings for use in a gaming environment or for a VRML application. The entire scene is quite simple, yet added textures makes it a detailed backdrop. The scene is compact enough to be interactively updated on most low-end 3D devices, including game consoles and home PCs with little or no 3D support. This project uses Chapter 14's earth-bound city as an element in an other-worldly landscape scene.

To compose the new scene, you will create a landscape that will surround your city elements. The terrain should look barren and unearthly. There should be relief in the distance to add visual appeal, and there needs to be flat areas where you can insert your domed cities. Use the terrain techniques covered in Chapter 12 to create a fractalized landscape. If you're rendering with Mental Ray, consider using displacement maps to add detail to this geometry. Layer some rocky, sandy, and gritty textures to create a harsh airless planet surface; instead of earth tones, use dark blues, purples, and grays to tinge the landscape. Determine where you will place domed cities on the landscape, and flatten out those regions by tagging their vertices and scaling them to level. Be careful not to shear your landscape by flattening out the side of a mountain.

Before adding city elements, set up the background. Add a large sphere to your scene and surround the landscape with it.

Scale the sphere to encompass your whole scene (including the camera) and then invert the sphere so that it renders properly from the inside. If you are using Mental Ray, apply one of the night sky environment shaders to the sphere; otherwise, paint up a texture to put on the sphere as a sky backdrop. (This process was covered in Chapter 2, in the cemetery scene.) Now that you have some decent surroundings, it's time to add some lighting. Use stark directional lights for your key lighting. They should be quite cool tones—on the blue side of white—and should cast sharp, dark shadows. Make sure the diffuse components of your scene elements are nearly black. Add some dark purple and bluish fill lights to punch up your shadows and add some detail and mystery to your landscape.

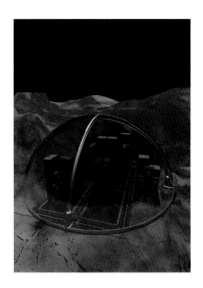

Now we'll add the cities. The central domed city will be the main element in the scene. Because the viewer's attention will be focused primarily on this element, spend some extra effort to nail it down. If you like, add some futuristic detail to the city at the street level, such as space craft or high-tech billboards. The structure that holds up the dome should look high tech and solid enough to hold the huge expanse of transparent material that covers the city. First, create the base that you will place the city block onto; a revolve of a single curve should suffice for a solid base. Then, construct a support element and an arch. Copy these objects as needed to complete the main structure. Finally, create the dome itself using a highly transparent and reflective half sphere. Adjust the specularity of the dome to get attractive highlights and, if you are using Mental Ray, make sure you use

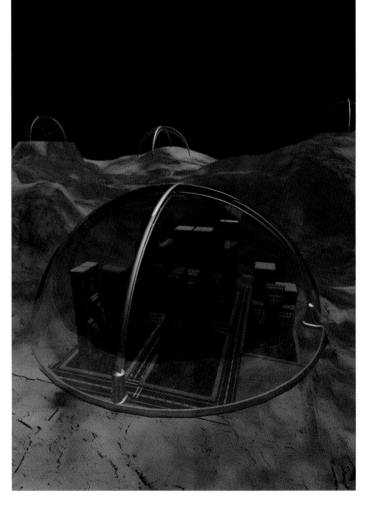

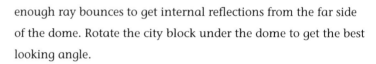

enough ray bounces to get internal reflections from the far side of the dome. Rotate the city block under the dome to get the best looking angle.

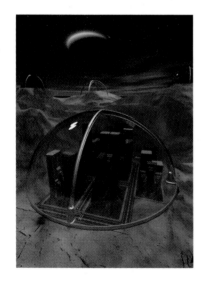

Now things are starting to come together. Copy the whole domed city and place smaller copies off in the distance, where you have flattened out the terrain. Add some small pickup lights to indicate the scale of your scene and to highlight any elements you think need attention. Position some high tech flying vehicles with obligatory plasma exhaust systems, and you're all set. You might also consider using some lens effects, or adding some glints and glimmers to other scene elements to add interest. Decide on your final scene composition and start tuning your elements to heighten the overall scene appearance or your final rendering. Adjust light positions so that the shadows look dramatic and the highlights off the dome are impressive. That's it. You now have a happening alien metropolis—good work!

These images were reconstructed from imagery produced by Gene Bodio and Steve Speer for B2 Engine Inc. They were created for SOK Industries, a Japanese security company, and were nominated for an International Broadcasting Award. Facial features were animated with clusters and IK was used for body movements. Images courtesy of PCA Graphics.

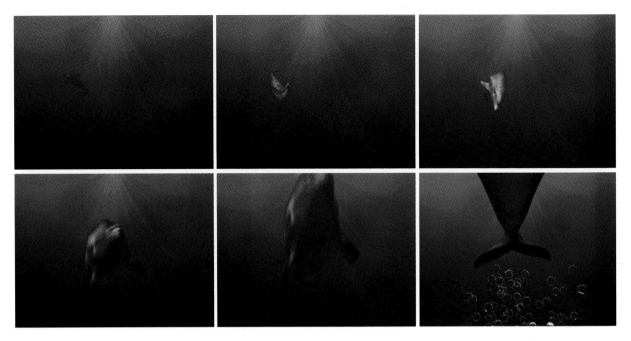

These are snapshots from the dolphin animation generated in Chapter 9. The dolphin barrel rolls off in the distance and then whooshes up over the camera.

Mental Ray shaders create atmospheric and glowing effects. Generated with a procedural output shader called Soft-FX.

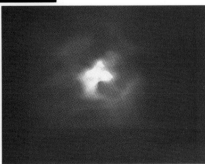

A lively character model, this frog was modeled to allow for a full range of motion without rips or tears where the legs merge with the body. His stylized lines, vibrant coloration, and energetic facial expression bring the frog to life. Created by Gene Bodio and Steve Webster.

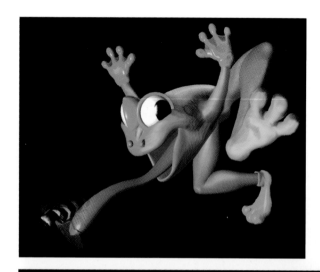

This dramatic still life was modeled and rendered by Rob Stein III.

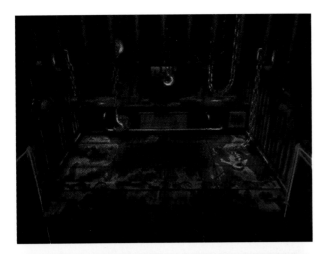

This dark environment was created for a game project. These shots were used as backgrounds for interactively placed sprites or simple 3D characters that can be controlled by a player. Note how layered textures have been used to change reflectance properties and add multiple layers of dirt, grunge, and erosion. Also, using the spreadsheet, the camera was tweaked to correct perspective distortions of the scene.

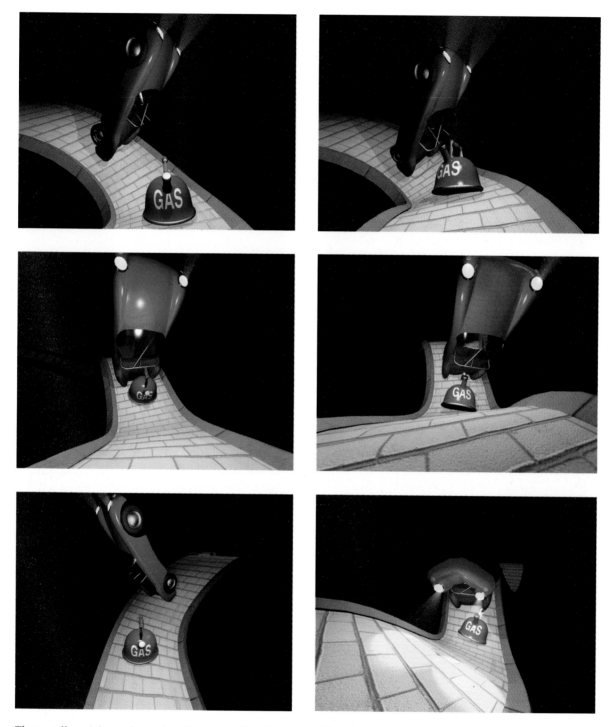

These stills are from the animation created in the Car Walk project from Chapter 13. Headlights and a starry night background have been added to the scene, as well as some additional character animation.

These images are part of an animation in which the viewer speeds down a tunnel lined with psychedelic cyber textures, used as an introductory animation on a CD-ROM project. The transparent textures are animated, as well as the underlying geometry. All images were created by PCA Graphics Inc. for the CD-ROM game by Hasbro Interactive.

The figures above are examples of what can be done with transparency maps. The geometry is composed of nurbs and spline grids.

The images on the left are made from the same cylinder using Matter| Polygon|AutoColorize and local 2D texture maps. AutoColorize will assign a material on every other 4-sided polygon. That material is then used as material for a local texture. A sky was mapped to the material on the top-left, and the other is an abstract image. The images on the right are also made from the same cylinder using Matter|Polygon|AutoColorize and local 2D texture maps. A sky was mapped to the material on the top, and a picture of a circuit board is mapped to the other material. The images were run through a Photoshop edge detection filter.

Here are a variety of images created in projects throughout the book. Use them as guides to tune your color selection and parameter tuning as you complete the projects.

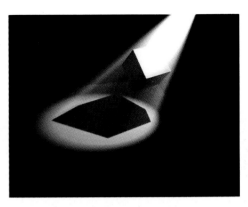

Volume lighting from Chapter 7.

Game interface rendering from Chapter 10.

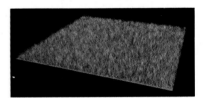

Grass shader from Chapter 7.

The cemetery scene from Chapter 2.

Example of static blur from Chapter 3.

The Nemo shader used in Chapter 3.

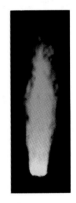

Flame created with Particle in Chapter 8.

Variations on a theme, these game interfaces are similar to
the Yahtzee interface developed in Chapter 10. The final rendering of the logo project from Chapter 11 is on the facing page.
Images are courtesy of Hasbro Interactive.

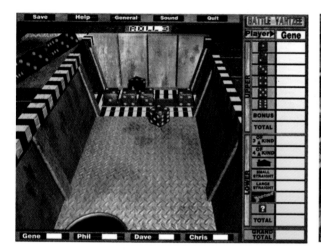

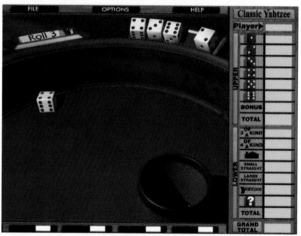

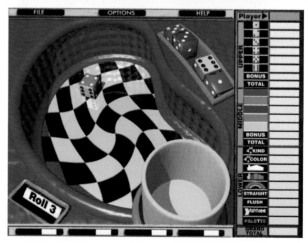

These images were created from the ant walk scene in Chapter 12. The ants were formed into a procession by turning animation on in the duplication setup dialog box and offsetting the copies out along the walking path. The ants make strong use of IK and animating them, as in the fight image shown, is a natural process of animating the proper end effectors.

3D models by Viewpoint DataLabs International, Inc.

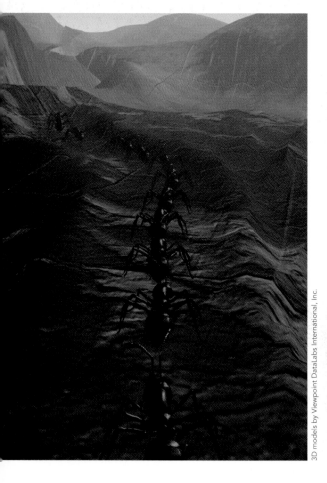

3D models by Viewpoint DataLabs International, Inc.

3D models by Viewpoint DataLabs International, Inc.

sample. Try adding some secondary particle emissions to this example. In other words, make the Particle_3 type decay into a particle of your making.

As one final example, let's look at a system with some more pyrotechnics. Load the system called "explosion." This system ejects debris in all directions and has an absorbing obstacle that catches the debris as it hits the ground. Figure 8.9 is a rendered still halfway through the explosion. Try adding some smoke and a second group of scattered particles that are lighter and somewhat agitated by turbulence as well.

Particle File Format

Just as Mental Ray has a text file format, so does Particle. Most folks never bother to tweak particle files, preferring instead to rely on the Particle user interface to meet their needs. If you consider yourself a hardened techster, however, and need the challenge of learning yet another scripting language, Particle won't let you down.

As with most scripting tools, you can achieve some powerful custom effects by editing your own files. You can also quickly change scene elements without opening Particle, and you can

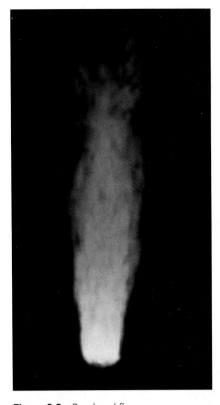

Figure 8.8 Rendered flame.

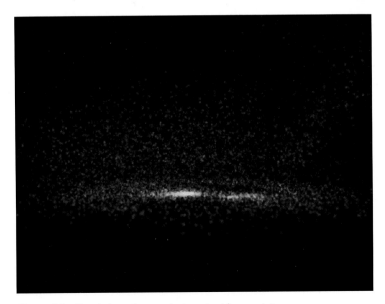

Figure 8.9 Rendering of an explosion at midway point.

render the final images or scenes directly from the command line.

When Particle writes out a file, it actually stores two files: a settings file and a description file. The settings file has all the camera and scene information. Here is a simple settings file:

```
Cameras {
  Settings:
    Type = Perspective
    Position = 0.0000 2.0000 20.0000
    Interest = 0.0000 0.0000 0.0000
    Field of View = 43.7000
    Twist = 0.0000
    Aspect = 1.3333
    Near = 0.1000
    Far = 32768.0000
  Settings:
    Type = Ortho
    Position = 20.0000 0.0000 0.0000
    Interest = 0.0000 0.0000 0.0000
    Field of View = 43.7000
    Twist = 0.0000
    Aspect = 1.3333
    Near = 0.1000
    Far = 32768.0000
  Settings:
    Type = Ortho
    Position = 0.0000 0.0000 20.0000
    Interest = 0.0000 0.0000 0.0000
    Field of View = 43.7000
    Twist = 0.0000
    Aspect = 1.3333
    Near = 0.1000
    Far = 32768.0000
  Settings:
    Type = Ortho
    Position = 0.0000 20.0000 0.0000
    Interest = 0.0000 0.0000 0.0000
    Field of View = 43.7000
    Twist = 0.0000
    Aspect = 1.3333
    Near = 0.1000
    Far = 32768.0000
  Current = 1
}

Setup {
```

```
    Oversampling = 1
    Sequence = 1 500 1 139
}

Images {
  Name = "default"
  Path = "/usr/people/softimage/
book_database/RENDER_PICTURES"
  OutputBpf = 0
  ZChannel = 0
  Resolution = 250 188
  Sequence = 1 100 1
  Pixel = 1.0000
  Background {
    Type = 0
    Color = 0.000000 0.000000 0.000000
    Path = ""
    Name = ""
    ZPic = 0
    ZPath = ""
    ZName = ""
  }
  Options {
    SortInZ = 0
    FieldRendering = 0 2
    Desaturation  = 0
    Fading {
      Active = 0
      Near = 0.000000
      Far = 20.000000
    }
  }
  Preview {
    Resolution = 250 188
    Sequence = 1 100 1
    DraftMode = 1
  }
}

PARTTYPE {
  SizeInPixel = 0
  AlphaInUse = 1
  Multiple {
    Active = 0
    Count = 0
    Size = 0.0000
    SizeJitter = 0.0000
    Rotation = 0.0000 0.0000
    Position = 0.0000 0.0000 0.0000
  }
```

```
    Image {
      Active = 0
      Name = ""
      Rotation = 0.0000
    }
    Shape {
      Type = 1
      Name = ""
      Resolution = 129 129
    }
    Brush = 1
    Parameters = {}
    Glow = 0
    BlurType = 1
    Blur = 0.0000
  }
```

Most of the parameters should look familiar. All the scene attributes are contained here, including where and how the imagery will be rendered. Be careful when modifying these files to maintain the Particle syntax. Next, here is a simple description file:

```
# Dexter version 1.0 (2.0.3)

def system "partest"
  scene = ""
  dbase = ""
  seed = 0
  range = 1
  source_rate = 1
  frame_rate = 30
  preroll = 0
  gravity_dir = { 0.0, 0.0}
  gravity_strength = 3
  force_dir = { 0.0, 0.0}
  force_strength = 0.0
  vortex_dir = { 0.0, 0.0}
  vortex_strength = 0.0
  drag_dir = { 0.0, 0.0}
  drag_strength = 0.0
  turbulence = { 0.0, 0.0}
  nearobst = DISABLE_COLLISION

  def particle "Particle_1"
    color_model = COLOR_RGB
    color_type = COLOR_STATIC
    trail_type = TRAIL_NONE
    trail_color_model = COLOR_RGB
```

```
    trail_color_type =
COLOR_INHERIT_DYNAMIC
    state = STATE_SIZE_0 | STATE_MASS_0
    lifetime = 4
    mass = 1
    force = 0.0
    vortex = 0.0
    drag = 0.0
    noise = 0.0
    vnoise = 0.0
    anoise = 0.0
    cnoise = { 0.0, 0.0, 0.0}
    size = 0.3
    collision_rate = 0.0
    color = { 1, 1, 1, 1}
    color_scale = { 0.0, 0.0, 0.0, 0.0}
    trail_life = 0.0
    trail_color = { 1, 1, 1, 1}
    trail_color_scale = { 0.0, 0.0, 0.0,
0.0}
    blur = 0.2
  enddef

  def source "Source_1"
    particle_type = "Particle_1"
    reference = ""
    gen = GEN_0_DIM
    emission_mode = MODE_STOCHASTIC
    state = STATE_STATIC_VEL
    geometry = GEOMETRY_POINT
    emission = EMISSION_RELATIVE
    pos = { 0.0, 0.0, 0.0}
    scale = { 1, 1, 1}
    rot = { 0.0, 0.0, 0.0}
    vel = { 0.0, 0.0, 0.0}
    dir = { 0.0, 0.0}
    speed = 5
    speed_min = 0.0
    speed_max = 1000
    rate = 100
    spread = 0.0
    spread = jitter box 0.0277778
  enddef
enddef
```

You can easily see the particle and source parameters. You can just as easily modify them for your needs and resave the files to render your new effects. If you've come this far, you have to try rendering directly from the command line. First, run Particle to make sure you have the path set correctly. Type *particle -R,* which should return with all the parameters for Particle. Now, to render a system, using full path names, type "X:\softimage\particle\bin\particle X:\softimage\particle\rsrc -R scenename", where *X* is the drive where you have Softimage installed and *scenename* is the name of your saved Particle file. The results will be rendered to the appropriate database.

Wrap-Up

Particle takes some practice to master, but it's well worth the effort. Push yourself a little further each time you use it. The effects you can create with forces and obstacles, for example, are mind boggling. Begin with simple systems, and evolve them to meet your production needs. Plan ahead, because you'll have to composite your results, and remember, that takes time, too.

This is the last chapter that covers specific tools and features. The rest of the book will focus on real-world projects and how to put what you've learned into practice. So, let's move on to the stuff that pays the bills.

PART 3

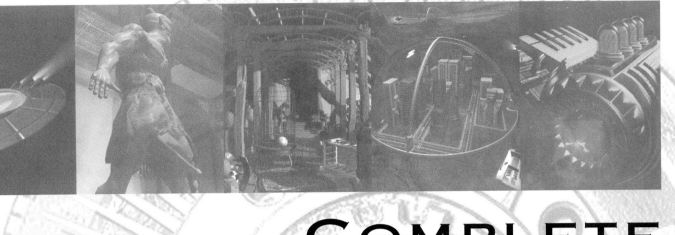

COMPLETE PROJECTS

DOLPHIN ANIMATION 9

Key topics:

- **Spline deformation**
- **Polygon reduction**
- **Model substitution**
- **Depth fading**
- **Flipbook preview**

In this project, you will create a short animation sequence of a dolphin swimming. The dolphin will swim forward, do a barrel roll, and whoosh up past the camera for a finale.

The main tool for this project is *spline deformation*, in which you use a spline as the Y axis for an attached object. Simply by translating along Y, you can make your model deform and contort to match the shape of your path. (Imagine a snake slithering along your spline, or a cartoon race car bending and stretching as it banks around turns.) Spline deformation will let you quickly create a swimming path for your dolphin while imparting a very natural-looking motion that allows for tail flipping and lots of energetic and fluid body moves.

To enhance interactivity during the creation process, use *model substitution*, which allows you to switch easily among multiple versions of your model. You can use Softimage's polygon reduction tools to create a lightweight model of your dolphin, then set up model substitution to switch between your low-polygon model and your high-end final version. This way, you can do all of your motion tests and animations with snappy efficiency, yet still be able to switch over at any point to preview the end product.

The last step will be to add some atmosphere by using *depth fading*, which lets you tinge the color in your scene based on how far away the rendered objects are. In this project, depth fading will be used to simulate light being absorbed and colored by ocean water. The dolphin will emerge from the murky depths and become less occluded as it approaches the viewer.

Getting Started

To get things rolling, set up your design environment and import or create the working elements. You will create a new database for this project and then add the main pieces—the dolphin model and the deformation path.

Create A New Database

Any project that you intend to save or use again, whatever its size, should have its own database *and* a meaningful name. Files pile up quickly, and that catchy model name you choose today (model1, polyobj, or the like) isn't going to mean much three weeks from now, especially if it's lumped in with twenty other ambiguously named models. So, rather than making a mess in your default database, you should create a new database for this project.

The Database Manager is available from Softimage's Model, Motion, Actor, and Matter modules. Because most of the first operations you'll perform are related to modeling, select Model from the server bar or press F1 to choose that software module. Open the Database Manager by selecting **Get|DB Manager**, then use the .. to move up the directory tree until you are at the Database level (.. is a filename for the directory above where you currently are, by selecting it you move up one level).

Here you will see all of the standard Softimage databases (like SI_material_lib and SI_DEMOS), and the New Database button will become active. See Figure 9.1. Click on New Database, select a path where you want your DB to reside, type chap9 in the name field, and click on Create. Click on OK to confirm the creation, then Exit the create dialog. Once you're back in the DB Manager, your database will be at the bottom of the list. To move it to the top, select the new database, click on the Default DB button, and click on Yes when the warning appears (see Figure 9.1).

Before you leave the DB Manager, let's add one more database to your list. In the path field, type the path that points to the CD-ROM

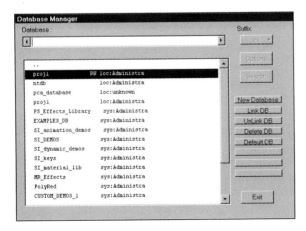

Figure 9.1 The Database Manager.

that is enclosed with this book. Browse down the directory tree until you reach Projects, and select Chapter9. Following the dialogs, add Chapter9 as a database, and then exit the DB Manager. All of your work will now be saved to your chap9 database, and you will be able to access elements out of the Chapter9 database on the CD-ROM.

Set Up The Dolphin Model

Now it's time to bring in the talent. Select **Get|Element** to view the various directories in your database, and then use .. to navigate up to the database level. Go down into the Chapter9 database on the CD-ROM, and then into MODELS. Select the Dolphin model and click on Load (see Figure 9.2).

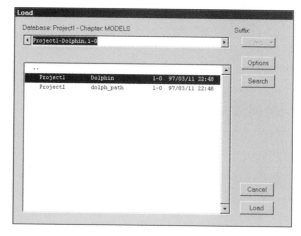

Figure 9.2 Load Project1.

This is the high-resolution model, which already has a texture associated with it (see Figure 9.3). To take a quick look at the dolphin's texture, switch to the Matter module, press F4, and then select **Preview|All**. Hit the middle mouse button to exit the preview mode. Press F1 to get back to the Model module.

The next step is to set up model substitution. To save the high-polygon dolphin into your database, make it the currently selected object by moving the cursor over the dolphin, holding down the spacebar, and clicking the left mouse button. The dolphin will be highlighted in white. Now choose **Save|Selected**

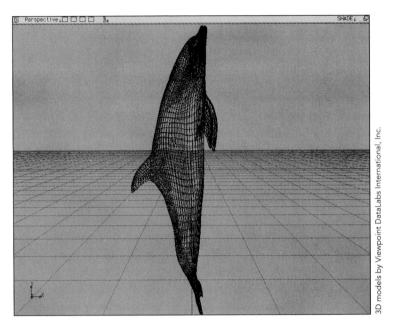

3D models by Viewpoint DataLabs International, Inc.

Figure 9.3 Perspective view of dolphin model.

Models and rename your model Dolphin with no prefix. (Model substitution will allow you to switch between models with the same name and different version numbers.)

To create a low-polygon version of the dolphin, select **Effect|PolygonRuleBased+** to bring up the polygon reduction dialog box. Check Preserve Boundaries and Preserve Materials, then click on OK (see Figure 9.4). Choose the model by left-clicking on it; after a brief pause, you will have your low-polygon version.

The cone that has been added to the scene is the icon for the polygon reduction. This icon can preserve the operations performed (so that later, for example, you could reset the percentage of how many polygons were reduced). Because you won't need to save this information, delete the cone by holding down the back-space key and left-clicking on the icon.

Now choose **Info|Elements** and go into the MODELS directory. Select the dolphin you had saved previously and click on Set Subst to set its substitution ID. Set it to 1 and exit (see Figure 9.5). Now select the low-polygon dolphin, choose **Save|Selected Models**, and

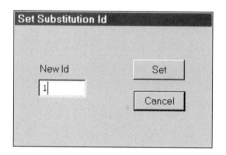

Figure 9.4 Polygon reduction.

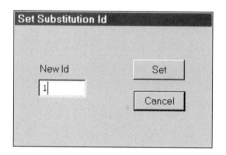

Figure 9.5 Set Substitution ID.

click on OK. This process will save the low-polygon dolphin using the same name as your high-polygon version, but with a different substitution level number. You can now switch back and forth easily between the models by using **Get|Substitution|Up** and **Get|Substitution|Down**.

Set Up The Deformation Path

The dolphin is going to swim along a path beginning off in the distance and proceeding up and over the camera. The path is just a standard Softimage B-spline created using **Draw|Curve|B-Spline**. Rather than explain where to place 20 control vertices, you can read the deformation path from the Chapter9 database on the CD-ROM enclosed with this book. To do this, choose **Get|Element**, move up into Chapter9, to MODELS, and select dolph_path. To see the whole path, press the a key when inside the Top and Front windows (see Figure 9.6).

You can use a similar process to load in a camera orientation for the scene. Select **Get|Element**, go into the CAMERAS directory, and select cam_intl; this will position the camera so that the path runs right up over the top of it. To save this camera view, click the middle mouse button in one of the empty squares to the right of the word "Perspective" in the Perspective window. The box will fill with black, signifying that a view has been stored (Figure 9.7). From now on, when you left-click on

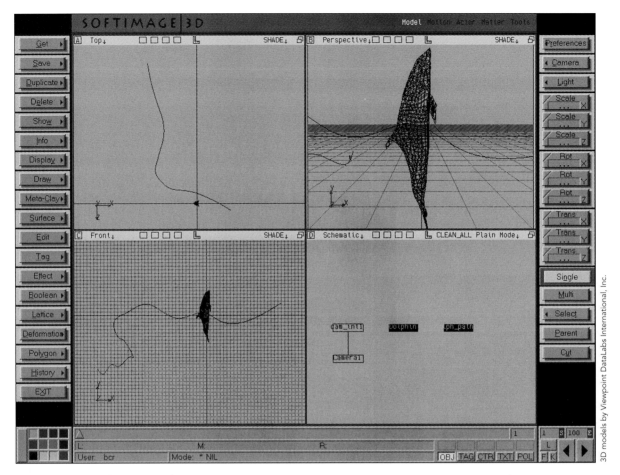

Figure 9.6 The deformation path.

the black box, the camera settings in that window will switch
back to the saved values.

Animating The Dolphin

Now that your initial elements are set up, it's animation time.
First, you'll attach the dolphin to the deformation path and animate the dolphin's translation along the path. Then, you'll add
some rotation keyframes to create a barrel roll in the middle of
the animation.

Attach The Dolphin To The Deformation Path

Select the dolphin model by holding down the spacebar and clicking on the object with the left mouse button. (You should be using

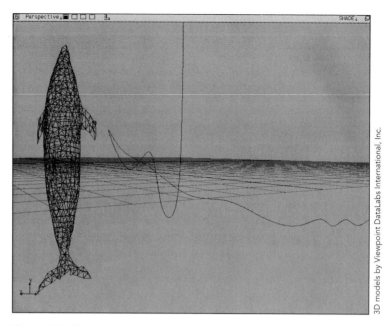

Figure 9.7 Camera view loaded.

the low-polygon version of the model now; if your model isn't substituting, make sure chap9 is still your default database in the DB Manager.) Note that the dolphin is oriented along the Y axis.

To replace the object's Y axis with the spline, select **Deformation|by Curve|Node|Create** and then left-click on the curve. Because your scale factors will reset when you set up the deformation, middle-click in the Y Scale box and change the value to 1. Also middle-click in the Y Translation box and change its value to 0.0 to start your dolphin at the beginning of the path. See Figure 9.8.

Next, press Shift-Z and drag out a rectangle around the dolphin in the Top window. This performs a window zoom. You will now rotate the dolphin so that the dorsal fin is pointing straight up. Middle-click in the Z Rotate box, then use your mouse keys to spin the dolphin. Rotate Z to about 146 degrees. Work in both the Top and Front windows to make sure the dolphin isn't upside down.

Translate The Dolphin Along The Path

Switch to the Motion module by pressing F2, and position the timeline at the bottom of the screen to frame 1. You will now set up the starting keyframe for the animation.

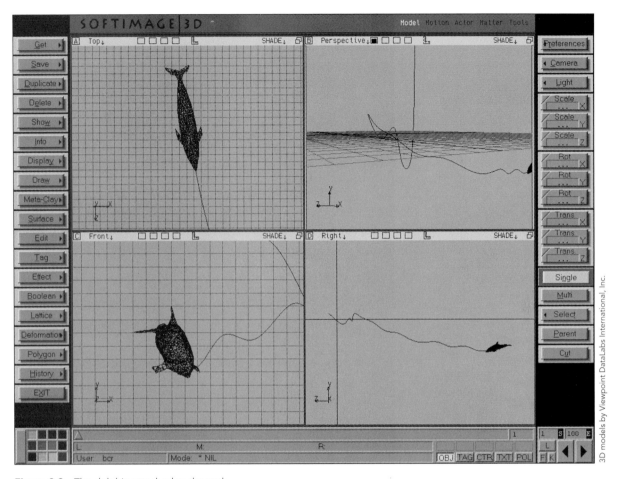

Figure 9.8 The dolphin attached to the path.

Select **Save Key|Object|Node Curve Deformation|Translation**.
Check the playback box to make sure that the endframe for the
animation is set to 300, and then move the timeline to frame
300. Now you will translate the dolphin along the Y axis to its
final destination in the animation, which is just beyond the view
of the camera. Middle-click in the Y Translate box and enter 145.
This should move the dolphin up just outside of the camera's
view. See Figure 9.9.

To set the final keyframe, select **Save Key|Object|Node Curve
Deformation|Translation**. (Note that Softimage saves your last
menu selection in a buffer for each button, and you can recall
your choice by clicking the middle mouse button. So for the current example, middle-clicking the mouse on the **Save Key** button

BEYOND PATH

When you translate along a deformation path, going off either end of the
path, your object position will be
extrapolated from the last direction
along the curve.

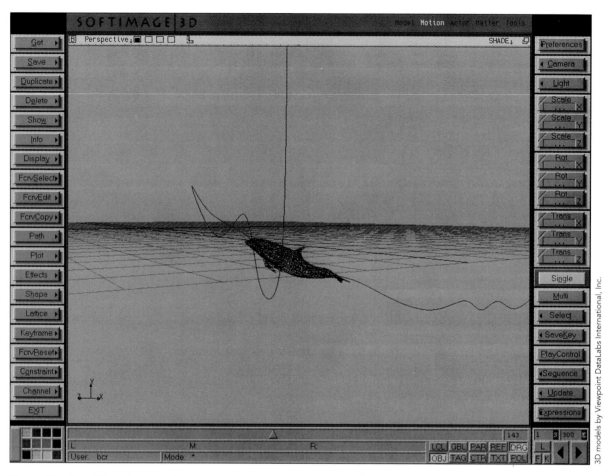

Figure 9.9   Translation along a path.

will automatically choose **Save Key|Object|Node Curve Deformation|Translation**.) Your dolphin is now animated across the entire path. Make the Perspective window full screen, drag the timeline around, and click on Play in the playback box to preview the motion. Set shading to on and switch back and forth between the high- and low-polygon model to get a better idea of how the final product will appear.

By now, you should start to get a good feel for what the playback will look like. In particular, take note of the motion at the beginning of the path. Zoom in on the Right window and scrub the timeline back and forth; you'll see how the humps in the deformation spline create gentle body arching and natural-looking tail kicks.

Create A Barrel Roll

Now, for some acrobatics, let's add a roll. Scroll the timeline to frame 235. Here the dolphin's body is right in front of the camera; this is where the roll will end. You want to rotate the dolphin slightly so that his belly is directly facing the camera at this frame. Middle-click the Z Rotate box and use the mouse to twist the dolphin flat at about 163 degrees. (If your numbers aren't matching exactly, don't worry—you probably twisted things differently when orienting the dolphin earlier. Just tune by eye to get a similar result.) Now set a key for the roll by selecting **Save Key|Object|Node Curve Deformation|Roll** to save the rotation you just set.

Now scroll the timeline back to frame 171, which will be the start of the roll. Middle-click the Z Rotate box, use the arrow key to get the cursor to the end of the number, then type -360 and hit Return; Softimage will calculate the new rotation (approx. -196 degrees). Middle-click on the **Save Key** button to repeat setting a keyframe for the deformation's roll. That's it—now you have a spiffy roll.

Play back the move with the Perspective window set to full screen. Things should look pretty good by now— but notice how the dolphin is slow at the beginning and end of the path. This is due to the default ease-in/ease-out settings for the translation keyframes.

Fortunately, this problem is easy to fix. While still in the Motion module, select **Fcrv Select|Object|Node Curve Deformation|Translation** to open up a Function Curve editor in the lower half of the screen. Now select Dolphin.nsftry with the left

mouse button (see Figure 9.10); this will highlight the function curve for the translation along Y. Left-clicking on LIN will change the curve into a linear ramp across time. (You can middle-click on Fcurve in the C window to revert back to the previous window settings.) Now play back the move in full screen again to see the dolphin's constant speed across the path.

Finishing Touches

Now that you've breathed life into the dolphin, take a few moments to polish things up. By adding depth fading and some better lighting, you'll have a much more dramatic animation. When you're done polishing, create a flipbook of the animation and preview the final rendering.

Lighting The Scene

First, establish the overall brightness of the scene. Hit F4 to get into the Matter module, and select **Get|Substitution|Up** so that you are working with the high-polygon dolphin. Go to frame 260, where the dolphin is very close to the camera. Select **Preview|All** to preview a rendering of this frame.

You'll probably notice that things are a bit dark. To add a light source to the scene, select **Light|Define**. In the color palette, press the RGB button twice to switch to HSV, then change the value (V) parameter from 1 to 3 and click on OK.

The light you have just created is currently selected; press the *v* key to drag the light into your window until it is slightly above the dolphin and toward the end of the motion path (see Figure 9.11). Scrub the timeline and select **Preview|All**

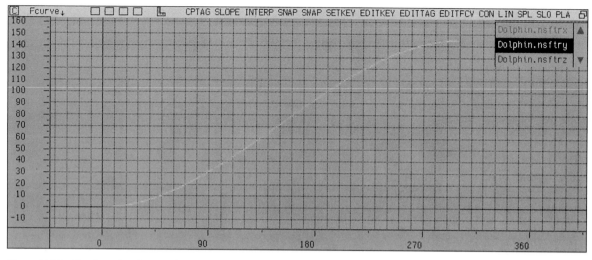

Figure 9.10 The Function Curve editor.

a few times to make sure the dolphin doesn't swim through or too close to your light. As you move the light to get the precise level of brightness you desire, remember not to make your imagery too dark, because you'll lose some color in the next step when you add depth fading.

Add Depth Fading

Now you should add some atmospherics to simulate the way light is absorbed as it travels through ocean water and how the light picks up the coloration of the water. In this case, you will adjust depth fading to simulate greenish ocean water that is dense and murky in the distance, with the lighter, bluish-gray of the dolphin breaking into view as it approaches.

First, you need to determine the distance from the start of the dolphin's path to the camera. Select **Info|Distance**, then middle-click in the Top window near the end of the path. Holding the middle button down, middle-click again near the camera; you'll see that the distance is roughly 110 units (Figure 9.12).

Now select **Atmosphere|Depth-Fading** and activate Depth Fading by clicking in the check box. Set the Starting Distance to -150 and the Ending Distance to 110. This will make objects beyond

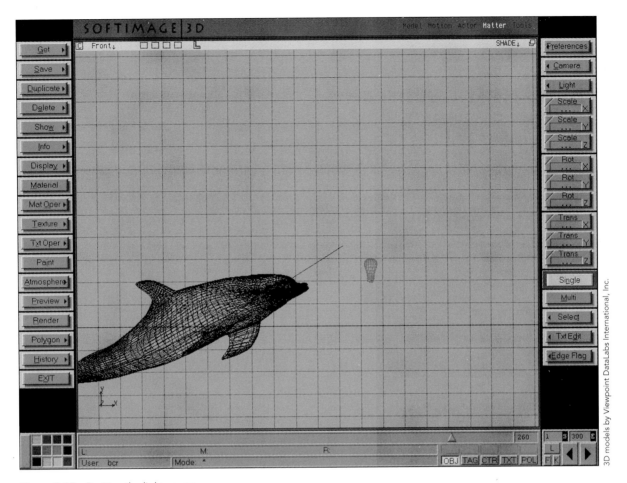

Figure 9.11   Position the light source.

110 opaque; at the end of the path (near the camera), they will
still be half tinted by the Depth Fade color. Set the Depth Fade
color to R = 0.169, G = 0.669, and B = 0.613 for a tropical green
(see Figure 9.13) and click on OK.

You may need to fine-tune the starting and ending distances
based on where you put your light and any other scene differences. To test your settings, do a few preview renderings at
various points along the path. At the farthest point from the
camera, the dolphin should just be coming into view, and it
should still look immersed in water as it gets close to the camera.
Remember that the majority of your motion is happening away
from the viewer, so don't concentrate on the last frames—be sure
that the middle of the path looks very natural as well.

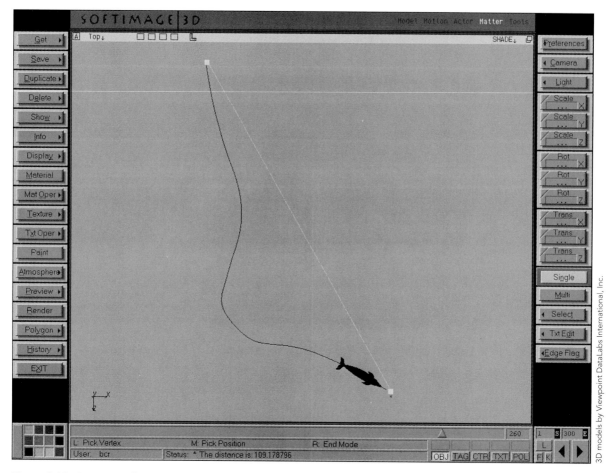

Figure 9.12 Determine distance.

Render Flipbook

Now is the time for a final rendering. To create a preview animation that you can play back on-screen, use Flipbook. Flipbook allows you to play rendered frames back in near realtime. While still in the Matter module, select **Render**; the Start and End frames should be set to 1 and 300. Set the step value to 2, which will only render every other frame. For resolution set X to 250, and Y will automatically be recalculated to 197. The database should be set to chap9 (if not, use Db List to set it). When all of these values are correct, set the filename to c9flipbook and select Render sequence as shown in Figure 9.14. (If you prefer to render to tape or a digital video device, you already know what settings you'll need.)

Frames will start rendering on-screen as they are saved to your database. When the rendering is complete, go to the Tools module by pressing F5, then select FlipBook and choose your chap9 database. Scroll down and select RENDER_PICTURES, then double left-click to find where your frames are stored. Select c9flipbook.1 as the first frame, and set Start frame to 1 and End frame to 300. Set the Step to 2, Frames per second to 15, Horizontal and Vertical scaling to 2 and then click on OK (see Figure 9.15). After the frames load, press Play to view the flipbook. You can also use the timeline to scroll to various points in the flipbook. To exit, click all three mouse keys at once.

Add-Ons

Great work—you've got a swimming dolphin! Read on for a few comments about the process and some additional elements you could add to make this animation worthy of your demo reel. First of all, forget for a moment that you just toiled on a dolphin project. By replacing your model and modifying the deformation path, you could easily make an ominously circling shark or a stylized biplane performing aerial acrobatics.

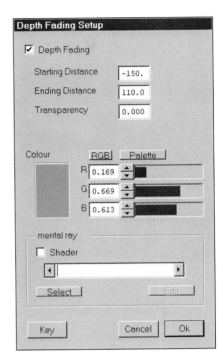

Figure 9.13 Depth Fading.

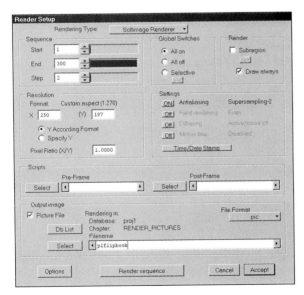

Figure 9.14 Render Setup dialog box.

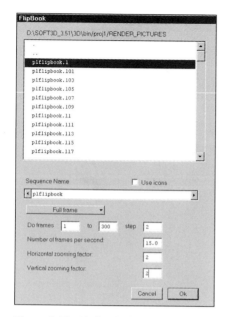

Figure 9.15 Flipbook playback.

Scenery

Throw in some scenery to create a more realistic environment for your dolphin. You might add some visual interest on the ocean floor, or make some bubbles that trail off from your dolphin's snout as he swims along the path. Experiment with the Flocking option to make the bubbles emanate from the snout and then backward to a Null that trails after your dolphin. (If you are new to Softimage and you haven't used these features before, don't worry—they will be covered in detail in later projects.)

Layers

Think in layers. This project was rendered in one pass, but it might be nice to have the dolphin rendered alone; you could then render bubbles in a separate pass and composite the results. Separate layers will give you a lot more flexibility when compiling a final piece, because you can easily try different

Figure 9.16 A close up shot.

3D models by Viewpoint DataLabs International, Inc.

Figure 9.17   A full-length shot.

backgrounds or run effects and filters over specific layers. This separation allows you to make changes to elements without having to render your whole scene again. For example, if your client decides that the bubbles need to be smaller, you can just re-render the bubble layer, re-composite the element, and be done in a fraction of the time it would have taken to re-render the entire scene.

Wrap-Up

This project covered a number of useful techniques, but the primary lesson is that paths are powerful. Animating along a path is very common. In later chapters, you'll use paths to define character position, camera location, and a host of other parameters that change over time.

BOGGLE INTERFACE 10

Key topics:

- **3D game interface**

- **Booleans**

- **Bevels**

- **Tagged vertices**

- **Exclusive lights**

This project creates the 3D interface for a game. You will construct beveled button boxes, a title bar, and a score display. After loading in some game elements (dice, an hourglass, and a marble game table), you'll then add some dramatic lighting and render the final result. You can easily manipulate the interface you create and update its materials to suit many CD-ROM, kiosk, and game console applications.

The techniques you use to build this interface also may be applied to many other types of projects. You could create imagery for use on the Web, for example, or export your interface to create a VRML touch pad. If you ever need to model an airplane cockpit or stereo console, you'll find many of the tips in this project useful.

Most of the interface geometry is constructed by creating a beveled frame that is copied and manipulated to create other shapes and forms. You will use tagged vertices extensively to reshape frames and to stretch buttons and boxes. In the course of this project, the mysteries of freezing transformations and texture mode manipulation will be revealed, and you will dabble in the art of fake perspective.

Wrapping up the project will require more basic lighting and rendering techniques as you apply materials and textures to the game elements, then use colored and exclusive lights to light the scene. The last step will be to render your final image.

Creating The Basic Elements

The first step is to create a new database for the project. You will then make a set of generic elements (a frame, a tray, and a button) that will be copied and scaled to build all of the interface elements.

A New Database

Press F1 to select the Model module. Open the Database Manager by selecting **Get|DB Manager**, and move up the directory structure to the Database level. Create a new database called chap10, and make it your default database.

Create The Frame

Before creating the frame, you should set the aspect ratio of your final scene. Select **Camera|Picture Format**, choose NTSC, and click on Accept. Then make the camera look directly down the Z axis by selecting **Camera|Settings** and setting the camera Y position at 0.

The first element to construct is a frame that encircles your entire interface. You will construct the frame from a default cube. Select **Get|Primitive|Cube**, and accept the default size of 10. Scale the cube in Z to make it thin (try a setting of 0.04). To make the cube fill the perspective camera view, scale X to 2 and Y to 1.5. Now select **Effect|Freeze|Scaling** to reset the cube's scaling factors back to 1,1,1; this step allows you to continue working relative to the full-screen size of the cube. Freezing renormalizes the transformations while maintaining the current state of your object. If you had moved the cube, you would also want to freeze translations so that the center of the object would return to 0,0,0.

Now create a second cube to cut out the center of the first, leaving a frame around the edge of your camera view. To do this, make a copy of the original cube by selecting **Duplicate|Immediate** or by pressing d (the supra key for duplicating; see the tip on this subject) and clicking on the cube. Scale the copy down in X and Y a small amount and make it larger in Z (values of .96, .96, and 2 would be good).

Make the outside cube the active object, and then select **Boolean|Static**. Switch the boolean operation to Difference and A And B Together, as shown in Figure 10.1. Click on OK and select the inner cube to perform the difference operation with. To hide the two cubes and see the resulting object, select **Display|Hide|Unselected**. Switch shading on in the Perspective window to see the boolean object.

Now apply a bevel to the frame by selecting **Effect|Bevel**. Accept the default bevel value of 0.1. When you're done, select **Info|Selection**, choose Faceted, and give the object the name outer_frame.

FREEZING

Freezing is especially useful if you have rotated an object. If you rotate an object 90 degrees around the Z axis and then try to scale it in Y, for example, the object will actually get longer along the Z axis. Freezing the object's rotations will reset its rotation angles to 0,0,0 and allow you to scale it naturally.

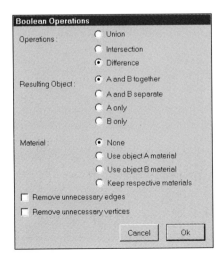

Figure 10.1 The Boolean Operations setup dialog box.

Create The Tray

You'll construct the tray from the same two original cubes as the frame. Instead of cutting the center out of the outside cube, however, the tray will notch out an indentation and leave a surrounding rim and back face. Craft this tray with care, because it will be the basis for most of the geometry in your scene.

Switch to multiple-selection mode by selecting **Multi**. Now select all three objects by holding down the spacebar and left-clicking on the two hidden cubes in a Schematic view. Select **Display|Hide|Toggle Desel Hidden** to unhide the two cubes and hide the frame instead. Switch back to single selection mode by selecting **Single** or using the control-n supra key.

Select the smaller interior cube, and change its X and Y scale values from 0.96 to 0.98. This will make the rim of your tray very compact. Now bring the Top window up to full screen and translate the interior cube forward in Z until its back face is at the center of the larger cube (Z = 0.4, as shown in Figure 10.2).

As with the frame, you will use a boolean difference operation to extract the center of the tray. Click on the exterior cube and

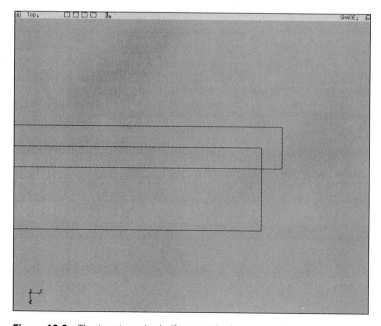

Figure 10.2 The interior cube halfway inside the outer cube.

select **Boolean|Static**. Leave the settings as Difference and A And B Together, as shown in Figure 10.1, and pick the inner cube to differencewith. Delete the two construction cubes, leaving the tray as the currently selected object. Select **Effect|Bevel** with a setting of 0.05. Now select **Info|Selection** (the swift key combination is q-s), change the boolean to Faceted, and name it tray1.

To make tray1 easy to find later, change its color in the Schematic view. To do this, deselect tray1, click on the vertical bar in the color box at the lower left of your screen, and select red. Now select the tray1 object by left-clicking on tray1 in the Schematic view; it (and its Wireframe representations) will turn red. Switch the selected color back to black for subsequent objects, and click on the vertical bar to exit the color box selection mode.

Create The Button

The final basic element is a button that you will create out of a cylinder. Select **Get|Primitive| Cylinder**, and set the Step and Base to 1. Rotate the cylinder 90 degrees around Z so it is horizontal, and then select **Effect|Freeze|Rotation** to lock in the rotation. Bevel the button by selecting **Effect|Bevel** with a value of 0.1. Now set the Z scale to 0.123 (flattening the button so it fits nicely into the tray), and freeze this value by selecting **Effect|Freeze|Scaling**. Select **Info|Selection**, rename the cylinder button1, and change its Wireframe color to blue the same way you changed the tray to red. When you're finished, hide the button until you need it later by selecting **Display|Hide|Toggle Desel Hidden**.

Building The Interface

Using the basic elements just created, you will now construct the main elements of the interface. The main elements consist of a frame on the right side of the screen (which will have some buttons and the wordpad), a score frame at the bottom of the scene (which will show player scores), and a title frame (which will be centered at the top of the display). If you haven't done so already, take a look at the finished rendering in the color gallery section of this book to see how all the parts fit together.

Create The Right Frame

The tray will be repeatedly copied and resized to build up the elements of the right frame. All of the major interface elements will be built this way. (Note that if you just scaled the copied objects, your frames and trays would have rims with varying thickness. Resizing with tags avoids this.)

First, make tray1 smaller and easy to get to so you can make copies of it quickly. Press F9 to select TAG mode (this will be shown at the bottom right of the screen, below the timeline), and then frame tray1 in the Front view by pressing the a key while the cursor is over that window. Press and hold the *t* key to get in Tag Rectangle Selection mode. You can now use the left mouse button to drag a rectangle over the top half of tray1, tagging all of the vertices in the top of the tray. Now hit the *v* key, and you will be able to move the selected elements. Hold down the right mouse button down and drag to move the tags down vertically.

If you hold the *t* key down again and use the right mouse button to drag a rectangle across the entire tray, the bottom vertices will be selected (the right mouse button toggles the tags on and off). Because you remain in drag mode after you release the *t* key, you can use the right mouse button now to drag the tags up, thereby making the frame smaller. To de-select tags, use the middle mouse button to drag a rectangle while pressing down the *t* key.

This basic operation of tagging and dragging is how you will construct most of the elements in this chapter. Experiment with tagging and dragging until you can quickly resize the tray to any size you like. Be careful, though, to drag only horizontally and vertically. If you accidentally ruin the shape of your tray, just select **History|Undo** to go back to an earlier version.

Reshape the tray until it is nearly square and centered in the upper left quadrant of the screen. Now unhide the outer frame by clicking on it in the Schematic view and selecting **Display|Hide|Toggle Selection**. Switch back to OBJ mode by pressing F8, and make the tray the selected object. Select **Duplicate|Immediate** (or hold the *d* key) and click on the tray to make a copy of it. If you aren't in drag mode anymore, press the *v* key; now drag the new tray over to the right half of the screen. Switch back to TAG mode by pressing F9 and resize the new tray so that it looks like Figure 10.3. (To get things positioned just right, switch into OBJ mode when you need to drag the whole object and then back to TAG to resize. Bring the shaded Perspective view to full screen while you drag, so that you can better see the end result.)

After this positioning and resizing, it will only take some simple duplications, tagging, and dragging

to finish up the frame. Make a duplicate of the right frame, tag its bottom vertices, and drag them up to create the first shelf in the tray. Copy the smaller shelf and drag the copy down until it is flush with the bottom of the frame, then tag its top vertices and drag them down to make the shelf thinner. To complete the frame structure, copy that object and drag it up to sit on top of the bottom shelf (see Figure 10.4).

One last item: The center of the right frame will hold a pad of paper. Simply create a default cube, to be the pad, and resize it to fit into the center tray. Do not bevel this cube.

Create The Score Frame

The score frame will be constructed in the same manner as the right frame. Start by selecting the bottom shelf of the right frame; make a duplicate of that object and drag it to the left. (This will ensure that the score frame is aligned with the bottom of the right frame.) Resize the shelf using tags so that it is close to the left side of the exterior frame, leaving enough space to the right to place a button between the score frame and right frame later. Duplicate this new shelf and move the copy up so that its bottom lines up with the top of the original.

Now create the frame for the button we just mentioned. Duplicate the top tray in the score frame, and drag it to the right until it nearly touches the right frame. Now tag its left vertices and drag them so that they mesh into the edge of the score frame. Tag the object's bottom points and drag them down to match the bottom of the score frame. Adjust the tags until the button box is square.

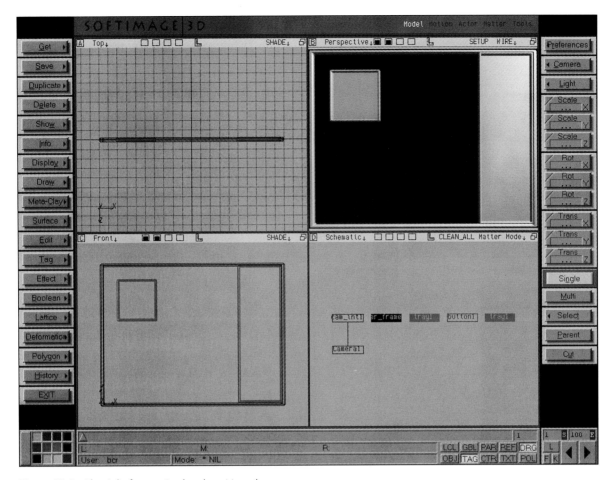

Figure 10.3 The right frame, sized and positioned.

To construct the top buttons in the score frame, duplicate the top shelf, resize it to the size of one button, then copy and drag those elements across to fill up the top shelf. To make the interface look less boxy, choose the **Multi** selection mode and tag all of the vertices in the bottoms of the buttons and the middle shelf parts. Drag them up to make the buttons look more sleek and to heighten the bottom tray (which is used in the game as a type-in field for Internet chat among players). The finished score frame is shown in Figure 10.5.

Before you construct the next object, clean up your Schematic view by merging spare parts into single objects. In **Multi** selection mode and with OBJ mode on, select all the elements that make up the score frame, then select **Effect|Merge** and accept

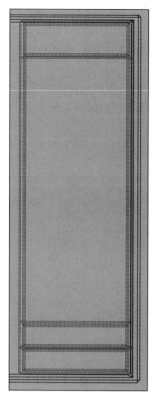

Figure 10.4 The completed right frame.

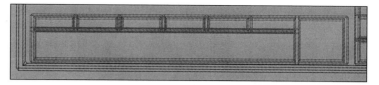

Figure 10.5 The completed score frame.

the default parameters. This will create a single object for the score frame. (You can still manipulate the elements of the frame with tags if necessary.) In the Schematic view, the new object has a set of children material nodes that you can delete by holding down the backspace key and left-clicking on each node. Delete from right to left, because the leftmost node is the global material for the object and can't be deleted until the others are gone.

Now delete the original components of the score frame, renaming the merge object score_frame when you are done. Do the same cleanup work for the right frame, selecting and merging its elements, deleting the materials and original components, and renaming the merge object right_frame. The Schematic view will be much easier to work with.

Create The Title Frame

The title frame is even easier to create than the last two frames. Select the original tray element, resize it to make a rectangular form, and drag it up to the top center of the screen (see Figure 10.6).

Now create a default cube by selecting **Get|Primitive|Cube**. Scale the cube in X and Y until it is close to the shape of the title frame. Select **Effect|Bevel** and set a value of 0.1 (it's easier to bevel objects large and then scale them down than it is to guess how small you should set the bevel size). Now scale down the object in Z so that it is thin enough to sit inside your title frame. Drag the cube into your title frame and resize it until it fits snugly and looks good in shade mode. Select **Info|Selection** and turn Faceting on. Select **Parent** and middle-click tray1 to make the cube a child of the tray, then

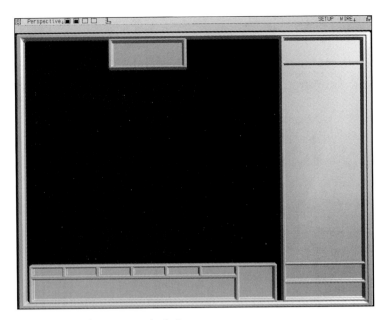

Figure 10.6   The positioned title frame.

select tray1 as the current object and use **Info|Selection** to change its name to title_frame.

Position Buttons

Now place buttons into the frames you have just finished. Select the blue button in your Schematic view, and use **Show|Hide|Toggle Keep Selected** to unhide the button. You can now set the material properties that you would like copies of the button to inherit. Switch to Matter mode by pressing F4, and select **Material**. Choose the color properties by left-clicking on the squares at the points of the color triangle. Set the RGB values as follows: Ambient 0,0,0.75; Diffuse 0,0.2,0.6; and Specular 0,0.1,0.5. Click on OK to accept the color changes, and then switch back to Model mode by pressing F1.

Duplicate the button, move it into the top of the right frame, and resize it to fit the shelf. Repeat this process until you have filled all the frames with buttons; use the original blue button as the last button. Press the f key to frame the buttons, and the a key to show everything in the window (this way you can quickly shift from gross movement to subtle positioning). See Figure 10.7 for the final layout.

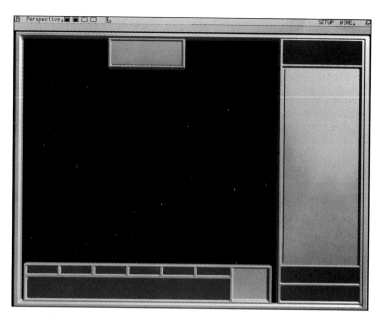

Figure 10.7 The final positioning for the basic interface elements.

Loading The Final Elements

The last elements to add to the scene are some buttons shaped like dice, an hourglass timer model, and a set of playing dice. Because this project is focused on the interface elements, we've pre-modeled these for you to load into the scene.

Load The Dice Buttons

Select **Get|Element**, and retrieve die_button4 from the project database MODELS directory on the CD-ROM enclosed with this book. Center the dice around the title frame, then select one die to use as a button in the score frame. (In the Schematic view, you can right-click while holding down the spacebar to isolate a single die.) Duplicate the die, move it down to the square in the score frame, and resize as necessary to get it to fit and maintain its shape.

Load The Game Elements

Select **Get|Element** and retrieve Boggle_tray from the CD-ROM. Load it into the scene and position it slightly to the right of the center of the screen. (You will place the hourglass timer to the left of the boggle tray.) Now select **Get|Element** and load hour_glass, followed by table_top.

The table is tipped to create a sense of false perspective, so that the table appears to recede in the distance. To make the objects on the table look correct, you must tilt them as well. The hourglass already matches the slant of the table top. Arrange the boggle tray so that its front bottom is barely resting on the table; this will make the tray look like it is sitting up on a pedestal (see Figure 10.8).

Final Steps

Now that you have all of the elements finished, it's time to set up the final materials, textures, and lighting for the scene. Then you can render your completed interface.

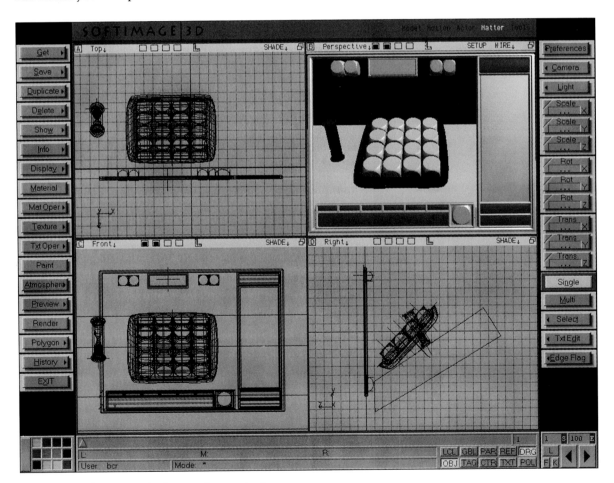

Figure 10.8 The scene with all game elements in place.

Applying Materials And Textures

To liven up the scene, select the right frame and go into Matter mode by pressing F4. Select **Material**, and click on Select to load in a material type. Go up to the database level and down into SI_material_lib. Go into METALS and click on the Options button; select Use Icons and click on OK. Select material Gold_001 and click on OK again to accept the material.

Now select the title frame (make sure to include the cube child), select **Mat_Oper|Copy Mat**, and click on the right frame to copy its gold material. Use this same procedure to copy the gold material quickly to the outer frame and the score frame.

Now apply the title texture to the title frame by clicking on the cube part of the frame and selecting **Texture|2D Global**. Click on the Select button under Picture Filename, go into the database on the CD-ROM enclosed with this book, and switch to the Pictures directory to retrieve the file named title. Use the left mouse button in the texture image to crop around the blue Classic Boggle text; set Blending to Alpha Channel Mask and set Roughness to -2.5 to create a raised-character look.

Apply textures for the buttons in the same way, using any texture you prefer on each button. For example, to put a name on the top button in the right frame, click on the button and select **Texture|2D Global**. Choose the picture titled David and crop the texture to select the name you prefer, then set Blendingto Alpha Channel Mask and click on OK. Use the Preview key from within the texture dialog box to see what the texture will look like on your object. Apply textures to as many or as few of the buttons as you wish.

The last texture to apply is the word set on the pad of paper in the right frame. Click on the wordpad cube and select **Texture|2D Global**. Load in the file named word, crop the blue Words text, and set Blending to Alpha Channel Mask. When you click on OK to accept these settings, the texture will be applied across the whole pad.

Now go into TXT (for Texture) mode (F11), which allows you to define the UV mapping of any layer of a texture to its object. Use the standard scaling and translation tools to resize where the texture will be placed on the pad, and center the heading *Words* at the top of the pad. Go back into **Texture|2D Global** and click on the Next button to create a second layer for your texture. Select the image file words and set its blending to Alpha Channel Mask, and then use scaling to position the text on the pad of paper. See Figure 10.9 for a sample preview.

Adding Lights

Unfortunately, it is very easy to create a poorly lit scene with computer graphics. Such scenes usually suffer from a few easily avoided pitfalls. Foremost among these is *ambient light*, which is added onto your objects after their shading has been calculated. It's an approximation of all the "bounce light" or indirect illumination in a scene, but its usual effect is to flatten the scene's appearance by washing out all of the subtle details, shadows, textures, and contrasts by adding a flat constant color. As the sole cinematographer of your scene, it's your responsibility to take control of the lighting. Use ambient light sparingly. Remember to paint with shadow as well as light.

Figure 10.9 A preview rendering of the scene, without lighting.

The second major problem area is *color temperature*. If you want a drab, plastic-looking scene, just leave all of the default light levels at an RGB setting of 1.0,1.0,1.0. Light is never this purely white in a real-world setting; usually a scene is bathed in two or three different types of light. Daylight is bluish and cool, for example, while incandescent light is warm and ruddy. Light bouncing off a colored surface picks up those tones, creating an intriguing melange of spectral interplay. To make your scenes as interesting as real life, tune the color of your lights to match their source, and add lights to the scene that approximate the bounce light you desire. Accent with both light and color.

The last danger to avoid is *sharp lighting distributions*. Real light drops off with distance, but in computer graphics it's all too easy to use lights that shine from infinity and radiate with an even brightness in all directions. Such lights tend to create stark, flat scenes with razor-sharp shadows and boring, harsh contrasts. Let your lights mix, using gentle drop-offs in intensity. Never light a scene with a single light unless you have a good reason; always know where your light is coming from and why you put it there.

In this scene, you'll start with two dramatic lights. Go to the Matter module, select **Lights|Define**, and create a red point

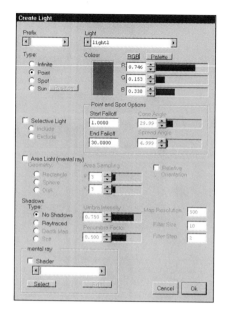

Figure 10.10 Defining a red light.

source (RGB values of .746,.153,.338) with a falloff ranging from 1 to 30, as shown in Figure 10.10. Move it behind your scene to the right and above, keeping it close enough that you see some kick from the light on your objects. Now create a light that is similar but bluish in color (RGB values of .246,.630,.823). Place it in front of and to the left of your scene, at a height slightly above the middle of the screen. Select Preview to see how the lights interact, and then adjust their positions until you are happy with the highlights.

To crank down the ambience, select **Atmosphere|Ambience** and set the RGB values to .15,.143,.16. For the key light, select **Lights|Define** and create a whitish infinite light (RGB values of .93,.961,.961). Check the Selective Light checkbox, leave it set to Include, and turn Raytraced Shadows on. Drag the light slightly up and to the right. (Remember, with an infinite light, distance doesn't matter; the angle is all that counts.)

A *selective light* shines only on certain objects, or prevents light from shining on certain objects. You will create two selective lights: one that shines only on the dice tray, hourglass, and table, and another that shines on everything except those objects. This combination will cast shadows on the table from the game elements but exclude shadows resulting from the interface framework. Select **Multi** and right-click on the dice tray, hourglass, and table top while holding down the spacebar; then select **Light|Associate** and click on the infinite light. That light will now shine only on the game elements—do a preview to prove it to yourself.

Next, duplicate the infinite light and drag the copy away from the dice tray. This will leave the new light pointing along the same direction as the first. Select **Light|Edit** and switch the light setting from include to exclude. Select **Multi** and pick the game elements (the dice tray, the hourglass, and the table) again, then select **Light|Associate** and click on the new infinite light. Preview the scene to make sure your exclusive lights are set up properly. If all is well, you should see a shadow beneath the dice tray, but not one being cast on the table by the frame.

Final Render

Congratulations! All your hard work has paid off. You've completed the scene, and now it's time to create the finished product. Select Render, and set Start, End, and Step to 1. Set the resolution at 640×480. Click on Select in the Output Image box, select your chap10 database, and save the result into RENDERED_PICTURES with a name like chap10_final. Now select Render Sequence, and switch to Tools by pressing F5 when the rendering is complete. Select Picture, change to the RENDERED_PICTURES directory in your database, select the image, and press Display.

Figure 10.11 A final rendering.

YAHTZEE LOGO
11

Key topics:

- **Beveled text**

- **PostScript elements**

- **Transparency mapping**

In this project, you will create a logo for a print advertisement. The logo we'll create here was used as the cover art for the Yahtzee CD-ROM game from Hasbro Interactive. The project will focus on creating the 3D letter forms from original 2D curves and applying textures and materials to create dramatic bevelled 3D text.

Setting Up The Project

As in previous projects, you'll get started by creating a database. With the database in place, you will set up the camera for the scene and load in the 2D curves of the logo text. The curves will be the starting point for creating the 3D characters of the logo.

Create A New Database

Start by pressing F1 to switch to the Model module. Choose **Get|DB Manager** from the left menu bar, go to the database level, and click on New Database. Name the database chap11 and link it to the Chapter11 database on the CD-ROM enclosed with this book. Although you will load elements from the CD-ROM Chapter11 into the scene as needed, chap11 should be set as the default database.

Set Up The Camera And Aspect Ratio

This scene will have a vertical aspect ratio similar to that of a small printed page, with its height greater than its width. To set up the proper aspect ratio and viewing parameters, load the scene ytz_logo_setup from the Chapter11 database.

Select **Camera|Settings** to view the parameters that have been loaded for the camera. Note that the camera has a custom aspect ratio of .833; this custom value can be set under the **Camera|Picture Format** menu.

A couple of other parameters were set when ytz_logo_setup was loaded: The grid in the Perspective window is turned off, and a Schematic view is enabled in the lower right window. Grids and other window-specific features can be reset by left-clicking on the ruler in the center of a window's title bar. This will bring up a layout dialog (as in Figure 11.1, where you can see that grids have been turned off).

Load In The Text Curves

The main element in the scene is the text that makes up the Yahtzee logo. There are a variety of ways to develop text inside Softimage. The internal Text primitive is very effective, but for many projects you will import logo elements and text. Often art will be provided in an easily manipulated electronic form, such as that generated by a vector illustration package. Nearly all these packages can output Encapsulated PostScript files, which Softimage can read easily (as you'll find out later in this chapter).

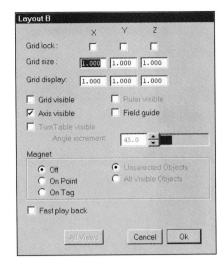

Figure 11.1 A window layout dialog box.

Sometimes, though, you may only have an image from which you wish to extract the geometry of some text or logo. In these cases, you can use **Tools|Autotrace** or some similar tools to extract shapes from the provided image.

This is the process that was used to create the curves for the Yahtzee text. To load in the generated curves, select **Get|Element**, go to the MODELS directory in Project3, and load the file ytz_curves. These curves will be the outlines for creating the Yahtzee 3D text. (See Figure 11.2)

Create The 3D Text

The 3D text is the heart of the scene. You'll first extrude and bevel the 2D curves, then apply separate materials to the text and its bevels. After that, you will use transparency mapping to fade in the Y character. Then you'll load the word "Ultimate" from a PostScript file, make it three-dimensional, and position it in the scene.

Extrude And Bevel The 2D Curves

Make the curves the currently selected item by holding down the spacebar and right-clicking in the Schematic view on the null that parents the curves. Doing this will select the entire tree of curves. Now select **Surface|Extrusion**, set bevelling to active, the

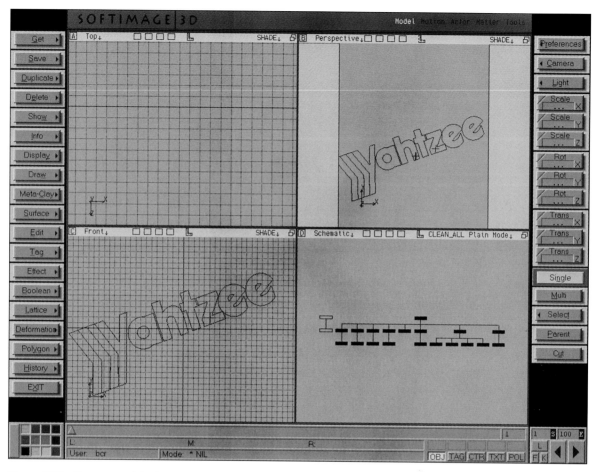

Figure 11.2 The curves of the logo.

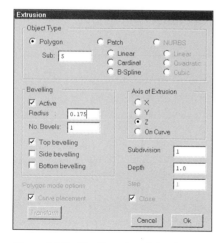

Figure 11.3 The Extrusion dialog box.

bevel radius to .175, and the number of bevels to 1; check the box for top bevelling only (see Figure 11.3). Once you have entered all of these values, click on OK to execute the extrusion.

At first glance, the extrusion looks good. If you zoom in on the letters "ee" in shade mode, however, you will see that the bevelling has produced some twisted faces that look like a tear in the 3D letters. Don't worry, this isn't difficult to fix.

You may be thinking, "Well, if the curves had been good to start with, I wouldn't have to fix *anything*." We admit that we could have provided picture-perfect curves that bevelled without a hitch, but in real life you will run up against lots of cases in which you have to figure out why something isn't rendering just right. So we decided not to candy-coat all of the gory details—pardon us, we mean all of the joys—of making production-quality graphics with Softimage.

Delete the original 2D curves by holding down the backspace key and right-clicking in the Schematic window on the null that parents the curves. Now only the extruded characters will be left in the scene. Zoom the Front window so you can easily see and adjust the letter *e* that immediately follows the *z*. Expand the Front window to the full screen and switch back and forth from Shade to Wireframe view.

In Figure 11.4, you'll see clearly that the bevel has twisted over itself, and the twist is causing the back of a triangle to be rendered. The result looks like a hole in the letter. To fix this problem, you will move the vertices of the *e* until the offending geometry is acceptable. With the *e* selected as the current object, select **Info|Selection** and change the object to faceted. Use TAG mode and the *t* key to select the leftmost point of the twisted bevel, then press the *v* key to drag the selected tag. Pull the tag to the right and up to clean up the bevel.

> ### DON'T PANIC
>
> There's no denying that Softimage is a very complex product. It has a personality all its own, and you'll need a while to get used to some of its quirks. As one veteran Softimage employee in Montreal was heard saying, "You don't learn Softimage, you experience it." So be willing to experiment, try features in new ways, and keep the documentation close. Enjoy the experience.

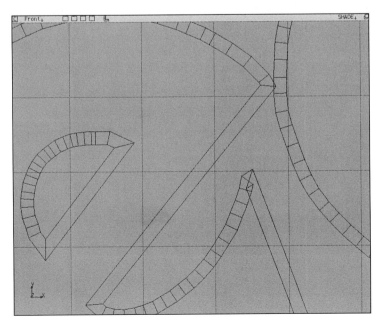

Figure 11.4 Twisted bevel polygons.

Now, switch back to OBJ mode by pressing F8. Duplicate the corrected *e* by holding down the *d* key and left-clicking the *e* character. Drag the copy so that it matches the position of the uncorrected *e*, then delete the *e* that still has twists in it.

Apply Materials To The Text And Bevels

Applying materials will be easier if the logo has hierarchical structure. By parenting the text elements, you will make it easier to select individual characters in the Schematic view.

Make the rightmost element of the *y* character the currently selected item. Select **Parent** and left-click the other three pieces to make them children of the letter. Now select **Get|Primitive|Null** to add a null object to the scene. This null will be the parent of the logo. Select **Parent** and then left-click the letters of the logo to make them children of the null object.

The characters still need a slight tune-up before applying materials. Take a close look at the characters in shade mode—the curved characters have clear faceting, and the straight characters don't look all that sharp. For each element of the logo, select **Info|Selection**, turn faceting on for all the straight elements (*y*, *t*, and *z*), and set the Automatic Discontinuity to 40.0 for the curved characters (*a*, *h*, and the *e*'s).

To distinguish between the bevels and the rest of the character, you will apply a different material to each. Make the whole logo active, and switch to the Matter module. Select **Material** and use the file browser to apply ytz_goldbase from the Materials in the Chapter11 database.

Now you will highlight the bevels in Polygon mode. Select **Polygon|Select By Rectangle** and use the left mouse button to drag a rectangle across the whole logo. This will highlight all of the polygons in purple. Now hold down the right mouse button and drag a rectangle from behind the logo to halfway through the bevel, followed by another rectangle from the front of the logo to halfway through the bevel. This will leave only the bevels highlighted in purple.

Now choose each element and select **Polygon|Assign New Material**, applying the material ytz_goldbevl to each. Although this step is somewhat time-consuming, the improved quality of the logo is well worth the effort.

Apply A Transparency Map

To create the appearance of the *y* character fading into view—from nearly invisible at left to fully opaque at right—you will apply a global 2D transparency map to the three left elements of the character. Make the leftmost element the currently active item and select **Texture|2D Global**.

Now use the picture file browser to retrieve the file trans_shade from the Pictures directory in database Chapter11. Set Ambient, Diffuse and Specular to 0, and Transparency to 0.85. (Fully transparent is 1.0, while opaque would be a value of 0.) Perform the same operations on the other two elements, giving them transparency values of 0.75 and 0.5.

Load A PostScript Element

Another common way to bring text into Softimage is to read in Encapsulated PostScript files generated by a vector illustration package. You will use this technique to add the word "Ultimate" into the scene.

Switch to the Model module and select **Get|Eps2Soft**. Click on the Browser button and select the file ultimate.ai from the Pictures directory of the Chapter11 database. Accept the default values to read the file into the scene. Leave the resulting curves highlighted.

Select **Draw|Convert To Face**, which will close the curves to create a solid 2D face set of the text. Select **Surface|Extrusion** and extrude the text 0.7 units, with no bevelling. Deselect the resulting object.

Now duplicate the null object (or create a new one), **Multi** select the extruded characters, select **Parent**, and middle-click the null to make it the parent of the extruded letters. Switch back to **Single** selection mode and select the null parent. Press the *v* key and drag the null object to the lower left of the word (see Figure 11.5). This will let you easily rotate the word to match the logo angle.

Delete the original face used to extrude the word. Then rotate and translate the word until it has the same angle as the logo

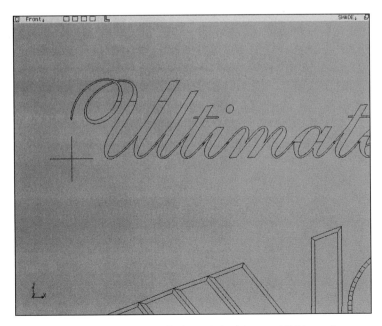

Figure 11.5   The null object to the lower left of the word "Ultimate."

and it looks good in the Perspective view; compare your positioning with the final image in the color gallery section of this book. Switch to the Matter module, select **Material**, and apply the ytz_goldbase material. Select **Texture|2D Global**, and apply the aluminum texture from SI_Materials/PICTURES/SURFACES.

Add Dice To The Scene

The final elements to complete the scene are some dice and a cup for shaking the dice. After you create a die using boolean operations, you will load some completed and positioned dice into the scene, followed by the dice cup.

Building A Die

The dice are constructed from a cube. Select **Multi** and click on the logo and word. Select **Display|Hide|Toggle Desel Hidden** to hide those elements. Now select **Get|Primitive|Cube** and accept the default cube size of 10. Select **Effect|Bevel** with a size of 0.6, and then bevel again with a value of 0.18.

Switch to the Matter module, and select **Material**. Change the color picker from RGB to HSV, then increase the Diffuse V value to 0.9, and the Ambient V value to 0.8. (HSV is the easiest color model to use when you are trying to make things lighter or whiter.)

Use Booleans To Create Dice Spots

To construct the spots, use the boolean difference operation to cut holes out of the cube. Go back to the Model module and select **Get|Primitive|Cone**. Set Radius to 1.0, Height to 2.0, Longitude Step to 12, and Latitude Step And Base to 1.0. Rotate the cone 180 degrees around the Z axis so that the tip points down. Select **Effect|Freeze|Rotation** to lock in the rotation.

Now move the cone up the Y axis until the base peeks over the top face of the cube. Select **Effect| Freeze|Translation** so the Y value goes back to zero. Make four duplicates of the cone and drag them to arrange the spots in the "five" pattern, as shown in Figure 11.6.

Using the **Multi** selection mode again, click on the five cones. Select **Effect|Merge** and accept the default values to combine the cones into a single object, then select **Single** and highlight the merged cones. Switch to the Matter module and select **Material**, then change the Diffuse value to 0.0 and the Ambient value to 0.1. Delete the original five cones and switch back to the Model module.

Make the die the currently selected object and select **Boolean|Static**. Set Operations to Difference, Resulting Object to A And B Together, and Keep Respective Materials, then click on OK; when prompted, select the merged cones. Hide the original die and the merged cones to view the result of the boolean operation.

Follow the above procedure to create the other faces of the die, arranging the spots so that you have the correct number on each side. Now that you can make a die on your own, hide or delete the dice elements, then unhide the logo and "Ultimate" text.

Load In The Dice And Cup

To finish up the scene elements, load in some dice and a throwing cup. Select **Get|Element** and choose the files revol1 and thrown_die from the

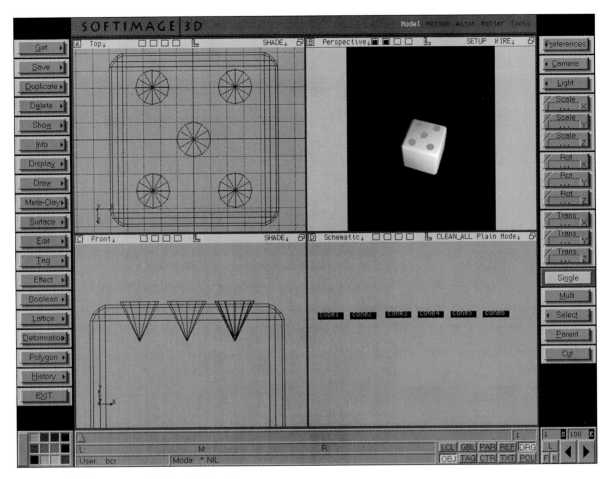

Figure 11.6 Spots arranged in the "five" pattern.

Chapter11 database. They are positioned to match your current scene. (The dice cup, a simple object to create, is made from a surface of revolution.)

Light And Render The Scene

Now that the scene is complete, set up some attractive lighting and render a final image for the chapter.

Add Lights To The Scene

Use multiple point lights to highlight the logo and dice (we used three, but you could do a decent job with two). Play around with varying light colors until you get the effect you want; look at the lighting section of Chapter 10 for some hints and guidelines.

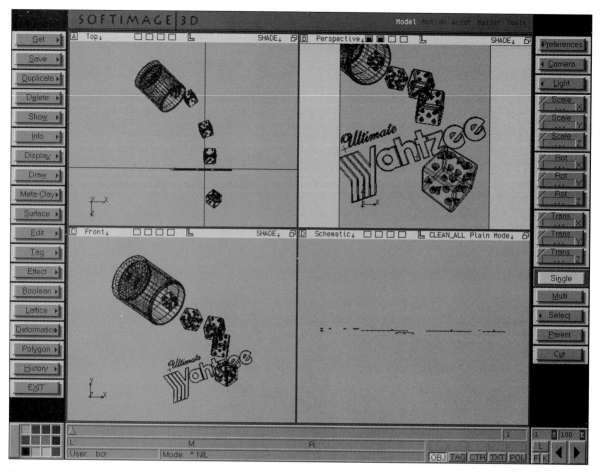

Figure 11.7 A Wireframe view of the entire scene.

If you aren't getting the results you want, load in the final scene from the CD-ROM enclosed with this book and edit the lights in that scene to see how things are set up.

Render A Final Image

Switch to the Matter module and select **Render**. Set the resolution of the image to 800×960. Set the filename to chap11_ytz, click on the Render Sequence button, and bask in the glory of your final rendered image.

If you want to add a kick to this final image, add a highlight or a star bouncing off the crest of the final letter *e*. If you have Softimage Extreme, this can be accomplished with the star lens shader for Mental Ray. If you don't have that package, load the final picture into your favorite image-editing software and add a starburst, sparkle, or highlight filter effect.

Wrap-Up

This project is deceptive. At first glance, it looks like some simple text and a few objects—but as you undoubtedly discovered, it takes a bit of sweat to get all of the details in place. Take the time to give each element of your scene the attention it deserves. Your satisfaction with the final image or animation will justify the effort.

Next, it's time to get back to some animating. Chapter 12 will cover some of the basics of putting together a character, giving it a skeleton, and making it walk.

Figure 11.8 A final rendering.

ANT WALK

12

Key topics:

- **Skeletons**

- **Envelopes**

- **MultiPed**

- **Fractal Terrain**

- **Constraints**

Softimage is an incredibly powerful tool for character animation. The project presented in this chapter will introduce methods and techniques for animating a character using skeletons. You will create the joints and bones for an ant and then use the MultiPed plug-in to walk the ant through a fractal landscape. The final animation will use some dramatic camera tracking to follow the ant through the scene.

Getting Started

Begin by setting up a new database for the project and loading an initial version of the ant model. This basic ant will be modified throughout the project to create a flexible character for animation.

Create The Ant Database

Start in the Model module (press F1 if you aren't already there). Select **Get|DB Manager**, then go to the database level and click on New Database. Name the database chap12. Link up the Chapter12 database on the CD-ROM included with this book. You will load project elements from the Chapter12 database, but be sure to make chap12 the default database so that all your work will be saved in the correct place.

Load The Ant Model

The star of this project is an unassuming insect model. It's up to you to bring this clump of polygons to life. Select **Get|Element** and load the file ant_model, which has the prefix "start". (See Figure 12.1.)

Originally, this model was a simple group of ant parts. The mandibles and antennae were single objects, and there was no hierarchy to the model. To make the model more flexible for character animation, the antennae and mandibles were split into left and right objects that can be separately manipulated and animated. More importantly, the elements of the ant have been grouped into a strong useful hierarchy, which will be examined in the following section.

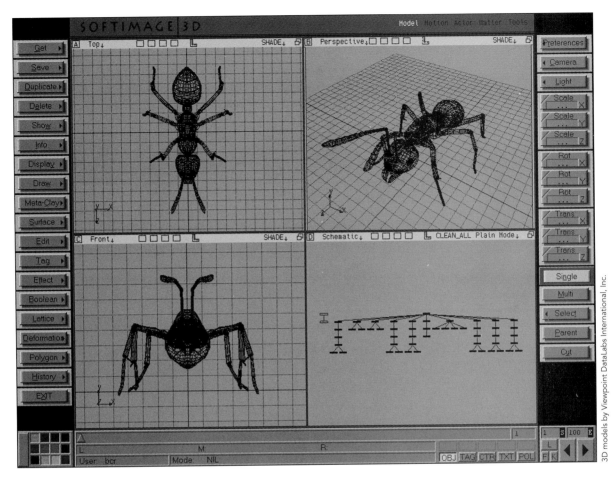

Figure 12.1 The initial ant model.

Analyze The Model Hierarchy

Open a Schematic view and look at how the elements of the model have been parented. The midsection, or thorax, of the ant is the root of the hierarchy. The components are grouped and parented in such a way that the outermost elements are at the bottom of the hierarchy.

Hold down the spacebar and middle-click on one of the elements connected to the root node. This selects all the elements in the branch of the tree below the node you have chosen. Middle-click across all the nodes connected to the root to see how the hierarchy is structured. As you select a branch, the selected sub-elements of the model are highlighted in white.

The main elements hanging off the root node are further grouped and parented. Each articulated leg is parented so that the top of the leg is nearest the top of the hierarchy and the outer elements are lower on the tree. Hold down the spacebar and left-click on parts of the model to examine where single nodes fit in the hierarchy.

The elements are grouped in anticipation of your adding a skeleton to the model. A skeleton will allow you to "pull" on elements lower in the hierarchy, affecting the nodes above them. For example, when you grab the ant's leg at the bottom, pulling it will move the element of the leg above it, and so on up the entire chain of the leg.

Prepare The Ant Model

To get the ant ready to animate, you'll first create a skeleton that connects the model elements with articulated joints. Then, you'll spruce up the ant's looks by adding some spiny hairs and setting the overall material properties of the model.

Create A Skeleton For The Ant

Switch to the Actor module and make the Right window full screen. Select **Skeleton|Draw 2D Chain**. Create a three-jointed chain for the antenna by left-clicking four times: at the base of the antenna, again at the bend, then two-thirds up the remainder, and a final click at the end of the antenna. Right-click to exit Draw mode. (See Figure 12.2.)

Make the Top window full screen. Press *v* and use the right mouse button to move the skeleton horizontally until it is over the base of the antenna. Press the *c* key and use the middle mouse button to rotate the skeleton around the Y axis until it is aligned with the antenna. Switch to Model mode. Select **Effect|Symmetry** and choose the YZ plane from the dialog box. (See Figure 12.3.)

Switch back to Actor mode and make the Right window full screen. Create a one-jointed skeleton for the head by selecting **Skeleton|Draw 2D Chain** and left-clicking once at the center

---

SYMMETRY

The Symmetry effect is invaluable when working with models that are mirrored across an axis—such as a car or a face. You need only to model one-half of the object and then mirror it to the other side to have a completed model. Symmetry is a big time-saver, but for organic models remember to make some slight changes in shape and size so your symmetric models don't look too perfect.

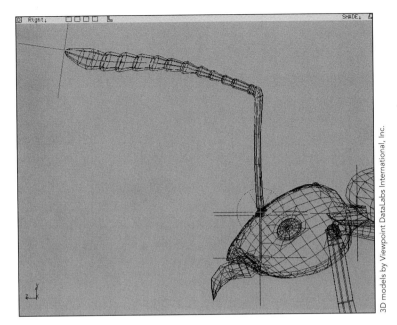

Figure 12.2 The antenna skeleton.

back of the neck, then again at the front of the head where the mandibles are. Right-click to exit Draw mode.

Middle-click on **Skeleton** to draw a two-jointed chain for the abdomen. Left-click on three points: first where the smaller element meets the thorax, then where the smaller element connects to the larger abdomen section, and, lastly, at the end tip of the abdomen. Right-click to exit Draw mode. For the thorax, create a null by selecting **Get|Primitive|Null** and move the null up vertically into the center of the thorax.

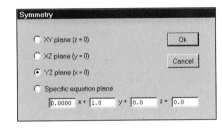

Figure 12.3 Symmetry dialog box.

Give the skeletons some hierarchy by adding parenting. With the null for the thorax highlighted, select **Parent** and then left-click on the chain with two joints in the Schematic view. This makes the thorax null the parent of the abdomen chain. Then, highlight just the thorax null again, select **Parent**, and left-click on the single-jointed head chain. Now, highlight the joint in the head chain, select **Parent**, and left-click on one of the antenna chains. Highlight the joint in the head chain again, select **Parent**, and left-click on the remaining antenna chain. The resulting hierarchy is shown in Figure 12.4.

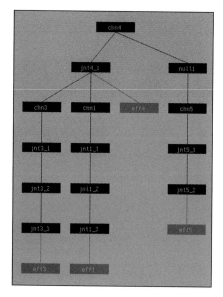

Figure 12.4 The skeleton hierarchy.

The time has come to bone the legs. Switch to **Multi** select mode, and highlight everything except the leg components. Select **Display|Hide|Toggle & Desel Hidden** to hide those elements. Switch back to **Single** mode. (You can draw skeleton chains only in **Single** mode.) In the Schematic view, hold down the spacebar and middle-click on the top node of one of the middle legs. This will highlight the leg so you can see where to draw its skeleton.

In the Actor module, select **Skeleton|Draw 2D Chain**. Create a three-jointed chain in the Front window by left-clicking on the hip of the leg, then on the first and second joints, and, lastly, on the tip of the foot. Make the Top view full screen and vertically drag the skeleton until the hip socket is in place. Then rotate around Y to line the joints up with the leg.

Bring the Front view to full screen and select **Skeleton|Move Joint|Pick Joint By Mouse**. Middle-click on the joints and adjust their positions. Select the effector at the end of the chain and drag it to line up with the tip of the foot. Switch to the Model module and select **Effect|Symmetry**, reflecting across the YZ plane.

Select **Duplicate|Immediate** to make a copy of the skeleton for the rear legs. Drag it vertically in the Top window until the hip is in place. Rotate it to line up with the leg. Select **Skeleton|Move Joint|Pick Joint By Mouse** and middle-click on the lower joints to drag them into position. Drag the effector again to the tip of the foot and use **Symmetry** to copy the resulting skeleton to the other side. **Duplicate** one of the middle legs again and drag it down vertically to line up with the front hip. Repeat as above to get the skeleton aligned and copied to the other side.

Now add the leg bones to the skeleton hierarchy. **Multi** select the top nodes of the leg skeletons, then select **Parent**, and middle-click the thorax null in the skeleton hierarchy. This makes all the legs children of the main skeleton. Right-click to exit **Parent** mode and then switch back to **Single** mode.

Attach The Skeleton To The Model

You now have two hierarchies: One contains the geometry of the model; the other is the skeleton. Combining the two will create an integrated model with a skeletal structure that you can easily animate. This attachment process is somewhat tedious, so take your time and test the parts as you create them.

Unhide the ant components and the skeleton hierarchy, starting with the abdomen. In the Schematic window, hold down the spacebar and middle-click to highlight the abdomen branch of the ant model. Make sure to include all three nodes that are under the thorax root. Select **Duplicate|Immediate**, then go back and hide the originals.

Highlight the center node of the duplicate abdomen and select **Cut**. This will sever the connection with the top node in the abdomen while keeping the bottom two connected to each other. Highlight the top node of the two connected abdomen parts. Select **Parent** and middle-click on the bottom joint in the abdomen chain, just above the red effector node in the Schematic view. Highlight the remaining abdomen part and **Parent** it to the joint just above the last one you selected. The resulting hierarchy for the abdomen is shown in Figure 12.5. To test your handiwork, highlight the effector on the end of the abdomen and drag it. The parts of the abdomen will now move with the skeleton.

Next, attach the antennae geometry to the proper joints. This is a slightly different process, using a local envelope. **Duplicate** the antennae and hide the originals. **Cut** the two stalks from the null they are grouped to and delete the null. Determine which antenna goes with which chain in your skeleton hierarchy, highlight the branch that has the chain, and select **Skin|Local Envelope**. Use the default values for the dialog box, as in Figure 12.6, then left-click on the antenna when prompted. This creates a local envelope, which attaches the geometry of the antenna to the chain.

Repeat the process for the second antenna and test the results by dragging the effector at the end of one of the antennae. Observe

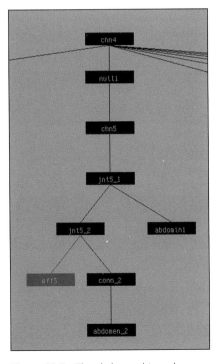

Figure 12.5 The abdomen hierarchy.

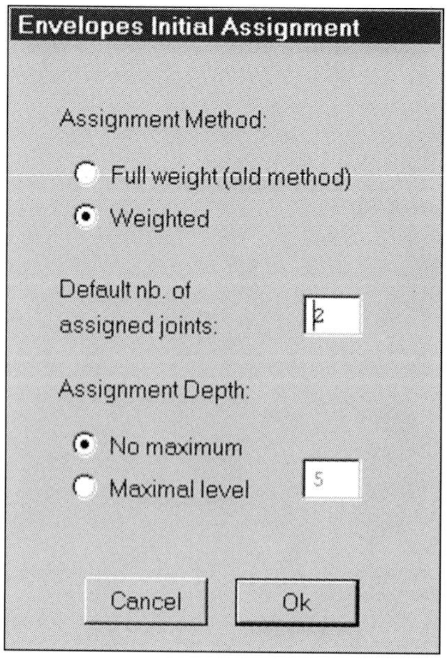

Figure 12.6 Local envelope dialog box.

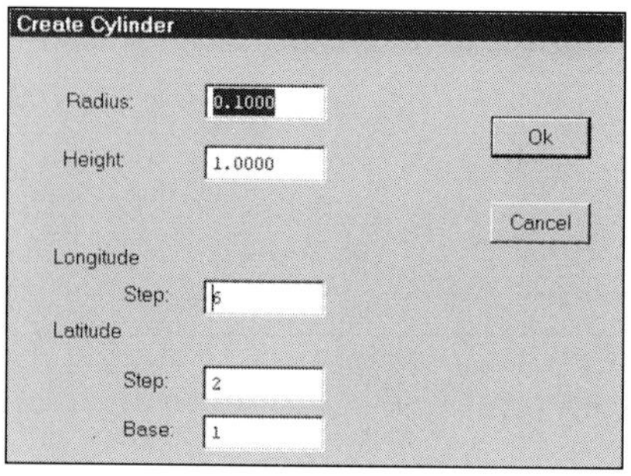

Figure 12.7 Cylinder settings.

how envelopes allow you to bend solid objects without having to split them into parts.

The legs should be attached in the same way the abdomen was. Copy the geometry, split it into pieces, and then reconnect the pieces to their respective joints in the skeleton hierarchy. If you have any trouble, just load in the boned ant from the MODELS database.

Add Hairs To The Model

To make the ant look a little more interesting, you'll add some spiny bristles over the model. These hairs give the ant a more menacing look and a more natural feel. You will create the hairs by duplicating a single bristle randomly over the surface of the model, using a very cool tool called the Duplicator.

Switch to the Model module and select **Get|Primitive|Cylinder**. Set the dialog box as shown in Figure 12.7. Scale the cylinder to make it very slender, then tag its top vertices and scale them down to a point. Drag this tip of the bristle slightly to the right to put a bend in the hair. (See Figure 12.8.)

Highlight the hair cylinder, then select **Duplicate|Duplicator**. Set the Duplicator to random, 200 copies, and check the rotate and scale boxes. Click on OK, then when asked to select a surface, left-click on the abdomen. When asked which object to use, left-click on the hair cylinder. After a short pause, the model will be updated with the bristled abdomen.

In a similar manner, add bristles to the thorax and head. Experiment with the number of hairs you add. If you don't like the result, just delete it and try again. Finally, **Parent** the hairs to the object they are placed on.

Apply Materials To The Ant

To complete the ant, you need to set some appropriate surface materials. Materials percolate down a hierarchy, so begin by setting a general material for the whole object. Switch to the Matter module

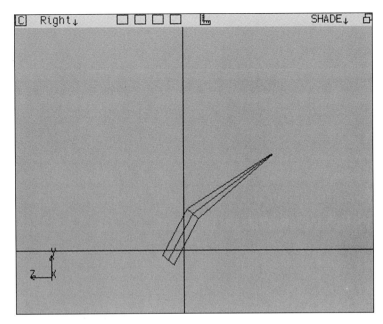

Figure 12.8 Close-up view of a single bristle.

and, with the entire ant model highlighted, select **Material**. Turn down the Ambient term, make the Diffuse component a blackish-red, and make the Specular a reddish-brown. Preview until you get a look you like. To see the materials better, you may want to turn on **Depth-Fading** with a light color for the background.

Highlight the eyes and select Material. Turn the Ambient and Diffuse terms down to black and crank the specular decay to 200. This will make for glassy black eyes. Next, highlight the antennae and mandibles, make them a little darker and more specular than the rest of the body. **Multi** select the hairs and give them a blackish shade. (See Figure 12.9.)

That completes the creation of the ant. The model is ready to animate, so you can now build a world for your character.

Create A Terrain

To make a simple landscape for the scene, you will build up some terrain using fractal offsets to scale elevations on a grid. Then you will cut a road through the fractal mountains for your ant to walk along.

Figure 12.9 Ant with materials applied.

Build The Landscape

If you haven't already saved your work from the previous section, do so now, saving the entire ant model into your database. Then, select **Delete|All** to start clean. Select **Get|Primitive|Grid** and make a polygonal 20×20 grid with a cell count of 1 by 1. With the grid still highlighted, select **Effect|Convert**, which will convert the grid to triangles. Select **Polygon|Fractalize** (Fractalize works only on triangles). Check the positive offset box in the dialog box that appears and set iterations to 7, magnitude to 1.5, and jagginess to .55. (See Figure 12.10.)

Figure 12.10 Fractalized terrain.

By adding a few textures, this fractal landscape can start to look quite nice. Select **Delete|All** and load the scene "start terrain" from the Chapter12 database. In addition to a fractalized grid, a half sphere and some basic lighting has been added. The sphere is textured to provide a cloudy skyline. Our progress is shown in Figure 12.11.

Flatten Out A Road

The fractal terrain is rather jagged for the ant to navigate, so to make life easier, flatten out a road for it to walk along. Begin by drawing a path that extends from behind the initial camera position and meanders off to the end of the terrain in the northwest. To see the viewing frustum of the camera, select **Camera|Show Camera**, toggle **Show|Cone** to on, and highlight

Figure 12.11 Terrain with textures.

the camera by holding down the spacebar and left-clicking on the camera node in the Schematic view.

Make the Top view full screen so you can see where to draw the path. Select **Draw|Curve|B-Spline** and create a road path from behind the camera that curves up to the upper left corner of the terrain. (See Figure 12.12.) Hold down the *m* key, and left-click and drag points on the spline to adjust the shape of the road.

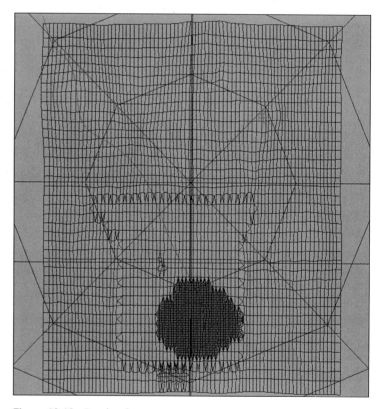

Figure 12.12 Road path.

Select **Draw|Curve|Pipe**, set the pipe width to 42, click on OK, and, when prompted, left-click on the road path. Zoom into the Top window to see the resulting road. Drag the road horizontally to the right, so that the original path travels down the center of the road. This will center the road in your Perspective view.

Select **Edit|Proportional Setup**, press the Exponential 2 button, set the Distance Limit to 30, and click on OK. Select **Tag|Spline Tag**, choose Top for the Projection Plane, and Tag for the Tagging operation, then click on OK. When prompted, select the road and the terrain. Highlight the terrain to see how all the tags for the road have been chosen.

Switch from OBJ to TAG mode and press the *x* key to scale the tagged points. Switch from XYZ to UNI mode and middle-click in the Y Scale box. Middle-drag in the Right window to flatten out the road. Drag until all the points are at the same level. Then press the *v* key and drag the tags up and down in Y until the road is at a natural level with the terrain. Experiment with this height to get gentle shoulders on the edges of the road.

In the craggy mountainous areas that have less geometry, you may have to tag some additional vertices. Just hold down the *t* key and drag around the points you wish to add to the road. Try to assure that at least three tags are placed both horizontally and vertically along the whole road. If there are too few tag points, the road will not flatten well. Once you've added tags, just rescale everything flat and then translate in Y to get the right height.

With the road completed and in place, select **Select|All**. This will highlight the entire scene, including the camera, lights, and models. Make the Right window full screen and turn on the Rulers. Highlight the terrain so you can see the tagged road, then zoom in until you can clearly read the height of the road. Switch from TAG to OBJ mode and vertically drag the whole scene so that the road is at 0 in Y. (See Figure 12.13.)

Develop Animation

Now that your character and environment are complete, you can get things moving. The ant will stroll down your newly excavated road into the foothills in the distance. The camera will follow the ant and swing around your character as if mounted on a moving boom. In addition to the walking, you'll add some jitter to the ant's antennae to make it look more alive.

Set Up MultiPed

MultiPed is a tool for creating walking animations. It attaches to a skeleton and a path, animating a multilimbed creature along the path and allowing you to set a variety of parameters that define the characteristics of the creature's gait and limb actions. MultiPed works with skeletons that have anywhere from two to eight appendages. Once you've mastered the settings, you can make people run or spiders crawl, but for now we'll focus on making an ant walk.

You will use the road as your walking path. Move it in the Schematic view so that it is near the head of the ant hierarchy. This will make both the ant and the road easy to select. Switch to the Motion module and select **Effects|MultiPed**. Figure 12.14 shows the MultiPed dialog box. Set the Frame Range End to 4000, Spread to 5, Spacing to 3.5, Step Length to 4, and the Body Offset to 5. Click on OK to accept these values.

MultiPed will now prompt you to select the floor. In this case, you can just use the road path as the floor. Next, select the road as the path for MultiPed to walk along. When prompted for the body, select the ant. You will then be prompted to select the various legs of the creature. Click on the effectors at the ends of each ant leg, starting with the left front, then right front, middle left, middle right, rear left, and rear right.

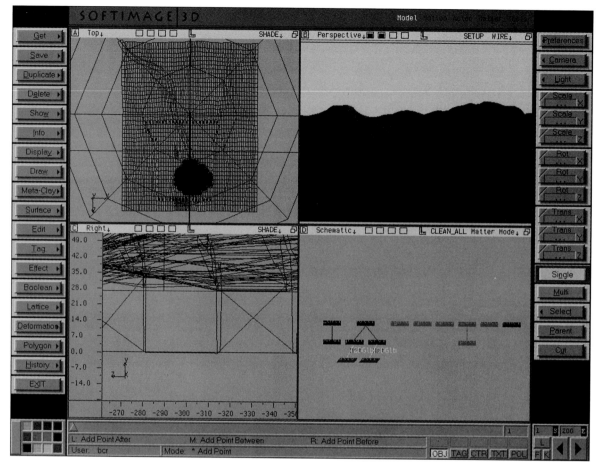

Figure 12.13 Scene with completed road.

At this point, MultiPed is ready to go, and the ant is transformed onto the road. Set the frame range of your animation to go from 1 to 4000. (You'll be rendering only part of this range for the final animation.) Now, one slight snafu must be adjusted to get the ant walking: You will need to edit MultiPed's translation function curve (Fcurve). Select **FcrvSelect\Motion\Multiped\TRANSLATION**, which will open an Fcurve edit window. Select EDITKEY and move the key up to 4000,1.0. Then select LIN to make the function curve linear. (See Figure 12.15.)

Now you're walking! In fact, your ant is probably walking out of your camera view as it heads merrily down the road. We'll deal with that momentarily, but first let's add one more touch to the ant before setting up the camera. Slide the timeline

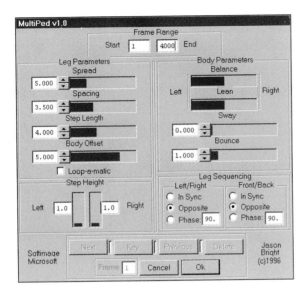

Figure 12.14 The MultiPed dialog box.

back to frame 1 and position the camera so you have a close-up view of the ant.

Add Jitter To The Antennae

To make the ant look a little more alive and insectlike, add motion (or *jitter*) to the antennae. You want some subtle swaying and sniffing-type movements. The antennae should be active throughout the animation, and you can treat their motion independently from the rest of the ant's movements.

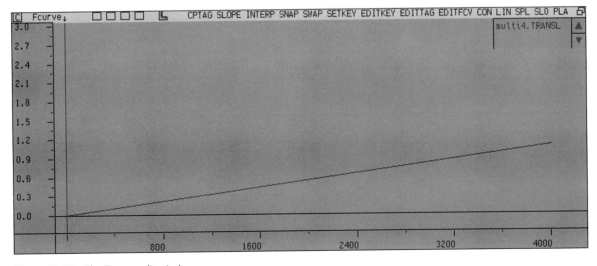

Figure 12.15 The Fcurve edit window.

Highlight one of the antennae and zoom into the Schematic view where the antenna parts are. To create motion, you will add a jitter effect to the effectors at the tip of each antenna by adding a null near each antenna tip. The effectors will be positioned constrained to the nulls, and you will make the nulls jitter over time. The nulls will be parented to the antenna skeleton, so that they move along with the ant's head.

Select **Get|Primitive|Null** and drag the null close to one of the antenna effectors. Duplicate the null and drag it over to the other effector. With the null still the currently selected item, left-click on **Parent** and middle-click on the skeleton element for the effector in the Schematic window. Repeat this for the other null. Now the nulls will track along with the ant's head motions. Move the nulls in the Schematic window so they are with the antennae parts. (See Figure 12.16.)

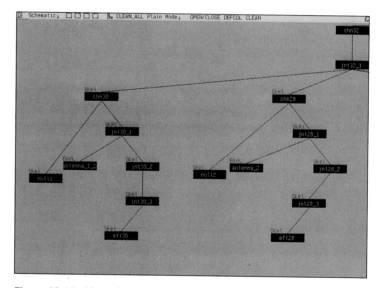

Figure 12.16 The nulls attached in the schematic view.

Highlight one of the effectors and switch to the Actor module. Select **Constraint|Position** and, when queried for the reference point, left-click on the null near that effector. Highlight the other effector and perform the same operation. Now the effectors are locked to the locations of the two nulls.

Switch back to the Motion module and highlight one of the nulls. Select **Effects|Jitter** to bring up the Jitter dialog box. Set the Frame End to 4000, check off only Translate, change the Seed value to 35, and set *x*, *y*, and *z* to 1.0. (See Figure 12.17.) When you click on OK, Jitter will ask you to choose an object to apply the effect to; left-click on the null. Highlight the other null and repeat the Jitter settings, but make the Seed value something other than 35. (The seed value sets up the randomness of the Jitter, so if you use the same seed, you'll get identical motion. Set it to 42.) That's it, your antennae are now waving about.

Add Camera Control

Now you're ready to track the action with the camera. You need to animate where the camera is and where it's looking. To accomplish this, you'll create two new paths with nulls attached. The camera itself will be constrained to one null, and the camera's interest to another.

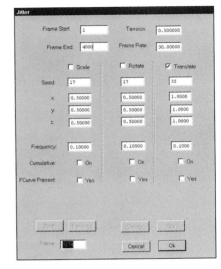

Figure 12.17   The Jitter dialog box.

Create the new paths by duplicating the road path twice. Drag one copy up slightly in Y so that it matches the body height of your ant, and drag the other duplicate up 9 to 10 units in height. Select **Get|Primitive|Null** and middle-click **Get** to create a second null. Position one null near each of the new curves.

Select **Camera|Select Interest**. Switch to the Actor module and select **Constraint|Position**. When asked to pick the reference, left-click on the null near the lower path. This constrains the camera interest to the lower null. Highlight the lower null and switch to the Motion module, then select **Path|Pick Path**. When prompted for a path, left-click on the lower path. Set the frame range from 1 to 4000. The camera interest will now be tracking with the null right along with your ant. Drag the timeline and watch your camera follow the ant.

Now, to make the camera chase after the ant and keep a good view of it, select **Camera|Select Camera**, switch to the Actor module, and select **Constraint|Position**, picking the upper null as the reference. The camera position is now locked onto the upper null. Highlight the upper null, switch to the Motion module, and middle-click on **Path**. Left-click on the upper path and set the frame range from 500 to 4500. Your camera now snaps up into position on the higher curve and stares down at your ant as it walks along.

To make the camera's motions more varied, highlight the upper null, switch to the Motion module, and select **FcrvSelect| Object|Translation** to edit the null's Fcurve. You can add and move points on this curve to vary the speed of the camera. You could also edit the shape of the upper curve to make a more interesting flight path. The same technique can be applied to the lower null to make the camera track in front of, or lag behind, the ant. Try to create some dramatic camera swoops that accent the mountains in the distance. (See Figure 12.18.)

3D models by Viewpoint DataLabs International, Inc.

Figure 12.18   Ant heading toward highlighted mountains.

Wrap-Up

Your scene is complete. Add some lighting as you see fit, and render away. Try playing around with the MultiPed parameters to modify the style of the ant's gait. Likewise, modifying the height of the road will vary how far the ant's legs have to bend to reach the ground. If the ant is low to the ground, it will bounce up and down as it walks. If the path is too high, the legs will have to stretch to reach the ground. Also experiment with some subtle motions. Try adding some head sway and possibly have the mandibles open and close occasionally.

Character animation is what Softimage is all about. If you've mastered all the techniques in this chapter, you'll have no problems creating a host of exciting, lively characters.

CAR WALK 13

Key topics:

- **Border**

- **StepMaker**

- **Ambulate**

In this chapter, you will bring a car to life. This project consists of a dreamlike sequence in which a car character, walking in an upright fashion, pursues a feisty gas container over a twisty road. You will construct the road and gas can and then animate the motions of the characters. The resulting animation is very cartoonish. Have fun with it.

Build The Set

The scene takes place on a twisty, winding road. In this section, you will create the road and a curb alongside the road. Then, you'll add textures to the surfaces to make them more lifelike.

Construct The Road

Begin by creating a new database called "chap13" for this project, then link up the Chapter13 database on the CD-ROM included with this book. Make chap13 the default database. Now, you can load model elements from the Chapter13 database, while saving your results to chap13.

Select **Get|Element|Models**, and navigate to the Chapter13 Models directory. Double-click on road_spline, which will load three spline elements: spline1_1, which will be used to model the road; gas_spline, to model the gas can; and square_1, to model the curbs on the sides of the road.

Highlight spline1_1, and center the object in the orthographic views by selecting **Camera|Frame Selection**. Use the **Camera|Zoom** and **Camera|Tracking** functions to center the selected object within the Perspective window. To view the selected B-Spline with its control points, select **Show|Points**. Viewing the spline through the Front and Perspective windows, you can easily see the numerous high and low points along the spline. This spline was originally planar (in the XZ plane), and the peaks and troughs were created by moving selected points up or down along the Y axis.

To start the actual road construction, make sure that spline1_1 is highlighted and that Modeling (F1) is the currently selected module.

Select **Draw|Curve|Border**. In the opened Border window, set the Distance of Border to 4, leave Linearize spline unchecked, put a check in the Preserve number of points checkbox, set Step size to 5, leave Thorough checking unchecked, and click on OK. (See Figure 13.1.) When queried, left-click on spline1_1, which creates a new spline that forms the outside edge of the road. At this point, you should deselect spline1_1 by holding down the space bar and pressing c.

With nothing selected, middle-click on **Draw**, and when the Border window reappears, change the 4 to a -4 for the border distance. Click on OK to close the Border window, and left-click on spline1_1 once again. This creates and highlights a spline forming the inside edge of the road. The two newly created splines will define the outer edges of the skinned road model and will also serve as extrusion paths for the road curbing.

Deselect all elements (space bar+C), and then select **Surface|Skin**. Left-click on both the outer and inner splines, then right-click to open the Skinning window. (See Figure 13.2.) Within the Skinning window, the Polygon option should not be selected, because UV coordinates will be needed to create a texture map of the road. If this were a polygon model, there would simply be no way to get the texture map to conform to the bends and curves of the road. Therefore, select Patch, and this function will automatically assign UV coordinates to the road. Next, select B-Spline, set the Step level to 3, and click on OK. You have created the road.

Depending on which spline was chosen first during the skin operation, however, the normals may be inverted. You can detect

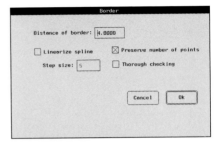

Figure 13.1 The Border dialog box.

Figure 13.2 The Skinning dialog box.

this problem by either setting the Perspective window to Shade mode and observing the poorly lit surface or selecting **Show|Normals** and observing which side of the surface the normals are facing. If the normals are pointing up from the road, everything is fine. If the normals are oriented away from your view, select **Effect|Inverse** to flip their direction.

Construct The Curb

To start curb construction, highlight square_1, and select **Surface|Extrusion**. With the Extrusion window open, select Patch and Linear under Object Types, select On Curve under Axis of Extrusion, and then click on OK. At this point, the command area at the bottom of the screen instructs you to choose a curve. Left-click on the outer, newly formed road-edge spline. This extrudes a new outer curb along the outer edge of the road.

Once again, after viewing the new object in the shaded Perspective window, the normals appear reversed. Select **Effect|Inverse** to flip the normals (or middle-click on **Effect**). To build the opposite curb, deselect all objects, highlight square_1, and follow the same procedure, using the opposite road spline as the extrusion path.

At this point, you should organize the Schematic window. Select **Get|Primitive|Null**, and leave the newly created null highlighted. Select **Parent**, then left-click on each of the extruded curbs and the road. These three objects are now grouped under the null. Rename this null by highlighting it and selecting **Info|Selection**. Once the Null Info window opens, enter "demo" next to Prefix and "road_grp" next to Name. (See Figure 13.3.)

The only object needed from the original generator curves is the gas_spline. Highlight the gas_spline, and then select **Cut**. This function separates the gas_spline from its parent group. Delete everything, saving only the gas_spline and road_grp. Select the Clean_All function from the top of the Schematic window to reorganize the nodes in the Schematic view.

Add Texture To The Road And Curb

The first object to be textured is the road, so make sure this is the only object highlighted. First, press F4 to enter the Matter module, then select **Texture|2D Global**. (See Figure 13.4.) Press the Select button next to Picture Filename and, in the picture directory, select Yellow Brick. In the upper-right corner, under View Mode, make sure On Material is selected.

To lessen the amount of shine on the texture, set the Specular level (lower-right corner) to .0010. The texture image cannot be stretched down the entire length of the road, so enter 20 in the Repeats box under the V coordinates column. Switch the Mapping Method to UV Coordinates, and add some roughness to the texture by entering 2 in the Roughness box. Select Preview to see how the texture looks on the road.

The road looks pretty good, so save these settings as a texture. In the top middle box under 2D Texture, enter "Yellow_Brk_Road_Tex", then select Save. In the Save Textures2D window, enter "car" under Prefix.

To add texture to the curbs, highlight one curb, then select **Texture|2D Global**. Next, in the 2D Texture box, press Select, and choose road_side_tex from the list of textures offered. Preview the

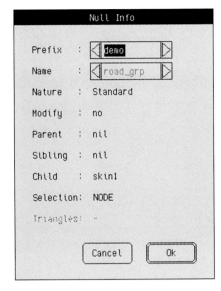

Figure 13.3 The Null Info dialog box.

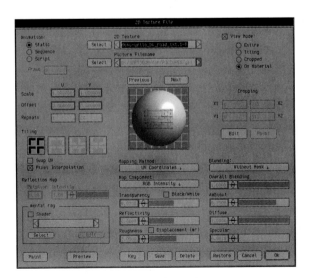

Figure 13.4 The 2D Texture File window.

mapped curb and, if satisfied with the image, click on OK to return to the Matter module. Use the same procedure to map the opposite curb. Your results should match Figure 13.5.

Figure 13.5 A preview image of the textured road and curbs.

Build The Gas Can

In this section, you'll construct the gas-can character from scratch. The can is primarily made from surfaces of revolution and extrusions. The main elements are the body of the can, the snout and cap, and the handle. After building the geometry of the object, you will apply some materials and textures to complete the character's look.

Create The Main Body Of The Can

Begin by retrieving the surface generation curves from the project database. Select **Get|Elements|Model**, and bring in the file gas_can_curves from the Model directory. These six curves are read in: bead_curve, bead_extru_curve, gas_main_curve, handle_curve, cap_curve, and snout_curve. Zoom into the Schematic view, so you can easily choose any of these curves.

Highlight the gas_main_curve in the Schematic window. Select **Surface|Revolution**, and within the opened Revolution window, under Object Type, make sure that Patch and B-Spline are selected and that the value 5 is entered for Sub. The Axis of Revolution is the Y axis, Degree is 360, Subdivision is 8, and Step is 3. (See Figure 13.6.) When these settings are correct, click on OK to create the main body of the gas can. Name the new object "main_body."

View main_body in the shaded Perspective window, and if the normals are reversed, select **Effect|Inverse** to flip them. The body of the can will look more realistic with a curved bead at its base. To accomplish this, first highlight the bead_extru_curve within the Schematic window. Next, select **Surface|Extrusion**. Within the Extrusion window, select Patch, B-Spline, and On Curve; then click on OK. The bottom command line instructs you to choose a curve, which will be the extrusion path for the bead_extru_curve. Left-clicking on the bead_curve from the Schematic window forms the bead at the base of the can. Name this object "bead_base". (See Figure 13.7.) Once again, if the normals are reversed, middle-click on **Effect**.

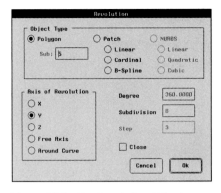

Figure 13.6 The Revolution dialog box.

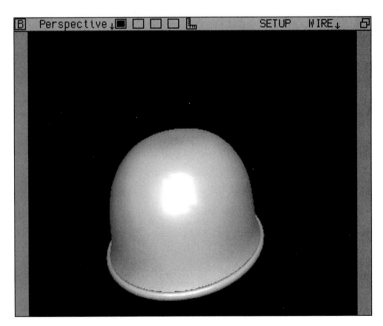

Figure 13.7 Preview image of the gas can with bead.

Create The Snout And Cap

The snout and cap will be created together, grouped, and then rotated into position onto the can. Highlight the snout_curve within the Schematic window, middle-click on **Surface** (or select

Surface|Revolution), and click on OK. Name the new object "snout". Follow the same procedure for cap_curve, naming the resulting object "cap".

At this point (in **Single** selection mode), highlight snout, select **Parent**, and then left-click on cap. You can now treat the cap and snout as a group. Prior to rotating this group, you must adjust the center point of the parent (snout). Highlight snout, press F10 to switch into CTR mode, select **TransY**, and move the center point to the middle base of the snout, in the Front window. You can now position the selected snout group (press the space bar, then middle-click on snout) on the right upper-third of the can, in the Front window. Return to OBJ mode by pressing F8, then use a combination of **RotZ** and translations to move the snout group into position on the can. (See Figure 13.8.)

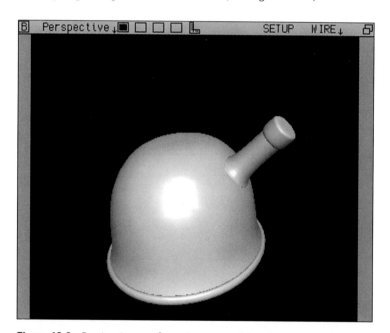

Figure 13.8   Preview image of snout group positioned onto can.

Create The Handle

The handle is made of three elements: the hand grip and two side parts. You create all three with handle_curve. Highlight handle_curve, middle-click on **Surface**, and click on OK to create a surface of revolution. This object is the hand grip. Name the resulting object "handle".

Select **Duplicate|Immediate**, and name the new object "handle_left". Select **TransX**, and move handle_left one unit to the left. Select **TransY**, and move handle_left down until it intersects main_body. Press F10, select **TransY**, and move the center point down to the base of handle_left. Return to OBJ mode by pressing F8. Select **ScaleX**, and scale handle_left on the X axis until it is nearly flat. Select **Duplicate|Immediate**, and name the copy "handle_right". Select **TransX**, and move handle_right two units to the right.

Make sure that **Single** mode is still activated, and highlight handle. Press F10, move the center point down two units to the center of the handle, then return to Object mode by pressing F8. Middle-click on the text box of **RotZ**, and enter a value of 90. The handle has now rotated 90 degrees and should be positioned between handle_left and handle_right. Switch to **Multi** mode, and make sure that only handle_left and handle_right are highlighted. Use **ScaleY** to scale these two objects down until they are appropriately positioned on the handle. (See Figure 13.9.)

Group handle_left and handle_right to handle, make handle a child of main_body, and make the snout group and bead_base

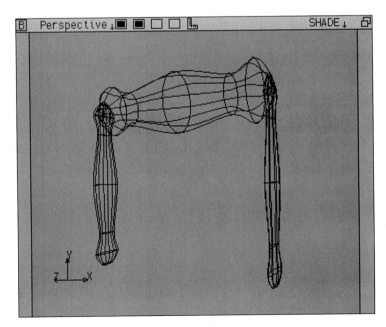

Figure 13.9 Wireframe view of the handle.

children of main_body. Select **Get|Primitive|Null**, and name the null "gas_can_all". Make it the parent of main_body. Select only the gas_can_all parent node, and press F10. Select **TransY**, and move the center point .5 units below the base of the gas can. Then, press F8 to switch back to OBJ mode. This center-point placement will be necessary for future animation of the can. Figure 13.10 shows how the completed handle looks on the can.

Figure 13.10 Preview image of the completed handle.

Apply Materials And Texture To The Gas Can

Highlight main_body only, press F4 to enter the Matter module, and select **Material**. In the Material Editor, make sure Phong is selected by left-clicking on the Ambient box. Under Palette, set R to .55, and leave G and B at 0. Left-click on and highlight Diffuse, then middle-click on Ambient to copy the Ambient palette settings. This results in a classic red gas-can look.

At this point, apply the gas texture map. Select **Texture|2D Global** to open the 2D Texture File. Under Picture Filename, select gas from the project texture directory; set Mapping Method to XY Coordinates, Map Component to Alpha Channel, and Blending to Alpha Channel Mask; then click on OK. This applies the word *Gas* to the side of the can.

The handle and snout both have the same material, so highlight only the handle, select **Mat_Oper|Copy Mat**, and then left-click on main_body. In the Schematic window (under Matter mode), you can see the material copying as new material nodes and links are added to the Schematic view. Use this same procedure to copy the red material from either main_body or handle to the snout.

To give a shiny, metallic look to some parts, highlight bead_base, then middle-click on **Material** to bring back the Material Editor. Press the Select button to choose from a list of scene materials. Choose Metals_silver, and select Load. Use the **Copy Mat** procedure to copy the silver material to cap, handle_left, and handle_right. (See Figure 13.11.)

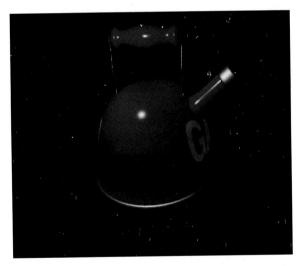

Figure 13.11 Preview image of the can with materials and texture applied.

Lights, Camera, Animation

With the construction phase completed, you can move on to the fun part of the project. In this section, you'll set up the motion of the main characters, add lighting to the scene, and set up some camera control.

Create Camera Paths

The first order of business is retrieving the center road path. Press F1, and switch back to the Model module. Highlight the road, and select **Draw|Extract**. When queried, left-click on the inside curve. This creates a new spline at this location. Next, select **Draw|Curve|Border** to open the Border window. Enter 4 for the Distance of Border, and click on OK. Parent the newly formed middle-of-the-road spline to road_grp. Name this object "middle_road_path".

Make sure the new spline is highlighted, and select **Duplicate|Immediate**. This duplicated spline will be used as a camera target path, so label the spline "cam_target_path". With the Front window active, middle-click on the **ScaleY** text box, and enter 0 for the scale value. This creates a perfectly flat 2D target spline. Now, select **TransY**, and move the cam_target_path spline up until it intersects the upper third of the road's high points.

With cam_target_path still highlighted, middle-click on **Duplicate** then on **Info**, and name the new spline "cam_path". Select **TransY**, and move the selected cam_path up to approximately 10 units above the peaks of the road. This spline will be used as a path for the camera and a light. (See Figure 13.12.)

Animate The Gas Can

Press F1 to enter the Model module. While in Single mode, highlight middle_road_path, and select **Effect|Inverse**. This step is necessary for the animation to begin on the far-left section of the road, as viewed in the Top view. This is also a good time to position the Perspective Camera close to the far-left section of the road, while maintaining a view of the majority of the road.

Press F2 to enter the Motion module. Set the number of frames (lower bar) from 1 to 900. Hold down the space bar, and middle-click on gas_can_all to select the entire group. Select **Path|Pick Path**, and then left-click on middle_road_path to attach the can to the road path. The entire gas can will move to the start of the road. Move the time slider back and forth across the timeline to see the can scamper along the road.

To achieve a macho walking motion for the gas can, you can use the Jitter effect. Highlight the gas_can_all group, and select **Effects|Jitter**. In the Jitter dialog box, shown in Figure 13.13, make sure Frame Start is 1, Frame End is 900, and Rotate and Translate (not Scale) are checked off. Under Rotate, change the Y value to 1.5, and under Translate, change the X value to 1. In Fcurve Present, check off Yes under Rotate and Translate, then click on OK.

With gas_can_all still highlighted, select **FcrvSelect|Object|Translation** to open the Fcurve window. Change this function curve to linear (select the LIN button at the top of the window). Then, select **Constraint|Tangency** for middle_road_path. Test the animation by pressing Play.

Set Up The Camera

Select **Get|Primitive|Null**, and name the null "can_target_null". With only can_target_null highlighted, select **Path|Pick Path**, and click on cam_target_path. This sequence attaches the null to the 900-frame cam_target_path. Try it out by pressing Play. The null appears to be lagging

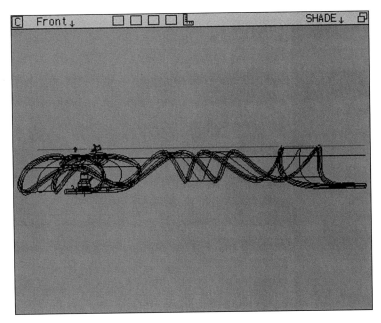

Figure 13.12 Wireframe view of the scene with new paths.

behind the gas can. You can correct this by making the Fcurve of can_target_null linear. Select **FcrvSelect|Object|Translation** to open the Fcurve window, and change the function curve to linear. Now, the null will keep up with the gas can.

The next step is to constrain the camera's target, or interest. Highlight the camera target (in Single mode), select **Constraint|Position**, and click on can_target_null. The camera target now tracks the gas can. Animate the camera using a similar procedure. Select **Get|Primitive|Null**, and name this object "camera_null". With only camera_null highlighted, select **Path|Pick Path**, and click on cam_path. When the Path Timing window opens, enter -30 as a Start Frame value and 870 as an End Frame value, then click on OK. These values are necessary for the camera to start ahead of and finish before the gas can. Once again, select **FcrvSelect|Object|Translation** to open the Fcurve window, and change this function curve to linear. Finally, highlight only the camera, select **Constraint|Position**, then left-click on camera_null. Play back the resulting motion, and see how you like it.

The can appears at some points to be passing through the road surface. This problem is probably a result of the Jitter settings.

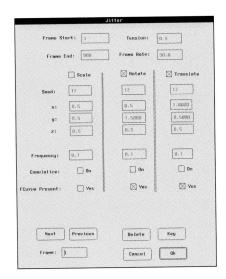

Figure 13.13 The Jitter dialog box.

Highlight the Jitter icon, and select **Effects|Custom| Edit Parameters** to open the Jitter window. Change the Y translation to .2.

Now, highlight the entire gas-can group, and select **FcrvSelect|Object|Translation** to open the Fcurve window. Manipulating this linear translation curve will cause the gas can to either slow down and move farther from the camera or speed up and pass in front of the camera. In general, adding a point (choose EditKey) and positioning it below the original curve will cause the can to pause, creating a greater distance between it and the camera. Adding a point and pulling it above the original curve will cause the can to speed up and pull in front of the camera. Experiment and adjust the motion to your liking. If you run into problems, read in the final translation curve for the gas can from the Models directory in the project database.

Add Lighting

Select **Light|Define** to open the Create Light window. Name the light "demo_light1", select Point for light type, enter 10 for Start Falloff and 20 for End Falloff, click on Raytraced shadows, and click on OK. With the light highlighted, select **Path|Pick Path**, and left-click on cam_path. Leave the Path Timing settings at 1 and 900. Once again, the light is lagging behind. Select **FcrvSelect|Light|Position|Translation**, and, inside the Fcurve window, select LIN.

Select **Atmosphere|Ambience** to open the Global Ambience window. Using the HSV parameters, set H to 0, S to 0, and V to .1. The dark ambient background, coupled with the short falloff of demo_light1, will create a localized lighting effect. (See Figure 13.14.)

Add some color to the scene by creating blue and red point lights. Place these lights about 20 units above the road, at opposite ends. Set Start Falloff to 30 and End Falloff to 70. Play with the lighting to create an optimum look.

Animate The Car

Finally, on to the star of the show. To load the car model, select **Get|Element|Models**, and choose car_clean from the project database. The model loads with all the materials preassigned and a skeleton already constructed for the vehicle. (See Figure 13.15.) The task at hand is to make the car walk.

The first step (pardon the pun) is to determine how far apart to make the stance. Select **Info|Distance**, and in the Top view, click from the middle of one tire to the middle of the other. The status line (at the bottom of the screen) reads 4.6 units. Half that distance, 2.3 units, will be approximately the length of each step. Press F1 to enter the Model module, and select **Effect|StepMaker**. Enter 4 for Step Width, and 2 for Step Length, then click on OK to exit the window. When queried, left-click on middle_road_path for the path. This creates two step paths on the road surface.

You now need to determine which path is for the left foot and which is for the right. In the Schematic window, move both paths so they are under and close to the car_clean group. Rectangular zoom in on the car_clean group and the parent null section of both step paths (this is necessary for attaching the effectors of the car group to the paths). Move the left step path to the left of center, to distinguish it from the right step path.

Figure 13.14 Preview image of the gas can with light and shadow.

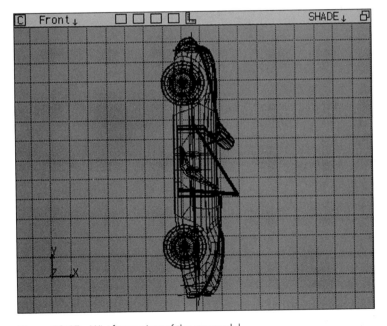

Figure 13.15 Wireframe view of the car model.

Press F2 to enter the Motion module, and select **Effects|Ambulate**. In the Ambulate window, accept all the defaults, and click on OK. Now, follow the prompts. First, select the left-foot hierarchy by clicking on the parent null of the left step path; second, select the right-foot hierarchy by clicking on the parent null of the right step path; third, choose the left-foot effector; fourth, choose the right-foot effector; and, finally, choose the torso by selecting the parent null for the car_clean group.

Check out the action. The car looks good walking, but it can't quite keep up with the gas can and camera. To remedy this situation, set the frame to 900, and view the entire project within the Top window. Notice how far the car is from the end of the road. Select **Effects|Custom|Edit Parameters** to open the Ambulate window, then enter a value of .16 in the top two boxes. Notice in the Top view how the car jumps nearer to the end of the road. This is the only way to edit the speed of the car, as you have no function curves to work with. Use the Key and Frame options to set the pace of the car at .18 sec/step from frame 100 to 300; then from frame 300 to 600, speed up the rate to .16 sec/step. Continue to experiment with these settings to fine-tune the pace of the animation. Likewise, revisit the camera, light, and gas-can function curves to get all the motions working together. Figure 13.16 shows a preview rendering of the two characters.

Figure 13.16 Preview image of the gas can and car.

Wrap-Up

This project was pretty straightforward. You could easily add a lot more to the scene. Consider putting some sort of background around the whole scene—say, a starry night sky or a dreamy blue sky with clouds wafting by. You could give the characters some more personalized expression and enhance their gestures. Perhaps you could add some motion blur or subtle smoke trails after the characters. Try to maintain a 'toon like quality to the piece, while in your head you hear a campy chase-scene soundtrack to go with the motion. In other words, just have some fun.

C I T Y

Key topics:

- **Low polygon modeling techniques**

- **Efficient textures**

- **Correcting perspective distortion**

This project will develop a low polygon count model that can be used for a VRML or gaming application. The emphasis is on economy and simplicity. The resulting scene must be efficient yet detailed enough for visual interest. You will leverage textures and low polygon modeling techniques to create an interactive city.

Planning Stages

Just as an architect or designer would approach a citywide project differently than a single-building project, Softimage users need to do the same. We need to be concerned with a number of different questions, including:

- How many polygons will the project need?

- How close will the camera need to be?

- Will the project be used in a still or an animation?

- Is the scene a main attraction or a set for the main attraction?

Because we are working in a limited universe—as far as CPU speed, memory, and time are concerned—all of these questions (and more) come into play and need to be addressed. In the case of a city, for example, you cannot just start building components as if they are to be used in the real world. You could put more detail into a car's tire than in a whole city by following this paradigm. We've heard of game developers who have attempted to construct scenes without heeding these questions; they ended up with 6 million to 10 million polygon scenes that could not be moved, used, or rendered—and, in the end, were thrown away.

Thinking artistically can often get you further than thinking analytically—after all, producing 3D art is not simply rebuilding real-world objects in 3D space. Even in a scene that calls for real-world objects, objects need to be approached in the way a painter would do it—not the way an architect or mechanic would approach them. You should be thinking: How can I save polygons here? Is anybody going to see each feature? Where is the camera?

3D art has its roots in mechanical and architectural drafting, CAD, and solid-modeling programs. As a result, architects and engineers were the types of users initially introduced to 3D graphics. They measured and planned out everything in real-world coordinates as if it were being built in the real world. This resulted in unnecessary elements. For example, do you really need to put an engine in an animated car if the hood will never be opened?

Consider the following: Suppose you are asked to model a railing. It should look like it is constructed from plumber-type piping. The intersection of a vertical pipe to a horizontal pipe should have a T joint with a bulge in the middle—essentially, a ball with three or four holes cut in it, depending on whether or not it is the top railing. The railing is to be used at the base of a 90-story skyscraper. How would you model this?

This example is from an actual project where conserving polygon count was the main consideration. Several modelers started on the project, making lengths of pipe and cutting holes into high-polygon-count T joints, and measuring the base of the building. Some even went so far as to cut threads into the pipes. In general, the project took each designer hours to complete, and the polygon counts ranged from a few hundred to a few thousand.

One person, however, hit on the winning formula. The posts consisted of one 6- or 8-sided cylinder, with no caps or subdivisions, and placed as needed around the periphery. The horizontal railings were made of a single 6- or 8-sided cylinder, no caps or divisions, with one length to the ball joints. The 3- and 4-way joints were simple 12-sided spheres with no holes cut in them. The total polygon count was less than 100. From the camera view, this railing

looks as good as a 10K polygon model made from a technical drawing.

With these caveats in place, let's start talking about our city project. This project is going to have two purposes:

- To serve as a VRML world for the Web. In this day and age, the sole defining word for the Web is *bandwidth*—i.e., *low* polygon count and *low*-resolution maps. Because this is a world that viewers will be exploring, adding detail at street level, like signs and street objects, will be necessary.

- To be a magazine ad in which the city will appear inside a bubble on a rocky foreign planet. Again, low-resolution bang for the buck is the motto here.

Construction

In a project of this size, you can't build everything from scratch as geometry. You'll need a variety of texture maps, and you better plan on some significant 2D paint time. The problem with images of large buildings is they are taken from either ground level or sky view. Either way, you could run into perspective problems when you map your objects. The buildings you construct are going to be based on rectangles, cubes, and other objects with parallel edges, so you will need maps with parallel edges.

Correcting Perspective Distortion

The odds are, you won't find maps of single buildings trimmed and perspective-corrected, ready to go. You will probably need to scrounge up whatever you can—often, a citywide shot. To make this work, you need an image with as high a resolution as possible. Bring it into a paint program, and start cropping out individual buildings by tracing around the building in question, copying the selection, and pasting it into a larger empty picture. Try to correct the perspective problems imposed by the camera's location at the time the image was shot.

The objective is to get parallel horizontal and vertical edges on the image. This is most often done using a distortion, warp, or perspective tool in your paint package. Keep in mind that this type of operation normally modifies every pixel on the image, so the lower the resolution, the less convincing the outcome will be. Use a high-resolution image from the outset. When your editing is finished, you can scale the resolution down to whatever is called for.

Once your images are in perspective, you can edit them to get different versions out of each building. For example, via copy and paste, you can add more stories or fix holes where other buildings cut into the building at hand. Then, crop the image down to the size of the building. This should give you a final image with very little, if any, black showing. Save your work as a PIC file for Softimage, and save all your maps into the Pictures directory of the Softimage database you are using.

Making Buildings

Once you have a few maps ready to go, start Softimage, and make the City database current. In the Front viewport, set the mode to Rotoscope (wire). Select one of the maps you just made. It will come up in the viewport. (See Figure 14.1.) Use this as a guide to the aspect ratio you need to create for your model to match. In the Pic field under the Roto setup, select the image building_map14c.

This will load a basic steel building map into the Roto viewport.

Because this is going to be a low-resolution project, remember to make your models as simple as possible. For the most part, a cube will suffice as a starting point; then, do a little point pushing and pulling to get things to conform to the picture in the Roto viewport. If you want, you can bevel the top and sides a bit. There is a scene in the building parts database called "steel_building_14c" on the CD-ROM enclosed with this book. This is a simple scene with a stretched bevelled cube that was done using **Model|Effects|Bevel** on a cube, then by tagging the top points and pulling them up to match the aspect ratio, as seen in the Roto viewport.

Because you have only a single side of the building, you will need to either apply the map to each side via 2D_local texture or apply one map and rotate it on the Y axis to cover front, back, and sides. As luck would have it, the map stretches along the sides and looks fine in this case, so you don't need to jump through any hoops to get this to work. You can see this when the scene is loaded in Texture mode, and you can move the position of the red map icon. (See Figure 14.2.)

Often, you'll need to nudge a map into position to get it to work. As an example, press the c supra key to move into Rotate mode. You'll rotate the map a few degrees about the Y axis while viewing the map's position in the Perspective view. Make sure the camera is in Shaded mode and texturing is turned on to show your mapped building.

Now, while holding the middle mouse button down, move the mouse to rotate the map icon about the Y axis. Note that the doors at the bottom

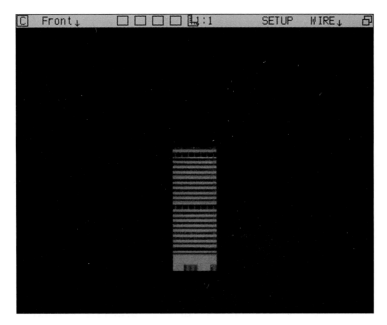

Figure 14.1 Front view Rotoscope (wire).

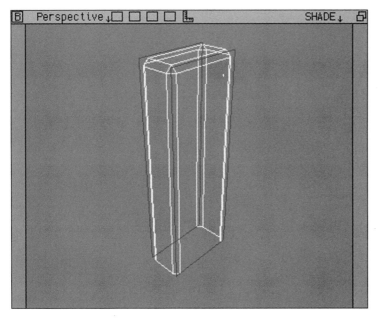

Figure 14.2 Red map icons in TXT mode.

of the structure move as the map twists. Find a position that looks the best. Paint a little detail into each texture, to make each structure appear a bit different. If you use **Paint** in the Matter module, the features will appear on the opposite side from where you are painting. Check both sides in the Shaded view from within **Paint**.

ASPECT RATIO

Don't worry if the models are coming out in different sizes. The aspect ratio is what's important here. Once the aspect is correct to the map, you can scale the model at will and maintain the aspect ratio of the model to the map.

A tip here is to rotate the map icon to allow any paint applied to one side to appear in the same area on the other side. Suppose you want to paint a gray line along the left front edge, top to bottom. Depending on how the map icon is positioned, that same line could appear in the middle of the back wall, which you don't want to happen. So, try to position the map to allow the line to appear on the back right edge, as well as the front left edge. Here again, you need to think how the project will be used. If the back is never going to be seen, don't worry about it. But always leave a little room in your decisions for wishy-washy clients and fussy directors. Now, you can continue creating buildings off the supplied texture maps, or you can load them in as needed.

At some point, you will need to choose some kind of scale for the scene. You'll quickly find that having a model that is perfect in every way does not guarantee a good-looking model. Try a scale of 1 Softimage unit = 1 meter.

Constructing The Block

Let's begin with the city block. The block size is roughly 60 by 40 meters. Go to the Model module, and select **GetElement|Model**. From the City_parts database, load Block_Curves. These are the curves you will use to build the block structure. Using **Draw| Convert to Face** and **Draw|Attach Hole,** you will create three 2D surfaces to extrude into three 3D surfaces.

Make sure you are in the Model module. Select the outer curve, and convert it to a face by selecting **Draw|Convert to Face.** If you shade the Top view, you'll see that the outer spline is now the edge of a solid. The icon in the Schematic view also has changed to read Face instead of Curve.

Because this is going to be the curb stone, you need to remove the whole interior. Select **Draw|Attach Hole.** Click on the next curve on the inside. If the Top view is still shaded, everything inside the curve you just clicked on will be gone. (See Figure 14.3.)

Perform the same steps on what will become the sidewalk. Select the middle curve. You should do so from the Schematic view

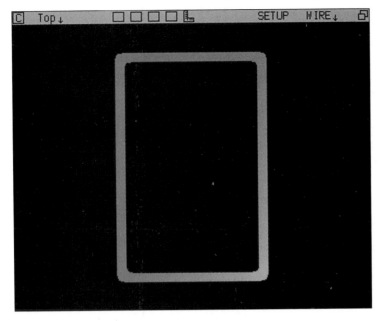

Figure 14.3 Top view of Attach Hole end product.

because the middle curve occupies the same space as the inner edge of the curb. Select **Draw|Convert to Face**. If the Top view is shaded, note that the whole interior is once again filled. This is not what you want, so remove the interior. With the new face still selected, click on **Draw|Attach Hole**, and at the prompt, click on the inner curve. A hole appears.

The last area to cover is the inner surface. This will require you only to convert it to a face. From the Schematic view, select the inner curve, and for the last time, select **Draw|Convert to Face**. This will fill in the inner area. All the former spline icons in the Schematic view are now faces.

You need to convert the flat 2D faces to real 3D objects. If you don't want to go through this, you can load the model Block-A. This is an hrc of three models—Curb, Sidewalk, and Base—under a null called Block-A. (See Figure 14.4.) If you want to go through the creation process, read on.

Fortunately, this can all be done in one pass. The three faces you just created should still be in a group. Select the group by either holding down the space bar and right-clicking on one of the

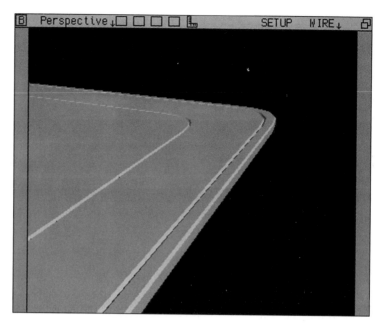

Figure 14.4   Shaded Perspective view of Curb, Sidewalk, and Base.

faces or holding down the space bar and middle-clicking on the
top icon in the Schematic view. All three faces and their parent
should be highlighted. Select **Surface|Extrusion**. Check the radio
button next to Polygon, as well as the Active button under Bevelling. The goal is to extrude your objects up about a foot and give
them a little bevel. This should result in a little separation between the three objects, because they are all sharing inner edges.
In the Radius field, enter a value of .05 units. Set the number of
Bevels to 1, and check Top Bevelling only—that is, uncheck Side
and Bottom Bevelling. Also, make sure the Axis of Extrusion is
set to Y, Subdivision to 1, and Depth to .3.

If your Top view is still shaded, you should see the bevels come in
as the three new objects are created. Hold the space bar down,
and press c to unselect everything. If you aren't seeing everything
and you think you should be, in the Schematic view, press the *a*
supra key.

Now, name the three new objects. Select the outer object, and
hold down the *s* key while pressing the *u* key to open the Polygon
Info dialog box. In the name field, replace whatever is there with
the name "Curb".

Make sure that the flat surfaces stay flat. To do this, select the Faceted radio button or the Automatic Discontinuity radio button, and change the field to contain a lower value. This value, which is in degrees, basically determines whether to treat the surface as a rounded or a flat surface. If the angle is *less* than the angle set in the Automatic Discontinuity field, there will be no break in the surface to indicate an edge. If the angle is more than the value set in this field, you will get an edge at the intersection. A value of 30 seems to work for this model.

Repeat these steps with the middle object—this time name the object "Sidewalk". Select the inner curve, and name it "Block_Base". Don't forget to set the Automatic Discontinuity to a value of 30 on both of these objects.

Put the three new objects in a hierarchy, so they are easier to move around. To begin, unselect everything, and click on **Parent**. At the prompt, click on the three objects, one at a time. Softimage will create a null for you after the first and group the objects you click on as children of that null. Be careful, once **Parent** is selected, it stays on until further notice. You may end up grouping objects you did not intend to. So, as soon as you click on the third object to add it to the group, right-click to end **Parent**.

With everything selected from the parenting operation, hold down the *s* key while pressing the *u* key to open the Polygon Info dialog box. In the name field, replace the null with Block-A, and click on OK to return to the main screen.

Using the **Effects|Alignment** tool, place the null and its center in the center of the Block in the XY axes, but leave the Y alone. First, unselect every-

thing by holding down the space bar and pressing *c*. Select the null (Block-A) by clicking on it while holding down the Space bar. Only the top icon should be highlighted in the Schematic viewport; the three objects under it should be unselected.

At this point, select **Effects|Alignment**, which opens the Alignment dialog box. On the left side are the selected object parameters, and on the right are the target object parameters. In this case, the selected object is your null (Block-A), and the target is any of its children. The center of the null needs to be moved from 0,0,0 (where it was placed when it was created) to the center of the children objects. You want Y to remain at 0, however, so check only the X and Z radio boxes on the selected object and the target. Y is not checked on either side. In addition, click on X and Z centers on *both* sides for both X and Z. (See Figure 14.5.) Click on OK to execute the command. At the prompt, click on any of the three objects. The null should go to the center of the block.

Before we get too far, you should be aware that, because this is to be a low-polygon-count scene, we decided to build the blocks with poly extrudes. If this were going to be a high-resolution scene, the better method would have been to make the sidewalk and curb objects from NURBS or splines. The reasons for this are many, the least of which is adjustable resolution via UV steps. More importantly, the UVs are set at creation time, so you can have texture maps wrap around the block.

We could have selected splines instead of polygons in the Extrusion dialog box, except we want bevels—and **Surfaces|Extrusions|Bevels** work with polygons only. Thus, we needed another way to

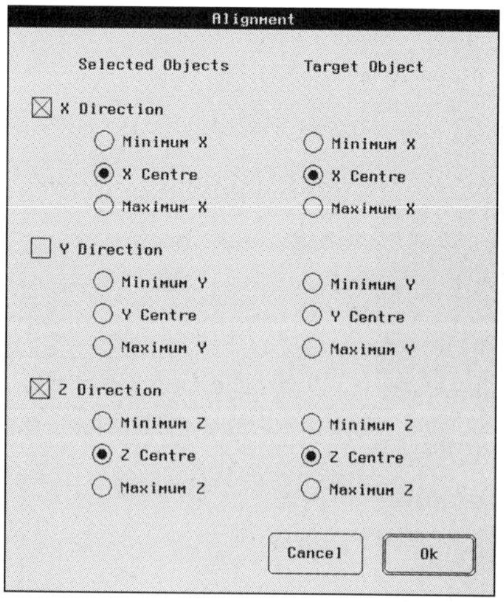

Figure 14.5 Alignment dialog box.

create our sidewalk and curb stones. We decided on creating a cross section out of linear splines. To see what these should look like, select **Get|Element|Model**, and choose Cross_curves. These splines are very small (see Figure 14.6), so zoom into the center of the Front view to see them, or simply select them, and, via supra *f*, click on the Front view. They will fill the frame.

You could use **Surfaces|Extrusion|By curve** to sweep our cross section around the block curves, except the corners would need adjustment. Because we already have our inner, middle, and outer curves, we're pretty much already set up for a Guided Extrude. To make the curb stone, the middle outer curves will force the sweep to maintain an inner and outer edge, as defined by these curves.

Select **Surface|Guided Extrude**, and check Scale Width Only. This will allow the extrude to scale the width of the cross section only, keeping the height as set by the cross section. Click on OK to return to the main screen. At the prompt for a cross section, click on the curb_cross icon in the Schematic viewport. When prompted for the left guide, click on the middle curve. Finally, when prompted for the right guide, click on the outer curve. After a second, a 3D object will appear centered at 0,0,0.

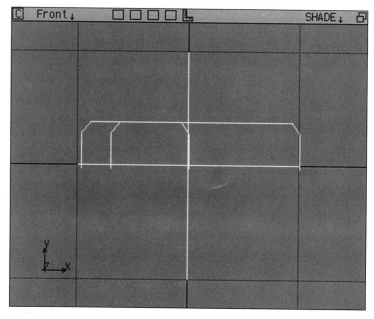

Figure 14.6 Front view of "Cross_curves".

Now, go back and repeat this operation, only this time, when prompted for the cross section, click on sidewalk_cross, and use the inner curve for the left guide and the middle curve for the right guide. Again, after a second, a new object will appear inside the curb stones you just created. If any of the newly created objects appear dark or black in the Shaded view, they can be easily corrected using **Model|Effects|Inverse.**

That leaves the base of the block. Because you are out of inner curves, you will need to create a face out of the inner curve. Then, following the previous steps, select **Surface|Extrusion.** Check the radio button next to Polygon, as well as the Active button under Bevelling. The goal is to extrude your objects up about a foot and give them a little bevel. In the Radius field, enter a value of .05 units. Set the number of Bevels to 1, and check Top Bevelling only—that is, uncheck Side and Bottom Bevelling. Also, make sure the Axis of Extrusion is set to Y, Subdivision to 1, and Depth to .3.

If you were going to continue with NURBS or splines, you would begin mapping them now. That is not your objective, however, so let's just save or hide the spline/NURBS objects and get back to low-polygon-count modeling. You can either load the hrc Block_A_Map that has all maps already applied or make sure the polygon model Block_A is in your viewport and ready to have maps and materials applied.

Applying Textures And Materials

To begin, select the inner object Base, and apply the texture "Base_Bricks" from the city database. This is basically a brick map projected from the

Top viewport, or XZ, and tiled three by three along the UV coordinates. Once the texture is assigned to the inner element of our block, go ahead and map the sidewalk, or middle element. Again, simply select the sidewalk, select **Texture|2D_Global,** and load the texture "Side-walk". This is a another top, or XZ, projected block map tiled six times along the U and four times along the V. Finally, select the outer element in the hrc block, named "Curb", and apply the texture "curb_stone". At this point, the whole block should be texture mapped. Check this by doing a preview in the Matter module.

Make sure that the block you just made is positioned so its upper-right corner as viewed in the Top viewport is four units away from both the X axis and the Z axis. You want to end up with four blocks. Either load them via **Element|Model|Quad_Block** or copy the current block three more times. If you are going to copy the current block, you will need to position the copies so all have their inner corners four units away from the X and Z axes. When finished, 0,0,0 should be positioned in the middle of the four blocks as viewed from the Top view. (See Figure 14.7.)

Select **Parent**, and once the cell is highlighted, proceed by selecting each of the blocks. They should all be highlighted and part of the same hierarchy, with the top null positioned at 0,0,0.

You now need to start thinking about the roads. Try the easiest method first—using a simple 2D grid or plane located under quad_block with a tar texture map. Load it via **Get|Elements|Models** "roads". (See Figure 14.8.) This grid should fit under the four blocks, leaving a margin around the

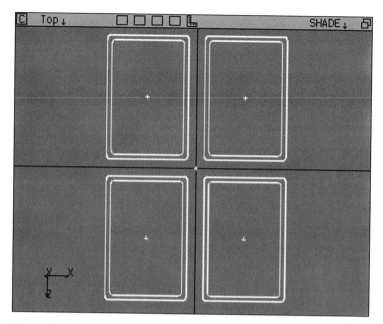

Figure 14.7   Top view of four "Quad_blocks".

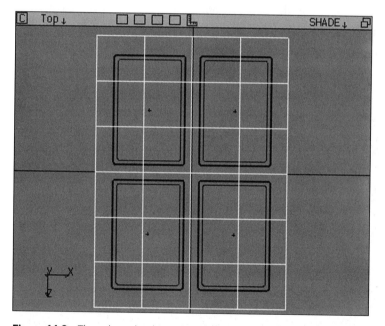

Figure 14.8   The selected polygon "roads" and the "Quad_Blocks".

outer edges. Position the camera, via the *o* (orbit) and *p* (pan) supra keys, down to ground level, looking down the middle road (Z axis). Do a **Preview|All**. If you have had any difficulties, load in the scene Quad_Blocks, via **Get|Scene** "Quad_Blocks". This is the base of the city.

The next item to deal with is street lines and crosswalks. You can do this with either geometry or maps. Because of the scale involved, laying geometry inches above the road surface could cause problems as the camera is pulled back. A Z-buffer has only so much resolution, and one of the most difficult things for the renderer to resolve is two planes butted up against each other. Often, as the camera is pulled back or just moved around, the two planes merge into one. Bearing this in mind, try using texture maps.

Because you can layer textures at will, add a map of lines running right down the middle. Make sure the grid is selected, and select **Textures|2D_Global**. The tar texture should be active in the dialog box. Click on the Next button to open a new, empty dialog box on top of the tar. Load the texture called "road_lines_vert" in the City database. Click on OK to return to the main screen, Matter module, and go into Texture mode by clicking on the TXT pad at the bottom right of the screen. The texture icon, which represents the current texture, should give you a good idea of what's going on with the map. You can see it is repeating 30 times along the Z axis and only once along the X axis, as well as being scaled down to the width of the road. (See Figure 14.9.) Preview it to see

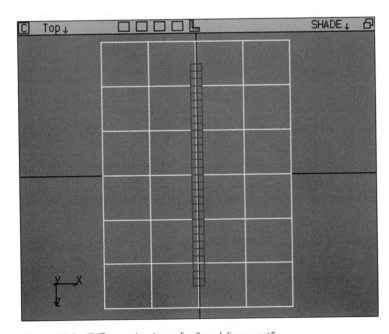

Figure 14.9 TXT mapping icons for "road_lines_vert".

the effect of the repeats. Textures are laid down for the other roads as well. All of them are made from the same texture maps, road_lines_vert and road_lines_horz.

For a better idea of what and how the maps are being used, make sure you are in TXT mode, and step through Next and Prev in **Matter|TxT_Edit**. The grid with maps, called "roads_and_lines", can be loaded as an element.

The City database's model directory contains many small objects clearly named, such as street signs, streetlights, and cross walks, as well as buildings. Many of them should load right into position when you bring them into the scene. You could add more to help bring your city to life—benches, advertisements, parking meters, bus stops, cars, and so on. A scene called "Ground_Clutter" shows some basic smaller models you could easily add.

This brings us back to where we started. We need buildings. So we've included about a half-dozen mapped buildings in the database. They all start with the name build_. You can bring them into the scene one by one, or just load in the scene Basic_City. Basic_City is the same as Ground_Clutter, except it has buildings and a little **Atmosphere|Depth_Fading**. This is vital to give a feeling of distance. In this case, a bluish fog is spread over 10 to 300 units, meaning the fog will start to show at 10 units and be completely solid by 300 units. (See Figure 14.10.)

Wrap-Up

This chapter only sketches out the structure of this project, so you can personalize it as you desire for your application needs. We will revisit this city in the *Do It In Color* section, making it part of an alien landscape. For now, flesh out the city as much as you like to make it your own.

Figure 14.10 Final rendering of city.

APPENDIX
SOFTIMAGE
INFORMATION
SOURCES

Key topics:

- **Discussion and newsgroups**

- **Web resources**

- **Third-party tools**

- **Training**

This appendix is designed to point you toward the wealth of information, products, and resources available within the Softimage community. The variety of tools and information matches the diversity and number of Softimage users.

Most of the information sources covered are available through the Internet in the form of email discussion groups, newsgroups, and, especially, Web sites. The Internet is a dynamic swirl of content. By the time you read this, some of these sources will have changed, and you can be guaranteed that lots of new materials will have been added. Overall, however, this snapshot of available sources should get you well on your way to finding what's out there and where to find it.

Email And Newsgroups

You are not alone. There are about 17,000 Softimage users. Being computer-savvy folks, like you, they tend to be wired to the outside world via the Internet. If you have an email account, you can partake in one of the most useful of Softimage resources—the discussion groups.

A discussion group is a subject-related email group. You subscribe, and articles posted to the discussion group start showing up in your mailbox. A number of Softimage discussion groups are ongoing, and they are alive with a constant stream of daily banter—most of it actually quite useful.

To subscribe, you must send an email request to the list server. To join the 3D list, send an email request to 3D-request@softimage.com. You will receive a reply instructing you how to post to the discussion and how to unsubscribe from the group. Another group is specifically for Mental Ray (mental-request@softimage.com); and there is a general-purpose group for open gabbing on all topics Softimage (discussion-request@softimage.com).

Once you have joined one of these groups, you can send email to it directly (3D@softimage.com, mental@softimage.com, and discussion@softimage.com). They are invaluable resources and provide up-to-the-minute information on Softimage topics.

Another timely Internet resource is the Softimage newsgroup (**comp.graphics.apps.softimage**). Use your favorite news browser to subscribe. The signal-to-noise ratio on the group can sometimes be a little distracting, but in the long run, you will find some good information there.

World Wide Web Resources

The Softimage Web Page
http://www.softimage.com

Let's start with the most obvious and useful resource. The Softimage Web page is a treasure trove of information. You can find product updates, third-party news, press releases, free downloads, and a wealth of other information, as well as links to a ton of other interesting sites. Bookmark this page quickly.

The Softimage User's Home Page
http://delphi.beckman.uiuc.edu/softimage

The Knowledge Base Index is a new part of this site, which allows you to browse the available Knowledge Base articles on Softimage without specific search criteria. This is a good way to get an idea of what Knowledge Base articles exist that might be of use. This site also contains the Softimage Mailing-List Archive, lists of related books and videos, and samples of student work done using Softimage.

Public Domain Plug-ins from the University of Manchester
http://www.man.ac.uk/MVC//software/soft.html

A small number of public-domain Softimage plug-ins are offered through the University of Manchester. These plug-ins are produced for Softimage 3.51, on SGIs only (no NT versions).

Two tools are currently available:

- *A Blending Tool*—Allows an animator to automatically construct a form of blend surface between two NURBS surfaces. This blend is updated as the connecting surfaces animate. It could be used to make seamless characters.

- *A Hyper-Surface Animating Tool*—Lets an animator construct the animation of a surface by providing several sections at points in time. These are then used to produce a hyper-surface, which can be used for such effects as metamorphosis.

Installation of each tool is straightforward, and the plug-ins are supplied as gzipped TAR files.

Jeremy Birn's Home Page
http://www.3drender.com

Jeremy Birn's Info Page provides a quick tutorial on modeling a head and recommends several texts covering anatomy, character animation, visual effects, and rendering. Check out his Thesis Page for some realistic character modeling and facial texturing. On the Production Page, take time to look at the Hippo and Piranha projects—excellent examples of Softimage modeling, animation, and texturing capabilities.

Also, check out Birn's new instructional video, "Secrets of Softimage," for learning advanced, hands-on Softimage techniques.

David Gallagher's Cineframe Animation
http://www.itsnet.com/~dgallagr

This Web page discusses in-house projects using Softimage. These projects include Cat in the Hat for the Universal Studios' Florida Theme Park's Islands of Adventure kiosk.

Gallagher also offers a video on making and animating characters in Softimage. This package should appeal to both beginning and intermediate users of Softimage, who are interested in character work. The four-hour tutorial, called "The Softimage Character Kit," starts with modeling, proceeds to character setup, and finally covers animation examples.

Scott Wilcox's Softimage Tutorials
http://dlf.future.com.au/scotty/TUTORIAL.html

Scott Wilcox discusses the success he has had using the Group as Skeleton feature found within the Actor module. This feature allows you to make any object into a skeleton for envelopes. He finds the best object to be a null, as it will not be included in the rendering process. This use of nulls as skeletons is also the basis for his method of driving lips for speech. Lip setup is the most complicated part of setting up the face. Although the setup takes some time, the user will be able to control the lips through one spline's shape animation.

Wilcox also discusses face setup. He says facial expressions can be achieved without the complex setups involved in the mouth. The user can create null skeletons to drive the various areas of the face quite easily. The more nulls you have, the finer the control—but the more elements you have to keyframe.

Lumis Softimage Page "Softimage-Stuff"
http://www.lumis.com/softimage/

This is a comprehensive, must-see Softimage Web page, featuring tutorials and how-tos, cool tools, videos, seminars, references, Softimage books, and a users' gallery.

The Asset Factory
http://www.assetfactory.com

Got a big animation project and an approaching deadline? No problem on the creation end, but do you lack the render horsepower? Check out the Asset Factory.

The Asset Factory is a digital media services company specializing in rendering and media asset management for 3D rendering, 2D compositing, digital media storage, sharing, and reuse. It gives graphics and animation professionals online access to a network of high-performance 3D graphics rendering and digital storage servers.

Third-Party Tools

Due to Softimage's success as a commercial animation package, a variety of developers have produced tools and applications to enhance your animating pleasure. This section presents a snapshot of many of the available solutions.

Marshall Graphics Systems' MegaFONTS
http://www.marshallgraphics.com

This company claims that the days of grabbing, tracing, extruding, and waiting for fonts are over. MegaFONTS is the oldest Softimage distribution source in the United States. It contains

1,001 professional-quality fonts from more than 400 font families officially licensed from Bitstream, AGFA, and ITC.

The Web page states that MegaFONTS' interface works seamlessly within Softimage 3D, both for NT and SGI. MegaFONTS has an intuitive design and visual preview that allows the user to find, compare, and select fonts instantly. Simply access the interface, and select your font.

Video Collage Inc.'s Texturemation
http://www.video-collage.com

Texturemation is a multivolume collection of animated textures on CD-ROM. Each Texturemation is a loop whose end blends perfectly with its beginning. This means that they can be concatenated, beginning to end, for use in projects of any duration. Each frame of every Texturemation is seamlessly tileable. Every Texturemation consists of a sequence of 720×480 true-color JPEG files.

Texturemation comes with all the tools you need, including a JPEG conversion utility that performs single-image or batch translations into many other file formats, and an image file list construction utility (for Softimage and 3D Studio Max) that can alter the speed of the Texturemation. You can easily select and preview the animation using the included 320×240 AVI and Quicktime movies of each Texturemation. Each volume consists of 25 animations, ranging in length from 60 to 180 frames.

Video Collage Inc. also makes a plug-in development tool called Softwish that allows you to quickly create your own tools. Access the entire

Softimage SDK with Softwish, an extension of the powerful and popular Tcl/Tk language. Build your tools only once; Softwish is an interpreter, so the same code runs on SGI and NT. No compiling and no linking mean fast development. Softwish supports all platforms that Softimage runs on.

SoftMan
http://www.ozemail.com.au/~softman

SoftMan is a converter that allows you to render Softimage scenes with RenderMan (Pixar). It is a great rendering alternative to the Softimage renderers and does not require you to change your Softimage scenes.

RenderMan has been tested and proven reliable on many platforms. It has been designed to be extremely memory efficient. This allows you to render huge amounts of model data, with many high-resolution textures, in a reasonable time and with very little memory penalty.

You can achieve the photorealistic look you are after with RenderMan. It renders patches as patches, which means that no matter how closely you zoom into a patch, you will never see a jagged edge. You can also apply a procedural shader and have the model get increasingly detailed as you zoom in. RenderMan supports advanced effects efficiently.

4Dvision's 4D Paint
http://www.4dvision.com

4D Paint is a 32-bit Windows-based 3D texturing package for the PC. It has been designed to work directly with Kinetix's 3D Studio MAX package and

Softimage NT. 4D Paint allows you to interactively position and paint directly onto the fully rendered surface of a 3D object built inside Softimage on NT.

Traditionally, one of the hardest jobs involved with rendering was the texturing of surfaces. Simple surfaces have always been moderately easy to texture, but when irregular surfaces are required, the limitations of trying to assign a 2D bitmap to a complex 3D surface become apparent. The solution appeared some years ago on Silicon Graphics machines with 3D paint packages that had the ability to paint onto a rendered surface and, thus, position texture correctly in relation to geometry.

These packages were available to only those with large budgets and fast machines. Until 4D Paint, no package for the PC could reproduce the features and speed of these packages. 4D Paint was developed by 4Dvision Asia with the intention of bringing the power of workstation 3D painting to the PC at an affordable price. Check out their demo software on the CD-ROM included with this book.

4Dvision also offers the LumeTools Collection, a series of shaders that provides a wide range of tools and natural effects for the Mental Ray renderer. The collection consists of five individual sets: LumeLandscape, LumeWater, LumeLight, LumeMatter, and LumeWorkbench. Developed in conjunction with the artists and animators of Cyan Inc. for use in Riven, the sequel to the hit CD-ROM Myst, the LumeTools Collection provides highly realistic natural effects for real-world 3D productions. The shaders are fast, easy to use, and produce stunning results.

Animats' Link to SD|FAST
http://www.animats.com

The people at Animats believe: "If it can't fall down, it isn't interesting." This group has linked Softimage|3D to the dynamics compiler SD/FAST from Symbolic Dynamics Inc. It is now demonstrating some of the first animations produced with this system. Falling down is hard to animate realistically, and motion capture of falls is hard on the actors. This is a job for dynamic simulation. These tools are expected to be available as a Softimage plug-in in late 1997.

Animation Science Corp.'s Kinema/Way
http://www.anisci.com

The physics experts at Animation Science are well-known for creating the powerful particle engine in Softimage Particle (a part of Softimage Extreme) used by thousands of animators. Animation Science Corp. now offers a product called "Kinema/Way", which can be used for animating crowds, complex pedestrian behavior, and flocks of motion. It goes far beyond simple deterministic simulations by modeling both the conscious and instinctive pedestrian behavior that leads to the elaborate movements of large numbers of people. A rich parameter set allows you to specify sources (e.g., entrances, such as doors), attraction points, obstacles (such as walls), events, and populations with different types of behavior.

Cinema Graphics' ShadeTree
http://www.cinegrfx.com

Cinema Graphics is marketing ShadeTree, which is an interactive shader builder that supports Pixar's

RenderMan renderer. Microsoft/Softimage Mental Ray will also be supported soon.

The Cinema Graphics Web page includes a guided tour through the ShadeTree software interface. The Web page also explains how to use the software to create shaders and images. An image gallery presents some example images and describes how ShadeTree was used to create them. You can download the software for a trial run.

Phoenix Tools' Plug-In Packages
http://www.phoeniximt.it

Phoenix Tools consists of a team of developers and specialists with years of experience in the computer graphics field. The developers are leaders in development of plug-ins for Softimage|3D and Mental Ray shaders. Their mission is to keep designing new tools to help the creativity of those who are working in the graphics field. Phoenix Tools also offers its customers a unique worldwide consulting service through its Quick Action Team. Its products include:

- *Plug-in Package 1*—Contains SetCameraInterest, OrthoRender, InteractiveLights, LightSilhouette, SwitchLights, CameraCut, ViewParticle, PolySubdivision, InteractiveRepetition, SetMultiKeys, and ShowTag.

- *Plug-in Package 2*—Has Dxf&IGES converters, CycleCurve, S-EllipsoidCreate, S-EllipsoidCtrl, S-EllipsoidGenerate, FakeFlares, ReadjustNormals, F-CurveTimeWarp, ScaleIcons, and SynchroLight.

- *Plug-in Package 3*—Includes MixerØne, NewRound, InterRound, DriveNorm, InvertNorm, SaveKeyMaterial, LightOnSpline, and MapGen.

Science-D-Visions' 3D-Equalizer V2
http://www.sci-d-vis.com

Science-D-Visions offers a product called "3D-Equalizer V2" for camera tracking. When a fixed camera is used in projects combining film or video with CG models in the proper perspective, you render images and use common compositing techniques to incorporate the CG content. If the camera performed more complicated movements, however, 3D-Equalizer V2 is the right tool for the job.

Using highly sophisticated mathematics, 3D-Equalizer V2 reconstructs the camera motion path relative to the recorded scenery. This data is then exported to your preferred animation package, and you use it for the animations. 3D-Equalizer V2 breaks the impenetrable barrier of perspective complexity between live action, computer animation, and compositing.

3D-Equalizer V2 imports the live-action material via standard image formats, such as Targa, SGI, Alias, and Wavefront. The user specifies a sufficient number of striking points in the real scene. These can be corners of objects or colored dots on surfaces, which are mutually fixed in 3D space. They can be easily recognizable points already available in the scene or markers introduced by hand. The motion path of each point has to be tracked on the screen for the entire sequence. You do so by specifying keyframes and using motion-tracking functionality.

Using this data and the motion path of each point, 3D-Equalizer V2 reconstructs the camera position and orientation with respect to the points, thus generating a camera/point motion path in 3D space. Nonlinear distortions appearing in realistic cameras are taken into account. Post-filtering can smooth out the camera motion path, if necessary.

The built-in previewer enables you to check the result quickly.

Finally, the camera/point motion path and the points are exported into the preferred animation package, such as Softimage|3D, using the respective file formats, so no file conversion is necessary. After rendering, the animation is combined with the real sequence using backdrop image techniques or any appropriate software.

Okino Computer Graphics' PolyTrans
http://www.okino.com/conv/exp_soft.htm

Okino Computer Graphics provides model converter software called "PolyTrans". One of Okino's premier export converters, it allows entire PolyTrans and NuGraf databases to be written out to a Softimage hrc model file, or, more conveniently, to a Softimage-compatible database. All geometry (polygonal mesh, NURB patches, and bicubic patches), hierarchy information, material, lights, cameras, PIC bitmaps, and texture mapping attributes are output.

These export plug-in modules have been developed to work with the data processing and user interface functions of Okino's NuGraf Rendering System and PolyTrans products. As such, they are not plug-in modules for Softimage but rather for Okino's software products. Demonstration software has been provided on the CD-ROM included with this book.

Production houses should find this converter invaluable in their daily work. Advanced features include tuned conversion of all texture modulation methods (ambient, diffuse, bump, etc.), alpha channel mapping, automatic or batch conversion of bitmaps to PIC format, direct database integration, accurate (UV) texture coordinate conversion, and dozens of export options.

Arete Image Software's NatureFX and RenderWorld
http://www.areteis.com

Arete Image Software offers two excellent plug-ins to create oceans or atmospheric effects: NatureFX and RenderWorld.

Features include speedy full-color near-photo-quality previews and easy-to-use interface, with parameter controls for every level of user expertise. It also provides full integration with Softimage|3D objects and choice of rendering engines.

RenderWorld is a procedural rendering engine that is able to create full-motion super-high-resolution images of oceanographic and atmospheric effects that are completely indistinguishable from photographic reality. RenderWorld has been used in many high-end professional applications, including Universal Pictures' *WaterWorld*, Sony Pictures' *The Fifth Element*, and Universal's *Commandments*.

RenderWorld's capabilities include: Completely photo-realistic renderings of oceans and atmospheric effects, such as volumetric clouds that your camera can fly through and boat wakes whose size and shape are automatically determined by your hull shape, displacement, and speed.

Although RenderWorld is available as a command-line program (lacking any GUI), the core technology remains consistent within Digital Nature Tools plug-ins. This technology provides a unique and powerful combination of advanced physics-based environmental modeling capabilities and state-of-the-art high-fidelity rendering techniques.

Animation Science's Kinema Products
http://www.anisci.com

Animation Science (previously ArSciMed) develops interactive simulation and animation software using dynamic elements—DYMENTS—combining modern physics with 3D imagery. The Kinema products include Kinema/Way for crowd animation, Kinema/Lighting for photometric simulation, and Kinema/SDK for application development.

3NAME3D's Cyberprops
http://www.ywd.com

3NAME3D offers a model library, Cyberprops, which has a full line of 3D models to populate cyberspace. The Cyberprops library consists of more than 2,000 models, primarily medium- to low-resolution, as well as a high-resolution collection of models suitable for the broadcast and film industries. Cyberprops is always expanding. Currently under development are two new additions: VRMLprops and a realtime collection.

VRMLprops are optimized VRML 2-compliant, low-polygon, textured models with attributes. The realtime library is a collection of low-polygon-count models with economic textures.

TOPIXCLOTH
http://www.topix.com/cloth

TOPIXCLOTH is a free cloth-simulation plug-in for Softimage version 3.7. It was developed in December 1996 for a shot in a recent Honeycomb Craver commercial, where the Craver character, making his entrance as a ghost, is featured pulling a bedsheet off his head. The SGI executable is available for downloading, along with installation instructions and demonstration files. The plug-in has been written for SGI R10000s running IRIX 6.2. Source code is included with the plug-in executable. The NT version has not been compiled, but, hopefully, someone out there will do that. You will need version 1.7 of the Sapphire SDK enabler, available from the Softimage Web site.

Mental Ray Shaders
http://softimage.lumis.com/out/si-mrshaders.html

The following Mental Ray shaders are offered at this site:

- *Bump Glass*—Simulates the distortion you would get looking through uneven glass—that rolling, rippling effect that you see in old mirrors.

- *Shadow Separator*—Makes a material visible only where it receives shadow cast from particular lights. It can also make a material invisible where the shadow falls (so where the shadow appears, there's a hole).

- *Captain Nemo*—Simulates underwater lighting.

- *Smear*—Generates the diffuse lighting interaction you get from imperfect surfaces.

- *Dusty*—Deposits "dust" on surfaces, to give them an old, dirty look. The dust is deposited according to the surface angle in world coordinates, +Y being up. A horizontal surface gets the most dust, tapering off to none for a vertical surface, and none for inverted surfaces.

- *Static Cling*—Provides a cheap, funky lightning effect. Somebody always wants to do lightning and static electricity all over an object—with the accompanying glow, of course.

- *Fuzzy*—Manipulates surface normals, viewing angles, and object transparency to achieve soft edges. It provides better control than static blur and works best with convex, smoothly curved objects (such as spheres). It allows the falloff to be gradual or to have a visible "step" for more of a glow-type effect around the object.

- *Tri-Alpha*—Controls transparency on individual color channels. Standard materials allow manipulation of object transparency only as a global parameter. This shader allows the user to control the transparency of an object on a per-color-channel basis.

- *Good Witch*—Makes "bubbles" that are clear through the center, with the color creeping in at the edges.

- *Turmoil*—A simple noise shader for funky results.

- *Heat Shimmer*—Simulates the shimmering quality of hot air (for example, the heat rising off the road on a hazy summer day, or the warm air coming out of a chimney or a vent on a cold winter day).

- *Cylindrical Spot*—As opposed to conical spot.

- *Volumic Lights Jr.*—Began as an attempt to optimize the volumic lights shader provided in the sample library for the cylindrical spotlights, and ended up also including an attempt to optimize for the conical spots. For the conical spotlights, this version is somewhere on the order of two to four times faster,

if you go by the user time statistics (from the verbose option), and depending on the parameters and the scene.

Standalone Gifts
http://softimage.lumis.com/out/
si-standalone.html

The following standalone gifts are offered at this site:

- *AddZeroPF*—Postframe/command-line script for padding PIC file numbers.

- *AlphaExtractPF*—Postframe/command-line script that applies alpha channel information to the RGB channels of a PIC file.

- *DDR*—Grabs and records Abekas, Accom, and Diskus DDR frames according to parameters entered in a standalone graphic interface. Supports alpha channel and true black in NTSC and PAL formats. Ethernet connection.

- *ddr_grab*—Postframe/command-line script version of DDR **grab** function. Grabs frames from DDR according to parameters entered in a DOS prompt window. Includes a verbose option.

- *ddr_record*—Postframe/command-line script version of DDR **record** function. Records frames to DDR according to parameters entered in a DOS prompt window. Includes a verbose option.

- *InterleavePF*—Postframe/command-line script to interleave field-rendered image PIC files.

- *Parse*—Postframe/command-line script. Prints out pre- and postframe variables to the prompt used to start Softimage|3D.

- *PVRField*—Records field-rendered image files that respect the Softimage naming scheme (image.1.1.pic) to a perception board. Parameters are entered in a standalone graphic interface. To run properly, be sure to have $SI_LOCATION\3d\bin included in the set path variable of your Setenv.bat file.

- *Raybatch*—Postframe/command-line script to batch-render Mental Ray (MI) files per frame (one MI file per frame).

- *Rename*—Renames files using a standalone graphic interface. Supports addition and removal of special characters (such as periods), Pad Zero, Unpad Zero, and Duplicate.

- *RenameSeq*—Renames files using DOS prompt. Supports addition and removal of special characters (such as periods), Pad Zero, Unpad Zero, and Duplicate.

- *Soft2tgaSC.zip*—Converts a sequence of PIC files to the TGA format. A limitation for the alpha platform in currently released versions of soft2tga.zip restricts PIC-to-TGA conversions to one frame at a time.

- *Soft2YuvPF*—Postframe/command-line script for converting PIC files to YUV format.

LambSoft's MoveTools
http://www.lambsoft.com/movetools.html

LambSoft's MoveTools is a translation and conversion utility that allows you to move geometry, motion data, and motion hierarchies between 3D animation packages without data loss or degradation. The MoveTools system is derived from LambSoft core technology called "LSCMP" (an abbreviation for LambSoft Scene Composition). The user saves an LSCMP database from the initial 3D animation package. The database, which contains all the geometry

and animation information, is then imported into the destination 3D package in the appropriate format. LambSoft supports the following input and output formats: 3D Studio MAX, Alias PowerAnimator, Wavefront TAV, and Softimage.

Viewpoint's InterChange
http://www.viewpoint.com/InterChange

Viewpoint has acquired the full InterChange product line from Syndesis Corporation. InterChange is for those of us who use more than one 3D program. It can convert an entire scene, including sub-objects and their parent-child hierarchical relationships and rotational centers. It also preserves material information, such as diffuse, ambient, and specular color; smoothing; glossiness; and refraction. InterChange preserves texture UV coordinates and texture map file names when translating popular formats.

Digital Image Design's Monkey 2
http://www.didi.com

The Monkey 2 digital input device with Softimage drivers is a hands-on desktop input device for keyframing and performance capture. Engineered to provide exceptional freedom in designing motion, Monkey 2 can be manipulated any way you want. Monkey 2 is entirely modular: You can take apart his Monkey Bones and reassemble them to make all sorts of Monkey creatures, from quadrupeds to imaginary life forms.

Kaydara's FiLMBOX
http://www.login.net/kaydara/products.htm

Kaydara's FiLMBOX is motion-capture processing software for Softimage. It supports a multitude of production devices, including 3D capture systems, DMX lighting, MIDI instruments, video decks, and motion-control rigs. Just set up the devices you have, plug them into FiLMBOX, and start recording. Each of the supported devices has its own set of calibration tools, to ensure that the data you are capturing is as error-free as possible.

With FiLMBOX, all captured animation data is synchronized to the reference timecode of your choice. You'll have no worries concerning slow sampling rates from capture devices, because FiLMBOX makes sure the data is sample-accurate, down to the last second.

FiLMBOX lets you manipulate data and devices in all manner of ways. You can define complex relations between devices and data streams, even establish connections between actual hardware devices and 3D software packages.

Altered Perceptions
http://www.vir.com/~altered

Altered Perceptions was founded in Montreal, Canada, in 1995 by veteran Softimage expert Keven Fedirko, after two years of accumulating and organizing textures intended for Softimage users. The database includes Environ_DB, Gaseous_DB, Hard_DB, Liquid_DB, Rugged_DB, Back_DB, and Dirt_DB. The textures are quality photographs that will wrap well.

Training Centers And Courses

As you are well aware, it takes a while to become proficient in Softimage. One of the best ways to get up to speed quickly is to take a course or two from one of the many training centers around the world.

We've highlighted some of the programs, but Softimage has some great training available as well. They also usually hold some daylong tutorial sessions at the NAB and SIGGRAPH trade shows.

Digital Media Institute
http://www.rfx.com/dmi/index.html

Digital Media Institute (DMI) offers a variety of classes geared to the production professional. As an authorized training center for Softimage (one of four), DMI is able to train individuals in many of the skills and tools necessary for producing visual effects for film and broadcast.

Besides holding regularly scheduled courses, DMI works with organizations and studios to create programs and classes tailored to their needs. Its classroom may also be rented for training you put together. DMI's two main courses are:

- *Softimage 3D Level I*—Whether you're new to 3D or simply adding Softimage|3D to your arsenal of tools, this class is the place to start. This introduction to modeling, animation, and rendering through the use of Softimage|3D software is an intensive one-week daytime or five-week evening course. These courses are designed with production in mind, learning through lectures, demonstrations, and extensive hands-on practice. Classes are small, with one student per workstation. Each student receives a training workbook and certificate of completion.

  Subjects covered include user interface, modeling fundamentals, hierarchies, splines, NURBS, motion fundamentals, deformation, wave, shape animation, channels, path animation, constraints, matter and textures, rendering tools, Mental Ray, inverse kinematics, skeletons, flexible envelopes, simulations, and collisions.

- *Softimage 3D Level II*—This class focuses in-depth on many of the high-end functions available in Softimage 3D. Intensive one-week daytime or five-week evening courses are available.

  Subjects covered during the classes include intermediate modeling and animation, combining custom effects for complex effects, expressions, Minerva and Ray Rebels effects, Mental Ray issues and shaders, and the Particle system.

Future Media Concepts
http://www.fmctraining.com

Future Media Concepts now offers two distinct week-long courses, as well as two new two-day courses. Level 0 is an introductory 3D animation course. Level I is for professionals with some knowledge of 3D animation. Level II is for professionals with a higher proficiency on the product. Level III concentrates on character animation.

- *Softimage 3D Level 0*—Designed for those who have used a computer but have never ventured into the world of 3D. This two-day introductory class introduces the student to the 3D environment, focusing on some key terminology and the concepts necessary to proceed into the more intensive 3D classes. Short tutorials and generous hands-on practice time are designed to make the user feel more at ease with the tools required for 3D animation.

- *Softimage 3D Level I*—Provides an introduction to Softimage as a complete animation package. The course focuses on short tutorials and small hands-on productions that encourage students to develop their own creative solutions to the problems posed. Each session builds on previously taught material and provides increasingly greater room for individual creative expression. Students develop a thorough understanding of the interface, 3D environment tool integration, and their use in a commercial production environment. With the aid of hands-on projects, students learn how to use Softimage for attacking animation projects from multiple viewpoints and in multiple ways.

- *Softimage 3D Level II*—Designed for those who wish to master the enhanced features available from Softimage. Exposure to various tools for the purpose of efficient modeling and effective animation gives students a comparative overview. Students learn complex modeling, animating, and rendering. The course features such topics as particles, character animation, instantiation, spline modeling, and Q-Stretch.

- *Softimage 3D Level III*—A two-day course (typically a weekend) designed for those who have completed Level II (or have equivalent experience) but would like to address more specifically the problems associated with character animation. The course looks at the pros and cons of shape, cluster, and forward or reverse kinematics in controlling both human and nonhuman forms. Facial and hand modeling techniques, virtual sliders, and preparing for lip-sync are among the exercises provided, as well as giving expression to inanimate objects and copying animations from one model to another.

Mesmer Animation Labs
http://www.mesmer.com/lab/training.html

Mesmer offers three courses in Softimage:

- *Introduction to 3D Animation using Softimage*—Appropriate for users without prior Softimage or 3D animation experience. Topics include: 3D/Cartesian space; the Softimage interface; modeling basics; hierarchies; basics of matter, texture, light, camera, and rendering techniques; and motion fundamentals.

- *Intermediate (Level I) Softimage*—Tailored for users who have completed Introduction to Softimage and/or have some Softimage|3D experience. This level concentrates on modeling, texture mapping and animation, motion (IK), constraints, basic expressions and channels, dynamic properties, and atmospheric effects.

- *Advanced (Level II) Softimage*—Concentrates on optimizing rendering, Mental Ray, motion (walk cycles, character development), particles, expressions and channels, and advanced lighting techniques.

Video Central
http://www.videocentral.com

Video Central is an authorized Softimage training center. It also provides professional training on Avid systems, Adobe software, mFactory, Fractal Design, and other products. The Softimage courses are Intro to 3D, 3D Level 1, and 3D Level 2.

Alex Colls
http://www.vfs.com/~alejandp/botuto.htm

Alex Colls provides two Softimage tutorials:

- *Boris Tutorial*—Starts head construction using B-Splines that originate at the mouth and end at the back of the head. A guided extrude with three splines forms the mesh. Splines on one side of the head are extracted and skinned. The half head is then shaped. More splines are added during the reshaping; when the model looks good, copy the splines using X-axis symmetry and then skin.

- *Texture Tutorial*—Shows a sequence of textures that were hand-drawn in Photoshop and applied to the model.

RenderMan
http://softimage.ancientfuture.net/tut1.html

The first light tutorial on the RenderMan's site is Lens Flares Tutorial. The 20K zipped database starts out with a raytraced point light, grid plane, and a few primitive cubes. Edit the properties of the Flares shader (found in the Shader_Lib database) as instructed. The properties and settings of the light are discussed, and a final image is provided.

http://softimage.ancientfuture.net/tut2.html
Also on the RenderMan Web site is the Area Lights Tutorial. It discusses the differences between a raytraced point light and an area light with the corresponding softer shadows. It provides images demonstrating the differences in lighting.

http://softimage.ancientfuture.net/tut3.html
The RenderMan's Web site offers a **Volumic Lights Tutorial** with a 21K zipped database. Create a

raytraced light, and set the parameters as instructed. The rest of the tutorial explains the editing parameters and the use of Volumic_LightsJr Shader, which is found in the Shader_Gifts database. Five rendered images with different parameter settings are also provided.

School of Television and Imaging
http://www.imaging.dundee.ac.uk/school/
softimage/index.html

School of Television and Imaging offers Softimage courses and examples of work by postgraduate students in 1997. The site features 15 animation projects with file sizes ranging up to 36MB. Also featured are links to a Channel 5 project and Softimage courses.

MSJC News Media Center
http://www.msjcnewmedia.com/si.html

MSJC News Media Center offers the following training in Softimage|3D:

- *Introduction to Softimage|3D*—A 2-day (10-hour) module that provides an overall context for the study of 3D animation and digital effects. It introduces students to the applications of 3D animation and digital effects using Softimage|3D, the structure of the industry, common software/hardware systems, and the production process.

- *Softimage I, II, and III*—Intensive 3-day (15 hours lecture/15 hours lab) modules. Students learn 3D animation tools and techniques using Softimage|3D. Basic through advanced 3D animation is covered (Windows NT).

Index

N

DESIGN GUIDE SERIES

For Today's Creative Professionals

Geared towards art and design professionals who work with electronic graphics tools, Design Guides present original and diverse techniques developed by a team of professional artists and graphics designers.

The Design Guide Series includes highly visual and practical books with detailed step-by-step techniques. Computer-accomplished graphics professionals can learn to create cutting-edge, commercial quality graphics for games, Web presentations, VRML, video, and numerous other uses.

Digital Camera Design Guide
Peter Aitken
1-57610-184-3 • $45.00/$64.00 (US/CAN)
Available Now

NetObject's Fusion 2 Design Guide
Dan Shafer and Ed Smith
1-57610-212-2 • $44.99/$62.00 (US/CAN)
November 1997

HTML Style Sheets Design Guide
Pitts, Tittel, James
1-57610-211-4 • $39.99/$55.99 (US/CAN)
November 1997

Softimage 3D Design Guide
Barry Ruff and Gene Bodio
1-57610-147-9 • $39.99/$55.99 (US/CAN)
November 1997

3D Studio MAX2 Clay Sculpture, Digitizing & Facial Animation Design
Guide Stephanie Reese
1-57610-150-9 • $49.99/$69.99 (US/CAN)
January 1998

CORIOLIS GROUP BOOKS

An International Thomson Publishing Company I T P

(800) 410-0192 • International Callers (602) 483-0192 • Fax (602) 483-0193 • www.coriolis.com

The Ultimate Technical Cheat Sheets

Out of every advanced technology comes a body of "black art." The Black Book Series captures that black art into the ultimate high-tech "cheat sheet." This is where the unknown network configuration magic, or blistering server performance expertise, resides. Where other titles may present advanced projects, Black Book presents advanced knowledge.

Encyclopedic and organized by topic, with superb indexes, Black Books allow readers to access information quickly and easily.

The Black Book Series

1-57610-114-2	1-57610-149-5	1-57610-174-6	1-57610-162-2	1-57610-189-4	1-57610-185-1	1-57610-187-8	1-57610-188-6
$39.99/$55.99	$39.99/$55.99	$59.99/$83.99	$39.99/$55.99	$49.99/$69.99	$49.99/$69.99	$49.99/$69.99	$49.99/$69.99
(US/CAN)	(US/CAN)	(US/CAN)	(US/CAN)	(US/CAN)	(US/CAN)	(US/CAN)	(US/CAN)
Available Now	*Available Now*	*Available Now*	*Available Now*	*November '97*	*December '97*	*December '97*	*February '98*

CORIOLIS GROUP BOOKS

An International Thomson Publishing Company I T P

(800) 410-0192 • International Callers (602) 483-0192 • Fax (602) 483-0193 • www.coriolis.com

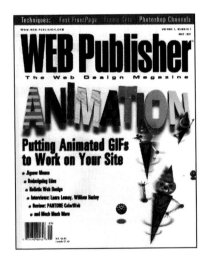

VP 6005
Runner, Male

Hit the ground running.

Let's face facts, you own one of the most powerful 3D animation software packages on the market today, AND you've got 3D project deadlines staring you in the face. You probably want to get right to work.

Jump-start those projects with 3D models from Viewpoint. With more than 10,000 high-fidelity, broadcast-quality NURBS and polygonal models to choose from, you'll save hours, perhaps days, in modeling time.

And our new file translation system, Interchange™ can translate your existing models into and out of Softimage quickly and accurately.

Call Viewpoint, and get a running start on your 3D projects.

VIEWPOINT
D A T A L A B S

1.800.DATASET   **801.229.3000**   **www.viewpoint.com**